Insurance Law in South Africa

Insurance Law in South Africa

Daleen Millard
Birgit Kuschke

This book was originally published as a monograph in the International Encyclopaedia of Laws/Insurance Law.

Founding Editor: Roger Blanpain
General Editor: Frank Hendrickx
Volume Editor: Herman Cousy

Wolters Kluwer

Published by:
Kluwer Law International B.V.
PO Box 316
2400 AH Alphen aan den Rijn
The Netherlands
E-mail: international-sales@wolterskluwer.com
Website: lrus.wolterskluwer.com

Sold and distributed in North, Central and South America by:
Wolters Kluwer Legal & Regulatory U.S.
7201 McKinney Circle
Frederick, MD 21704
United States of America
Email: customer.service@wolterskluwer.com

Sold and distributed in all other countries by:
Air Business Subscriptions
Rockwood House
Haywards Heath
West Sussex
RH16 3DH
United Kingdom
Email: international-customerservice@wolterskluwer.com

Printed on acid-free paper

ISBN 978-94-035-0000-3

e-Book: ISBN 978-94-035-0001-0
web-PDF: ISBN 978-94-035-0002-7

Printed in the United Kingdom.

The Authors

Prof. Daleen Millard obtained the LLD degree from the University of Johannesburg in 2005/06. She also obtained the degrees B Iuris (1994), LLB (1997) and LLM (1999) from the University of Pretoria, Pretoria and a Diploma in Insolvency Law from the Association of Insolvency Law Practitioners.
After starting her career as an administrative clerk in the Department of Justice in 1991, she proceeded to work as a claims handler at the Multilateral Motor Vehicle Accident Fund (as it then was). She started her academic career with Vista University, Mamelodi and was then appointed as a senior lecturer in the Department of Mercantile Law, University of Pretoria. She is currently employed as a Professor of Law in the Department of Private Law, University of Johannesburg and is vice dean. She specializes in Law of Delict, Law of Damages and Insurance Law, and she lectures Law of Delict to LLB students and Interpretation of Contracts to LLM students. She had practised as an advocate and had been a full member of the Pretoria Society of Advocates and when time permits, she drafts legal opinions. She has presented papers at several national and international conferences. She is the author and co-author of various national and international articles in accredited journals. She is a member of the International Insurance Law Association and is a member of the Association's editorial board of the AIDA Europe Research Series on Insurance Law and Regulation. She is the author of the student text Modern Insurance Law in South Africa (Juta, Cape Town) and the co-author of The FAIS Act Explained (LexisNexis Butterworths, Durban) with Wendy Hattingh.

The Authors

Prof. Birgit Kuschke is an Associate Professor in the Department of Private Law, University of Pretoria. She holds the degrees BLC (cum laude) (1986) and LLB (cum laude) (1988) from the University of Pretoria, and completed her LLD degree in 2009 at the University of South Africa. She completed her articles at VDT Attorneys in Pretoria and was admitted as an attorney, notary and advocate of the High Court of South Africa in 1994 and practises for her own account, specializing in insurance, construction and engineering contracts. She has been a member of the International Insurance Law Association since 1998 and has held memberships in its Consumer Protection and Dispute Resolution Working party, the Climate and Catastrophic Events Working Party and the Working Party on New Technologies, Prevention and Insurance. She currently serves as a councillor on the Presidential Council of the Association. She is a principal member of the Drafting Committee for the drafting of *Transnational Insurance Law: Principles of Reinsurance Contract Law* (PRICL), a project under the auspices of the Universities of Zürich, Vienna and Frankfurt and in official cooperation with UNIDROIT and is a corresponding member of the Project Group responsible for the *Restatement of European Insurance Contract Law: Principles of European Insurance Contract Law* (PEICL). She serves on the Editorial Board of the AIDA Europe Research Series on Insurance Law and Regulation. She has published widely in accredited journals, contributed to various textbooks, acted as a national rapporteur and has chaired and presented papers at national and international conferences.

Table of Contents

Table of Contents

List of Abbreviations

ASB	Accounting Standards Board
CGE	Commission for Gender Equality
CGT	Capital Gains Tax
CoFI	Conduct of Financial Institutions
COIDA	Compensation for Occupational Injuries and Diseases Act 130 of 1993
CPF	Company Policyholder Fund
DBSA	Development Bank of Southern Africa
EU	European Union
FAIS Act	Financial Advisory and Intermediary Services Act 37 of 2002
FASB	Financial Accounting Standards Board
FRSC	Financial Reporting Standards Council
FSA	Friendly Societies Act 25 of 1956
FSAP	Financial Sector Assessment Program
FSB	Financial Services Board
FSCA	Financial Sector Conduct Authority
FSP	Financial Services Provider
FSRB	Financial Services Regulation Bill
GCC	General Code of Conduct for Authorized Financial Services Providers and Representatives
IAIS	International Association of Insurance Supervisors
IASB	International Accounting Standards Board
ICC	International Chamber of Commerce
ICESCR	International Covenant on Economic, Social and Cultural Rights
ICP	Insurance Core Principles
IDC	Industrial Development Corporation
IFRS	International Financial Reporting Standards
IMR	Infant Mortality Rate
IPF	Individual Policyholder Fund

LTIA	Long-Term Insurance Act 52 of 1998
MPC	Monetary Policy Committee
MSA	Medical Schemes Act 131 of 1998
NCA	National Credit Act 34 of 2005
NCOP	National Council of Provinces
PAJA	Promotion of Administrative Justice Act 3 of 2000
PFA	Pension Funds Act 24 of 1996
PPR	Policyholder Protection Rules
RABS	Road Accident Benefit System
SACCI	South African Chamber of Commerce and Industry
SAM	Solvency Assessment and Management
SARB	South African Reserve Bank
SARS	South African Revenue Service
SA GAAP	South African Statements of Generally Accepted Accounting Practice
SME	Small and Medium Enterprise
STIA	Short-Term Insurance Act 53 of 1998
TCF	Treating Customers Fairly
UIF	Unemployment Insurance Fund
UPF	Untaxed Policyholder Fund
VAT	Value Added Tax
WCO	World Customs Organization
WTO	World Trade Organization

Preface

Statistics South Africa (Stats SA) estimates the population of South Africa to be 56.52 million as at July 2017. Approximately 30% of the population is aged younger than 15 years and approximately 8.4% (4.54 million) is 60 years or older. The division between male and female is almost equal, with 51% female. As far as race is concerned, about 80.2% of the population are Black African.[1]

Factors that influence mortality in South Africa are varied. It is estimated that the overall HIV prevalence rate is approximately 12.6% of the total South African population. The total number of people living with HIV is estimated at approximately 7.06 million in 2016, and it is estimated that one-fifth of South African women in their reproductive ages are HIV positive. Another important fact about the population pertains to infant mortality.[2]

Another important fact about the South African population is that there has been a constant decline in the infant mortality rate (IMR), with an estimated IMR at 34.4 per 1,000 live births. In addition, the average South African's total life expectancy at birth in South Africa is improving and is estimated at 61.2 years for males and 66.7 for females in 2017.[3]

As far as demographics is concerned, the forecast is that for the period 2011–2016, it is estimated that Gauteng has the largest share of the population followed by KwaZulu-Natal, Western Cape and Eastern Cape. In 2017 approximately 11.5% of South Africa's population live in Western Cape and Northern Cape has the smallest share of the population (2.1%). The Free State has the second smallest share of the South African population constituting 5.1% of the population.[4]

Geographically, South Africa occupies the southern tip of Africa with a coastline of more than 2,500 kilometres, bordering with Namibia on the Atlantic (western) coast southwards around the tip of Africa and then north to the border with Mozambique on the Indian Ocean. South Africa has only two major rivers, namely the Limpopo and the Orange. A predominantly dry country, South Africa's agricultural activities are further hindered by the fact that only 7% of land is arable and that the soil is of poor quality. These factors, together with poor farming practices and soil erosion make agriculture a difficult endeavour. However, there are also factors that favour agriculture,

1. Statistics South Africa accessed at http://www.statssa.gov.za/publications/P0302/P03022017.pdf, 6 Dec. 2015.
2. Statistics South Africa accessed at http://www.statssa.gov.za/publications/P0302/P03022017.pdf, 6 Dec. 2015.
3. Statistics South Africa accessed at http://www.statssa.gov.za/publications/P0302/P03022017.pdf, 6 Dec. 2015.
4. Statistics South Africa accessed at http://www.statssa.gov.za/publications/P0302/P03022017.pdf, 6 Dec. 2015.

such as a range of climates that allow for a wide variety of crops, a long growing season with many frost-free days and river networks for irrigation.[5]

South Africa boasts a sophisticated infrastructure of roads and railway lines. Although power and water supply systems have come under strain in 2014 onwards and frequent power outages had a negative impact on the economy,[6] it seems that these challenges are being met and that risks are being mitigated. The recent drought in the Western Cape has had a negative impact on agriculture and on the tourism industry.[7] Health care and education are further sectors where there are great imbalances between the poor and the wealthy.[8]

Speaking from a risk perspective, there are many adversarial events that may befall the average South African. A state-funded social security system seems inadequate to provide for basic education, food and shelter. Despite the radical and political change that was brought about by the new political dispensation that was founded and 1994 and the democratic Constitution of 1996,[9] de facto inequality seems to have a negative impact on living standards.

The South African legal system has experienced a revolution with the adoption of the 1996 Constitution. The most important change that took place was that the Constitution, and not parliament, is supreme.[10] It is furthermore generally accepted that the Chapter 2 (the Bill of Rights) is applicable to all law, including insurance law, and therefore binds the state (the legislature, the executive, the judiciary and all organs of the state), as well as all natural and juristic persons.[11] While the influence of the Constitution is perhaps less evident in some areas than in other, it remains important to understand that all law must be developed in accordance with Constitutional values. This aspect is discussed in more detail below.

5. Mindset accessed at www.learn.mindset.co.za, 10 Feb. 2015.
6. ENCA accessed at www.enca.com/coverage/power-outages-sa, 10 Feb. 2015.
7. https://www.westerncape.gov.za/general-publication/latest-western-cape-dam-levels (accessed 6 Dec. 2017).
8. http://hsf.org.za/resource-centre/hsf-briefs/the-distribution-of-income-and-the-distribution-of-wealth-in-south-africa-part-i-the-facts (accessed 5 Dec. 2017).
9. Constitution of the Republic of South Africa, 1996.
10. Section 2 of the Constitution.
11. Section 8(1) of the Constitution.

General Introduction

§1. General Background Information

I. Political System

1. South Africa is a constitutional democracy with a three-tier system of government and an independent judiciary. The national, provincial and local levels of government all have legislative and executive authority in their own spheres and are defined in the Constitution as 'distinctive, interdependent and interrelated'. Operating at both national and provincial levels are advisory bodies drawn from South Africa's traditional leaders. It is the aim of the Constitution that the country be run on a system of cooperative governance.[12]

2. South Africa's legislative authority is vested in Parliament, which is situated in Cape Town and consists of two houses, the National Assembly and the National Council of Provinces (NCOP). Parliament is bound by the Constitution and must act within its limits. The National Assembly consists of no fewer than 350 and no more than 400 members elected for a five-year term on the basis of a common voters' roll. It is presided over by a Speaker, assisted by a Deputy Speaker. The number of National Assembly seats awarded to each political party is in proportion to the outcome of the national election, which is held every five years.

3. The NCOP also participates in the legislative process. It is a body created to achieve cooperative governance and participatory democracy through which national and provincial interests are aligned in national legislation that affects the provinces. The NCOP consists of fifty-four permanent members and thirty-six special delegates, and elects its own chairperson. Each of South Africa's nine provinces sends ten representatives to the NCOP – six permanent members and four special delegates headed by the provincial premier or a member of the provincial legislature designated by the premier. There is a formula to ensure that each province's delegation includes representation by minority parties. In addition, local (municipal) government representatives may participate in the NCOP but not vote. Ten part-time members represent different categories of local governments or municipalities.

4. The President, elected by the National Assembly from among its members, is the executive Head of State and leads the Cabinet. The President may not serve more than two five-year terms in office. The Cabinet consists of the President, the Deputy President and twenty-five Ministers. The President appoints the Deputy President and Ministers, assigns their powers and functions and may dismiss them.

---

12. http://oldgov.gcis.gov.za/aboutgovt/structure/structure.htm (accessed 6 Dec 2017).

All but two Ministers must be selected from among the members of the National Assembly. The members of Cabinet are accountable individually and collectively to Parliament. Deputy Ministers are also appointed by the President from among the members of the National Assembly.

5. Legislation may be introduced in the National Assembly only by Cabinet members, Deputy Ministers, or a member of a National Assembly committee. Any Bill may be introduced in the National Assembly. In the NCOP, legislation may be introduced only by a member or committee, and it must fall within certain constitutionally defined areas. Bills passed in the National Assembly must be referred to the NCOP for consideration. The NCOP may pass, propose amendments to or reject a Bill. The National Assembly must reconsider a Bill in cases of amendments or rejections, and pass it again with or without amendments. This process is simple with regard to Bills affecting national functions such as defence, foreign affairs and justice, when each NCOP delegate has one vote. However, when the NCOP considers a Bill that affects the provinces – on functions such as security, welfare, education and health – each province has one vote. This is to ensure that provinces first reach consensus individually on the Bill. Such Bills may be introduced in either the National Assembly or the NCOP. Bills first passed by the NCOP must be referred to the National Assembly, and a mediation committee exists to resolve any disagreements between the two houses. It consists of nine members elected from and by the National Assembly, and nine (one representing each province) from the NCOP. Ultimately, the National Assembly may override the NCOP by a two-thirds majority. Bills amending the Constitution require a two-thirds majority in the National Assembly as well as a supporting vote of six of the nine provinces represented in the NCOP. It should be noted that any Bill amending section 1 of the Constitution, which sets out the state's founding values, requires a 75% majority in the National Assembly. (Serious violation of the Constitution is one of the grounds on which the President may be removed from office, also on a two-thirds majority.)

6. State institutions created to support constitutional democracy are the Public Protector; the Human Rights Commission; the Commission for the Promotion and Protection of the Rights of Cultural, Religious and Linguistic Communities; the Commission for Gender Equality (CGE); the Auditor-General and the Electoral Commission.

II. Commerce and Industry

7. The South African governmental Department of Trade and Industry is responsible for the national trade and industry. It is assisted by South African Revenue Service (SARS) and the South African Reserve Bank (SARB). Development is facilitated by the Industrial Development Corporation of South Africa (IDC) and the Development Bank of Southern Africa (DBSA). South Africa also holds membership in the World Trade Organization (WTO), the World Customs Organization (WCO), the International Chamber of Commerce (ICC) and the South African Chamber of Commerce and Industry (SACCI).

III. Financial Institutions

8. The SARS is the revenue service is the tax-collecting agency of the South African government. It was established by legislation to collect revenue and ensure compliance with tax law. Its vision is to be an innovative revenue and customs agency that enhances economic growth and social development and supports South Africa's integration into the global economy in a way that benefits all citizens. In accordance with the South African Revenue Service Act 34 of 1997, the service is an administratively autonomous organ of the state. This means that it is outside the public service, but within the public administration. So although South Africa's tax regime is set by the National Treasury, it is managed by SARS, who aims to provide an enhanced, transparent and client-orientated service to ensure optimum and equitable collection of revenue. Its main functions are to: collect and administer all national taxes, duties and levies; collect revenue that may be imposed under any other legislation, as agreed on between SARS and an organ of state or institution entitled to the revenue; provide protection against the illegal importation and exportation of goods; facilitate trade; and advise the Minister of Finance on all revenue matters.[13]

9. The SARB is the central bank of South Africa. The SARB was established by section 9 of the Currency and Banking Act, 1920 (Act No. 31 of 1920). It was established as a direct result of the abnormal monetary and financial conditions following World War I. It is governed by the South African Reserve Bank Act, 1989 (Act No. 90 of 1989), as amended. Unlike the Bank of England, which provided the model for establishing the SARB, the SARB is privately owned.[14]

10. The SARB has a board of directors consisting of a Governor, three Deputy Governors and eleven directors. The Governor and Deputy Governors are appointed for five-year terms by the President of the Republic of South Africa in consultation with the Minister of Finance. Four of the directors are also appointed by the President for terms of three years. The remaining seven directors are appointed by the Shareholders of the Bank, also for a three-year term. As stated above, the Reserve Bank is privately owned, with 2 million issued shares. The only limitation on shareholding is that no single shareholder may own more than 10,000 shares individually. Currently there are more than 660 shareholders owning shares in the SARB.

11. Shareholders are entitled a dividend of not more than 10 South African Cents per share per annum (the total maximum dividend is therefore South African Rand (ZAR) 200,000 or a maximum of ZAR 1,000 for any individual shareholder), with the remaining profits being paid to the South African government.

IV. Currency Legislation and Monetary Regulations

12. The Rand is the currency of South Africa. The Rand has the symbol 'R' and is subdivided into 100 cents, symbol 'c'. The ISO 4217 code is ZAR, from Dutch *Zuid-Afrikaanse Rand* (South African Rand). The currency is managed by the Bank as prescribed in Schedule 2 of the South African Reserve Bank Act. The Rand is also the

---

13. https://www.sars.gov.za (accessed 6 Dec. 2017).
14. https://www.resbank.co.za (accessed 6 Dec. 2017).

currency of the Common Monetary Area between South Africa, Swaziland and Lesotho. Although Namibia withdrew from this union, the Rand is still legal tender in that country.[15]

13. The SARB has full operational autonomy. Monetary policy is set by the Bank's Monetary Policy Committee (MPC), which conducts monetary policy within a flexible inflation-targeting framework. The primary objective of monetary policy in South Africa is to achieve and maintain price stability in the interest of sustainable and balanced economic development and growth. Price stability reduces uncertainty in the economy and, therefore, provides a favourable environment for growth and employment creation. Furthermore, low inflation contributes to the protection of the purchasing power of all South Africans, particularly the poor who have no means of defending themselves against continually rising prices.

14. The Minister of Finance issues Orders and Rules under the Exchange Control Regulations. The current set was published on 1 December 1961 and is amended from time to time. The Orders and Rules contain various orders, rules, exemptions, forms and procedural arrangements. In terms of the Exchange Control Regulations, the control over South Africa's foreign currency reserves, as well as the accruals and spending thereof, is vested in the Treasury. The Treasury is defined as '... in relation to any matter contemplated in these regulations, means the Minister of Finance or an officer in the Department of Finance (National Treasury) who, by virtue of the division of work in that Department, deals with the matter on the authority of the Minister of Finance'. The official Exchange Control Manual was first issued by the Bank during October 1990 to assist Authorized Dealers in foreign exchange and Authorized Dealers in foreign exchange with limited authority, their customers and other interested parties, by providing a general understanding of the purpose, scope and operation of the exchange control system in the Republic and in the Common Monetary Area. The exchange control manual merely serves as a general guideline and does not replace or supersede the Exchange Control Regulations, Orders and Rules, nor the norms and policies as applied by the Financial Surveillance Department from time to time. The Financial Surveillance Department continuously updates the exchange control manual to reflect current policies and norms.[16]

V. Insurance Business, General Organization and Special Features

15. An insurance contract can be defined as 'a contract to compensate the insured for a patrimonial loss proximately caused by the uncertain event insured against, or as a contract to satisfy the insured for a non-patrimonial loss consequent upon the occurrence of the uncertain event insured against'.[17]

16. The primary distinction of insurance business is between indemnity insurance (short-term insurance) and capital insurance (long-term insurance). Where indemnity

15. https://www.resbank.co.za (accessed 6 Dec. 2017).
16. https://www.justice.gov.za (accessed 6 Dec. 2017).
17. P.M. Nienaber & M.F.B. Reinecke, *Life Insurance in South Africa: A Compendium* para. 18 (Durban: LexisNexis, 2009); M.F.B. Reinecke, J.P. van Niekerk & P.M. Nienaber, *South African Insurance Law* para. 1.17. (LexisNexis 2013).

insurance aims to compensate for patrimonial loss in the wide sense of the word, capital insurance is aimed at non-indemnity insurance. The use of the terms 'short-term insurance' for indemnity insurance and 'long-term insurance' for what is essentially non-indemnity insurance has been described as 'anachronistic', 'curious' and 'uniquely South African'.[18]

17. Even so, these terms serve to classify the products that are categorized under the Long-Term Insurance Act[19] (LTIA) and the Short-Term Insurance Act[20] (STIA) respectively. Following this classification, long-term insurance refers to assistance policies, disability policies, fund policies, life policies, sinking fund policies and policies that combine these policies.[21] By contrast, short-term insurance comprises engineering policies, guarantee policies, liability policies, miscellaneous policies, motor policies, accident and health policies, health policies, property policies, transportation policies or contracts that constitute a combination of any of these policies. International and national insurers and reinsurers provide insurance business within the country.

18. The Financial Services Board (FSB) is the supervisory authority who oversees the insurance industry. The Board was established by the provisions of the Financial Services Board Act.[22] This corporate body lies outside the public service and its members are appointed by the Minister of Finance. At first, the function of the FSB was to supervise non-banking financial institutions which had been created by various acts of parliament but increasingly more functions were added to the FSB, such as supervisory powers over financial institutions through its executive officer and as statutory registrar of a variety of financial institutions in terms of their founding legislation. Currently, the FSB oversees a number of statutes, including the LTIA, the STIA, The Financial Advisory and Intermediary Services Act (FAIS Act), the Medical Schemes Act (MSA), the Pension Funds Act[23] (PFA) and the Friendly Societies Act (FSA).[24]

19. The FSB's objectives are to ensure the fair treatment of consumers' financial services and products, to promote the financial soundness of financial institutions and the systemic stability of financial services industries and to protect the integrity of financial markets and institutions. To this end, the FSB is empowered to use those enforcement measures provided for in Part II of Chapter VI of the FAIS Act as well as other enforcement measures employed by the FSB. These disciplinary measures against errant financial services providers (FSP) and role players in the industry include the suspensions and withdrawals of authorized FSPs or representatives, voluntary sequestration, winding-up and closure of authorized FSPs or representatives, removal of directors, section 14A debarment of persons, civil remedies in terms of section 33 of the Act, undesirable practices in terms of section 34 of the Act and offences and penalties in terms of section 36 of the Act. These measures may be taken by the FSB

18. Reinecke et al., 8–9.
19. Act 52 of 1998.
20. Act 53 of 1998.
21. Reinecke et al., 11.
22. Act 97 of 1990.
23. Act 24 of 1956.
24. Act 25 of 1956.

against role players in the industry who breach the relevant statutory requirements and do not include remedies that aggrieved clients may bring by way of civil actions against insurers, brokers or other role players who caused them to suffer harm. The rules pertaining to civil remedies are discussed below.[25] The much-anticipated Financial Sector Regulation Act was signed into law on 21 August 2017.[26] Different sections will commence on different dates and provisions that repeal or amend other statutes will also commence on dates as determined by the Minister of Finance[27] but the main aim of the Twin Peaks Act is to create a prudential regulator, the Prudential Authority, while the current FSB will be transformed into a dedicated market conduct regulator known as the Financial Sector Conduct Authority (FSCA). The Prudential Authority will be housed within the SARB. The main aim of the implementation of the Twin Peaks model in South Africa is to create a more resilient and stable financial system and to strengthen the country's approach to consumer protection and market conduct in the financial services industry.[28] National Treasury describes this aim as follows:

> A stable and more inclusive financial sector is needed to support increased economic growth in South Africa. At a macroeconomic level, a stable and well-developed financial sector supports real economic activity through the efficient channelling of savings into productive forms of investment, contributing to the country's objectives on job creation and a more inclusive economy (as set out in the National Development Plan). For individuals and firms, access to affordable and reliable financial products and services enables people to engage in economic transactions on a daily basis, to save for retirement and other long-term goals, to insure against varied risks, and to avoid an over-reliance on debt and exploitative or reckless lending practices. Access to appropriate financial products and services in South Africa is necessary if economic growth and well-being is to be genuinely inclusive.[29]

In order to achieve these goals the Prudential Authority's main task will be to promote and enhance the safety and soundness of regulated financial institutions while the FSCA will protect consumers of financial services by supervising market conduct.[30]

25. *See* in general on remedies, D. Millard & W. Hattingh, *The FAIS Act Explained* 32, 205, 212–215 (LexisNexis 2017).
26. This statute was preceded by the Financial Sector Regulation Bill that was published in December 2014. The Bill was the first step towards the implementation of the Twin Peaks model. The two policy papers that informed the Bill were: National Treasury *A Safer Financial Sector to Serve South Africa Better* (February 2011) (www.treasury.gov.za (visited 23 Sept. 2017)) and Financial Regulatory Reform Steering Committee *Implementing a Twin Peak Model of Financial Regulation in South Africa* (February 2013) (www.treasury.gov.za (visited 23 Sept. 2017)).
27. www.treasury.gov.za (visited 23 Sept. 2017).
28. www.fsb.co.za (visited 12 Sept. 2017).
29. National Treasury *Media Statement: Publication Update for Twin Peaks Financial Sector Regulatory Reform Programme* (21 Jul. 2016) (www.treasury.gov.za (visited 5 Oct. 2017)).
30. D Millard, CoFI and T(CF): Further along the road to Twin Peaks paper delivered at the University of Johannesburg's Annual Banking Law Update, Johannesburg, South Africa, 25 Oct. 2017.

Fairness will play an ever-increasing role due to the incorporation of the so-called Treating Customers Fairly (TCF) principles.[31]

§2. Historical Background of Insurance and Insurance Legislation

20. Insurance as a commercial contract has a history as old as that of the country and as such, has developed according to the needs of consumers. In South Africa, there is a discrepancy between the need for and the uptake of private insurance and that is but one of the issues that will hopefully be addressed by future law reforms when microinsurance is introduced. This innovation, together with reforms to the regulatory regime and other, more insurance-specific matters are on Government's legislative agenda. These changes will no doubt have an impact on the insurance industry and will hopefully enhance consumer protection.

21. Joubert JA in *Mutual and Federal Insurance Co v. Oudtshoorn Municipality*[32] explains that the contract of insurance was unknown to Roman law. In fact, the Romans relied on societies such as *sodalitates*, *collegia* and military societies as forms of mutual assistance with benefits such as proper burial rites, financial contributions towards burial costs and contributions towards the travelling expenses of members of the army. These are not true forms of insurance. As far as Roman-Dutch law is concerned, the old writers relied on the *lex mercatoria* of the Middle Ages and it dealt almost exclusively with marine insurance and indemnity insurance and it was this system that was introduced in the Cape of Good Hope in 1652. The connection with English insurance law commenced after the British occupation of the Cape at the beginning of the nineteenth century. English insurance law was formally introduced in the Cape Colony in 1879 and in 1902 in the Orange River Colony. Even though English law was never formally introduced in Natal and the Transvaal, courts in these two colonies often relied on English precedents. Colonial (English) legislation was only formally repealed in 1977, hence the significant influence English insurance law has had on the development of South African insurance law.[33]

22. One has to bear in mind that the insurance contract is a truly international contract and English insurance law can be ascribed to an earlier source, namely the *lex mercatoria*, which is of Italian origin. As well as forming the basis of the English and Roman-Dutch insurance systems, the *lex mercatoria* has, in addition, influenced the insurance law of other countries.[34]

23. Despite the pronounced influence of English law in South African insurance law, the court in *Mutual and Federal Insurance Co v. Oudtshoorn Municipality* ruled that by repealing the colonial legislation, Roman-Dutch law was restored as the main source of insurance. Therefore, even though the courts did rely on English precedents, after *Mutual and Federal* it can be accepted that matters not peculiar to insurance should be governed by the general principles of South African law. However, where

31. Millard, D. *Juta's Insurance Law Bulletin* 20 1–9 (2017).
32. 1985 (1) SA 419 (A) at 430G–H.
33. Reinecke et al., 7–11.
34. *Mutual and Federal Insurance Co v. Oudtshoorn Municipality* at 430E–F.

English law yields a better solution, that solution should be followed despite the fact that it originated from English law.[35]

§3. Sources of Insurance Law

I. Legislation

24. Generally speaking, South Africa has an uncodified legal system, which means legislation is not the only source of law. It is impossible to understand the insurance framework without having regard to all the sources of South African law. Sources include statutory law, common law, positive law (case law), customs and trade usages.

25. The Constitution is the supreme law of the Republic.[36] Any law that is in conflict with the Constitution is invalid. Furthermore, section 39(2) of the Constitution stipulates that in the interpretation of any legislation and the development of the common law and customary law, a court must promote the spirit, purport and objective of the Bill of Rights.[37]

26. Legislation is written law laid down by an organ of the State or enacted by a person or a body empowered by the Constitution or other legislation to do so. In South Africa, Parliament is responsible for the enactment or original legislation.[38] These laws are embodied in writing and are known as statutes or acts. There are also other designated bodies that can pass subordinate legislation, such as regulations or rules. This happens where the technical nature of these rules and regulations require expert research and drafting. Legislation is a powerful source of law and in principle it binds the whole society.[39] As was indicated in the previous paragraph, the Constitution is the most important statute and law, including statutes, must comply with the Constitution.

27. There are a large number and variety of statutes in South Africa. These include acts, ordinances, proclamations, by-laws, rules and regulations. Section 1 of the Interpretation Act[40] defines it as 'any law, proclamation and ordinance, Act of Parliament or other enactment having the force of law'. The hierarchical classification of legislation follows the level of government (national, provincial or local) whereat it is passed. Statutes which prevail over others can be either original or delegated even within one level of government. In certain circumstances, however, in certain levels of government, delegated legislation is always subordinate. Statutes derive binding

---

35. D. Millard, *Modern Insurance Law in South Africa* 5 (Juta 2013).
36. Section 2 of the Constitution. *See also* I. Currie & J De Waal, *The Bill of Rights Handbook* 30–31, 138–140 (Juta 2013).
37. D. Kleyn & F. Viljoen, *Beginner's Guide for Law Students* 40 (Juta 2010) and I. Currie & J. De Waal, *The Bill of Rights Handbook* 133 (Juta, 2013).
38. C. Botha, *Statutory Interpretation: An Introduction for Students* Ch. 3 (Juta 2012).
39. Kleyn & Viljoen, 41–42.
40. Act 33 of 1957.

force from their creators or legislators, who are empowered by the Constitution, and serve broadly to regulate the modern state.

28. The Constitution provides guidance on how to read statutes and construe the common law in section 39: 'When interpreting any legislation, and when developing the common law or customary law, every court, tribunal or forum must promote the spirit, purport and objects of the Bill of Rights.' In general, its function is to promote the public interest and legal certainty. A clear disadvantage of legislation under a common-law system is that legal certainty is frequently an illusion and it falls to the courts to give and official interpretation or meaning. There is also a danger of over-legislating, which can limit the development of a legal system and sometimes even undermine basic principles of fairness and justice, as with the misuse or abuse of legislative power for the ends of social engineering.[41]

29. Old-order legislation is legislation enacted before the interim Constitution of 1993 took effect. It still forms a substantial part of the current body of statute law in South Africa as is illustrated by the discussion of insurance legislation below. New-order legislation refers to the whole body statute law enacted in South Africa since 1994 on the era of constitutionalism. Some Acts of Parliament give effect to specific human rights and are created by specific mandate in the Constitution. These are superior to all other legislation, but subordinate to the Constitution.

30. Provincial legislation is a category of original legislation, enacted by an elected body that can alter the common law and could even have retrospective force. The original power for new Provincial Acts is derived directly from the Constitution. Some older provincial ordinances, passed between 1961 and 1986, are still in force. A provincial ordinance only applies now in the 'old' geographical region of the relevant former province. Subordinate existing provincial proclamations and regulations (1968–1994) include those issued by the Provincial Councils and, since 1986, the Provincial Administrator. New provincial proclamations and regulations (since 1994) are issued to fulfil the requirements of the prescribing provincial act. A further tier of subordinate legislation is local government or municipal legislation called 'by-laws'. Those that were enacted since 1993 also derive their original power from the Constitution. Other proclamations and regulations may be made or issued by the conferral of delegated powers.

31. Legislation is cited by its short title, and number and the year in which it was signed by the President. This does not reflect the year of its implementation. The final Constitution of 1996 is not cited with its original statute number. In the citation 'section 5(2)(b)(ii)(aa)', '5' refers to the section number; '(2)' refers to the subsection; '(b)' refers to the paragraph; '(ii)' refers to the subparagraph; and '(aa)' refers to the item.

32. The South African insurance industry is highly regulated, which means that, apart from the common law, legislation together with regulations and rules in terms of these statutes, are a very important source of insurance law. That means that in interpreting insurance contracts, the starting point is always the applicable statute, for example, the STIA.[42] But insurance legislation also regulates the way in which insurance

41. In general *see* C. Botha, *Statutory Interpretation: An Introduction for Students* (Juta and Company Ltd. 2012).
42. Act 53 of 1998.

companies should operate and the greater part of the statute may be dedicated to these matters. These statutes are discussed in the table below. If a particular statute is silent on a contractual matter, one looks to the common law for a solution.[43] Precedents are a further, indispensable source of law in interpreting contracts of insurance.[44]

33. The system of judicial precedent, also called the doctrine of stare decisis, applies in South Africa. The application of the doctrine of precedent means that courts must apply their previous judgments in similar cases and in South Africa, both reported and unreported cases of the higher courts (Supreme Court of Appeal and the High Courts) and the Constitutional Court are considered as precedents.[45]

34. When a specific matter is not governed by legislation, common law applies. South African common law is mainly the seventeenth and eighteenth century Roman-Dutch law that was transplanted to the Cape in 1652.[46] Roman-Dutch law forms the basis of modern South African law and has binding authority.[47] In contract law, principles pertaining to consensus and fairness have their roots in Roman-Dutch law. Although South African common law is mainly Roman-Dutch law, English law had a pronounced influence on Roman-Dutch law and this is particularly evident in insurance law with principles pertaining to subrogation.[48] In addition, changing circumstances called for statutory reform and that means that the seventeenth and eighteenth century Roman-Dutch principles have changed significantly over the years.

35. Customary law is generally unwritten law and in modern law, custom plays a small role.[49] In order for a custom to be recognized as a source of the law, that custom must be immemorial; it must be reasonable; it must have continued without exception since its immemorial origin; and its content and meaning must be certain and clear.[50] Currently, custom as a source of the law plays no role in insurance law.

36. Many Black communities live according to indigenous law and indigenous law can be written or unwritten customary law. South African courts recognize and apply indigenous law.[51] According to the Evidence Amendment Act[52] a court can take judicial notice of indigenous law, provided that it is not in conflict with the principles of public policy or natural justice. In addition, indigenous law must be developed in accordance with the spirit and purport of the Constitution.[53] Indigenous law does not recognize the concept of insurance and is therefore largely irrelevant as a source of insurance law.

37. Insurance in South Africa is primarily regulated by the LTIA, the STIA and the FAIS Act.[54] As insurance products are often used in conjunction with other financial

43. Millard, 5.
44. B. Prozesky-Kuschke, 'Introduction to Insurance and Insurance Contracts' in *Commercial Law* 335 (C.J. Nagel ed., LexisNexis 2011) and *Nafte v. Atlas Insurance Co Ltd* 1924 WLD 239.
45. Kleyn & Viljoen, 80–81. Ch. 7 of the Superior Courts Act 10 of 2013.
46. Kleyn & Viljoen, 80–81.
47. *Green v. Fitzgerald* 1914 AD 88.
48. Reinecke et al., 389–390.
49. Kleyn & Viljoen, 87.
50. *Van Breda v. Jacobs* 1921 AD 30.
51. Kleyn & Viljoen, 89.
52. Act 45 of 1988.
53. Section 39(2) of the Constitution.
54. Act 37 of 2002.

products, there are several other statutes that need to be taken into account in order to understand how insurance products and related financial services are regulated. The Acts in question are the MSA, the PFA[55] and to a lesser extent, the FSA.[56]

38. By way of a summary, the following table provides an overview of these statutes:[57]

	Name	*Objective*	*Important Subordinate Legislation*
1.	LTIA	Registration of long-term insurers; control of certain activities of long-term insurers and intermediaries.	– Regulations – Policyholder Protection Rules (PPR)
2.	STIA	Registration of short-term insurers; Control of certain activities of short-term insurers and intermediaries.	– Regulations – PPR
3.	FAIS	Regulates the rendering of certain financial advisory and intermediary services to clients.	– Regulations – General Code of Conduct – Code of Conduct for Discretionary Financial Services Providers – Code of Conduct for Administrative Financial Services Providers – Code of Conduct for Forex Investment Business Financial Services Providers
4.	MSA	Provides for the registration and control of certain activities of medical schemes; protects the interests of members of medical schemes; provides for measures for the coordination of medical schemes and the establishment of the Council for Medical Schemes.	– Regulations

55. Act 24 of 1956.
56. Act 25 of 1956.
57. Millard, 8–9.

5.	PFA	Provides for the registration, incorporation, regulation and dissolution of pension funds.	– Regulations
6.	FSA	Provides for the registration, incorporation, regulation and dissolution of friendly societies.	– Regulations

39. It is evident from the discussion above that the LTIA regulates the long-term insurance industry and that the STIA contains stipulations pertaining to the short-term insurance industry. Other than the LTIA and the STIA, the most important statute for purposes of insurance regulation is the FAIS Act. This statute regulates the activities of FSPs who advise or provide intermediary services to consumers of financial products. Key concepts for purposes of this Act include *advice, intermediary and intermediary service.* It is expected that the Twin Peak reforms will have a major impact on insurance regulation in South Africa. The ideal of Twin Peaks regulation necessitated a critical overview of all financial legislation, including insurance legislation, in order to anticipate and address a variety of issues, including overlaps, conceptual issues and the expected role of the various regulators. The promulgation of the Insurance Bill Act will necessitate future amendments to the LTIA and STIA, followed by the 'Tranche 2' amendments to the regulations in terms of the STIA and LTIA. These two statutes will be repealed after the promulgation of the envisaged Conduct of Financial Institutions (CoFI Act). The Bill, as tabled, clearly sets out its objectives in the preamble, which is to provide for a legal framework that is consistent with international standards and to introduce a legal framework for microinsurance to promote financial inclusion. The Insurance Bill has a strong prudential focus and this aspect is the most marked difference between the Insurance Bill and the current LTIA and STIA. The Bill further consolidates the prudential regulatory framework for long-term (non-indemnity or life) insurance and short-term (indemnity or non-life) insurance and the technical requirements (such as prudential standards) will be contained in the regulations. This Bill, once enacted, will repeal the prudential sections of the LTIA and the STIA. An important feature of the Bill is that all standards pertaining to financial soundness, governance and reporting differentiate between insurers, insurance groups, microinsurers. The stipulations on microinsurers recognize the need for microinsurers to market and sell products that are aimed at a niche market and it is expected that a proper prudential framework for microinsurance will strengthen this aspect of insurance law. Alongside the Bill, the new CoFI Act will regulate market conduct and will repeal the FAIS Act. The CoFI Act will in future regulate market conduct aspects such as advice. At present, the definitions that follow still form part of the FAIS Act.

40. Advice refers to any recommendation, guidance or proposal of a financial nature supplied by any means or medium, to any client or group of clients. The advice must apply to the purchase of any financial product or the investment in any financial product. Advice includes any recommendation, guidance or proposal of a financial nature on the conclusion of any other transaction, including a loan or cession, aimed at the incurring of any liability or the acquisition of any right or benefit in respect of any financial product. Furthermore, any recommendation, guidance or proposal made or given is included in the term 'advice', regardless of whether or not it is provided in the course of or is incidental to financial planning in connection with the affairs of the client; or whether it actually results in the purchase, investment, transaction, variation, replacement or termination of a financial product.[58]

41. The definition of 'advice' is not limited to advice relating to insurance products. Insurance products fall under the wider category of financial products, which is why advice concerning insurance products will fall within the ambit of the FAIS Act. The FAIS Act does not define the term *intermediary* but instead provides a definition of *intermediary service.* An intermediary, in the context of insurance, is someone who, as well as providing advice to a client regarding his or her insurance needs, negotiates an insurance contract between the client and an insurance company and in so doing, it can be said that the intermediary provides an intermediary service.

42. The statutory definition of an *intermediary service* includes any act other than the furnishing of advice that is performed by a person for or on behalf of a client or product supplier that results in the client entering into or offering to enter into any transaction in respect of a financial product with a product supplier.[59] It can also mean any act other than the furnishing of advice that is performed by a person for or on behalf of a client or product supplier with a view to one or more of the following acts, namely: buying, selling or otherwise dealing in, managing, administering, keeping in safe custody, maintaining or servicing a financial product purchased by a client from a product supplier or in which the client has invested; collecting or accounting for premiums or other moneys payable by the client to a product supplier in respect of a financial product; or receiving, submitting or processing the claims of a client against a product supplier.[60]

43. The MSA regulates medical schemes. Section 1 of the MSA defines a medical scheme as any such scheme registered under section 24(1) of the MSA, and the business of a medical scheme is defined as follows:

> [T]he business of undertaking liability in return for a premium or contribution—
>
> (a) to make provision for the obtaining of any relevant health service;
>
> (b) to grant assistance in defraying expenditure incurred in connection with the rendering of any relevant health service; and
>
> (c) where applicable, to render a relevant health service, either by the medical scheme itself, or by any supplier or group of suppliers of a relevant health service or by any person, in association with or in terms of an agreement with a medical scheme.

58. Section 1(1) of the FAIS Act, *sv* 'advice' and Millard, 49–50.
59. Section 1(1)(a) of the FAIS Act.
60. Section 1(1)(b)(i)–(iii) of the FAIS Act.

44. There is a distinct difference between medical schemes and products that insure certain risks pertaining to ill-health and disability. Despite this difference there is sometimes an overlap between the business of a medical scheme and some related insurance products. The business of a pension fund should be distinguished from insurance business. However, the PFA regulates aspects such as annuities which are sometimes combined with long-term insurance policies. This is a very complex issue that will not be discussed here.

45. The final statute and definitely one that has become less important over the years is the FSA.[61] This particular statute provides for the registration, incorporation, regulation and dissolution of friendly societies. A friendly society is 'any association of persons established for any of the objects specified in section two [of the Act]' or 'any business carried on under a scheme or arrangement instituted for any of those objects'.[62] The objects stipulated in section 2 of the FSA include the following, namely:

> (a) the relief or maintenance during minority, old age, widowhood, sickness or other infirmity, whether bodily or mental, of members or their husbands, wives, widows, widowers, children or other relatives or dependants;
>
> (b) the granting of annuities, whether immediate or deferred, to members or to nominees of members, or the endowment of members or nominees of members[.]
>
> […]
>
> (c) the insurance of a sum of money to be paid or other benefit to be provided—
>
> (i) on birth of a member's child; or
>
> (ii) on the death of a member or any person mentioned in paragraph (a) or in the form of an endowment insurance on the life of a member or such a person.

46. It also extends to the payment of a sum of money towards the expenses in connection with the death or funeral of any member or any person mentioned in section 2(a). Over the years, insurers have gradually taken over the business of friendly societies. It is expected that dedicated legislation pertaining to microinsurance will eventually usurp the ratio behind friendly societies and that this particular statute will eventually be repealed. Some long-term insurers still use the FSA to the extent that they assist existing societies in formalizing their business. They underwrite the risks and provide consumer education for the board members of these societies.

61. Act 25 of 1956.
62. Section 1 of the Friendly Societies Act.

II. Governmental Regulations

47. Legislative authority can also be delegated in terms of an Act of Parliament to a certain person or body of persons. Regulations may be made or issued by this conferral of delegated powers. Regulations are promulgated by Government Notices and are divided into (individual) regulations, sub-regulations and paragraphs. A cabinet Minister may be authorized to make regulations according to a prescribing statute. For example, the Minister of Trade and Industry in terms of the Consumer Protection Act 68 of 2008 (CPA) to pass regulations that carry the same weight as legislation regarding South African consumer agreements. The Minister may also empower or authorize another statutory body or person to make such regulations. The Policyholder Protection Rules (PPR) issued by the FSB serve as an example. Subordinate legislation must meet the following requirements in order to be valid and binding upon the community: (a) it must fall within the authority given to the specific subordinate legislator (otherwise it will be ultra vires); (b) it must be reasonable; (c) it must be impartial or unbiased; (d) it must be clear and certain; and (e) it must be promulgated, in other words published.

III. Regulation by Governmental Agencies

48. The FSB regulates the insurance industry. More specifically, enforcement measures are measures are provided for in Part II of Chapter VI of the FAIS Act. There are also other enforcement measures employed by the FSB and in the discussion that follows, these various actions are investigated.

49. The new Financial Sector Regulation Bill gives effect to the government decision in 2011 to shift to a Twin Peaks model of financial sector regulation for South Africa. Twin Peaks is a comprehensive and complete system for regulating the financial sector. It represents a decisive shift away from a fragmented regulatory approach to reduce the possibility of regulatory arbitrage or forum shopping and close gaps in the regulatory system. It is discussed extensively in the document: Implementing a Twin Peaks Model of Financial Regulation in South Africa (1 February 2013).[63] The idea is to separate prudential supervision from market conduct supervision. The prudential regulator will from part of the SARB and will be responsible for the prudential regulation and supervision of banks and insurers.

50. The market conduct regulator will aim to protect consumers of financial services and will promote confidence in the South African financial system. The prudential regulator's supervisory approach will be based on ten guidelines: (i) regulations will be designed to proactively identify and address possible market imperfections; (ii) regulations will mostly be principle-based; (iii) regulations will be aligned with international best practice; (iv) regulations will generally apply to financial institutions and their activities; (v) all activities or financial products that are consistent with the prescribed principles should be regarded as permissible unless the regulator specifies otherwise; (vi) registration, approval or licensing will be required before a person or institution can carry out specified regulated activities; (vii) the prudential

63. FSB, www.fsb.co.za, 7 Dec. 2017.

regulator will have the authority to set licensing, registration and approval criteria and reject applications that do not meet these requirements; (viii) the criteria for licensing, registration or granting approval will be consistent with those applied in prevailing legislation and supervisory practice; (ix) at the minimum, the registration, licensing or approval process will consist of an assessment of the ownership, structure and governance of an institution and its wider group; and (x) the prudential regulator will have the authority to implement timely corrective actions for regulation transgressions.[64]

51. The regulator will employ a variety of supervisory tools, such as on-site visits, reviewing compliance and other reports, 'mystery shopper' techniques where anonymous, independent observers posing as customers will test the quality of an institution's customer interactions and revised and enhanced reporting requirements.[65] In ensuring that regulatory principles are comprehensive and consistent, the market conduct regulator's regulatory and supervisory framework will aim to balance principles- and rules-based components.

52. Also being released is a discussion document '*Treating Customers Fairly in the Financial Sector: A Market Conduct Policy Framework for South Africa*' which proposes a comprehensive framework for how the market conduct regulator will operate, in order to ensure that financial institutions treat their customers fairly. The market conduct policy framework forms part of the Twin Peaks reform process, proposing a regulatory and supervisory framework for the new FSCA. Poor customer outcomes in South Africa's financial sector have highlighted the need for stronger oversight of how financial institutions conduct their business and treat their customers. To better protect customers, the financial sector must be held to higher standards than generic consumer protection, and standards must be applied consistently across the sector. As proposed in the policy documents, the various pieces of market conduct legislation applicable to the financial sector will be consolidated.

53. Principles-based components such as the duty to deliver TCF outcomes, will thus apply to the conduct of all regulated financial institutions. The six TCF outcomes that will form part of the new legislative framework are as follows:

(1) OUTCOME 1: Customers can be confident they are dealing with firms where TCF is central to the corporate culture.
(2) OUTCOME 2: Products and services marketed and sold in the retail market are designed to meet the needs of identified customer groups and are targeted accordingly.
(3) OUTCOME 3: Customers are provided with clear information and kept appropriately informed before, during and after point of sale.
(4) OUTCOME 4: Where advice is given, it is suitable and takes account of customer circumstances.
(5) OUTCOME 5: Products perform as firms have led customers to expect, and service is of an acceptable standard and as they have been led to expect.

64. Implementing a Twin Peaks Model of Financial Regulation in South Africa (1 Feb. 2013) 10.
65. Implementing a Twin Peaks Model of Financial Regulation in South Africa (1 Feb. 2013) 11.

(6) OUTCOME 6: Customers do not face unreasonable post-sale barriers imposed by firms to change product, switch providers, submit a claim or make a complaint.[66]

54. The law will also empower the FSCA to supervise institutions more intensively, and take strict corrective actions against financial institutions based on the breach of principles in addition to monitoring compliance with rules. The market conduct framework document also sets out proposals to support improved market conduct by better empowering financial customers. This includes improving the Ombud system so customers can easily and effectively lodge disputes against financial institutions, and refining financial education initiatives. It should be noted that SA also underwent a Financial Sector Assessment Program (FSAP) by the IMF this year, to assess the soundness of the financial sector in SA, and to assess compliance with global standards for banking, insurance and securities. The FSAP report is being released by the IMF as part of its Article IV report. The Financial Services Regulation Bill (FSRB) does not take into account the recommendations made in the FSAP, but will do so at the same time as public comments are incorporated. The revised third version of the FSRB is expected to be published for tabling in Parliament before the end of 2017. It is submitted that the current, rules-based framework will no doubt change. However, if one examines existing legislation, there is a good chance that one will find that many rules, both from common law and statutes, already support the six TCF Outcomes.

55. The above-mentioned amendments are *interim* measures, as a full review of both the LTIA and the STIA are underway. The aim is to give effect to the Solvency Assessment and Management Project ('SAM') framework for the South African insurance sector that is discussed under Solvency control below. The draft Bill was subject to consultation within the SAM framework, and is currently open for public comments.

56. As was indicated above,[67] the Insurance Bill now provides for a regulatory regime on microinsurance. This long overdue innovation is the result of the FSB's publication on the Policy Document on the South African Microinsurance Regulatory Framework on 28 July 2011.[68] According to the Policy Document, microinsurance refers to:

> Insurance that is accessed by the low-income population (also known as the mass market), provided by a variety of different providers and managed in accordance with generally accepted insurance practice.

The Policy Document proposed number of product features and standards, including:

- a microinsurance product should be a risk-only product;
- benefits should be provided on a sum assured or first loss basis;
- defined benefit caps;
- microinsurance policies should not exceed twelve months;

66. FSB proposed replacement of the PPR made under the LTIA, 1998 and STIA, 1998 – document supporting consultation (December 2016), www.fsb.co.za, 7 Dec. 2017.
67. Paragraph 39.
68. FSB, www.fsb.co.za, 7 Dec. 2017.

- microinsurance policies should certify initial and subsequent pricing;
- where policies are underwritten on a group basis, insurers should not be able to selectively cancel individual policies within the group;
- an actuarial technician should sign of initial pricing and subsequent price changes on microinsurance policies;
- microinsurers will have the discretion to underwrite policies on an individual or on a group basis;
- there will be a restriction or limitation of waiting periods;
- microinsurance products should prohibit exclusions for pre-existing conditions;
- policies should be simple and easy to understand and policy documentation must be provided in plain language;
- the client should have the right to a monetary benefit;
- all valid microinsurance claims should be paid within a period of forty-eight hours after receipt of all the documentation;
- cover will continue for one month after the due date of the premium and that the outstanding premium may be paid at any time during that month; however, if the premium is not paid within the month of grace, the cover will cease; the maximum period of grace will be six months.

57. Earlier attempts to introduce microinsurance legislation were halted by the implementation the twin peaks model of regulation. The idea was to ensure that new legislation on microinsurance should not only enable the informal sector to participate in the formal economy but also enable those who cannot afford traditional insurance to plan for adversarial events. It is now quite evident that the Insurance Bill has included provisions on microinsurance and that products that fall within this space will in future enjoy form part of the legislative framework for insurance. Only time will tell whether the legislation will be able to give effect to the ambitions that were set out by the Policy Document and whether it will in fact provide broader access to insurance products.

58. Enforcement measures in the insurance industry are in general provided for in Part II of Chapter VI of the FAIS Act. There are also other enforcement measures employed by the FSB and in the discussion that follows, these various actions are investigated.

59. Until the twin peaks model is implemented, section 9 empowers the Registrar to suspend or withdraw any licence (including the licence of a licensee under provisional or final suspension) at any time if the Registrar is satisfied, on the basis of available facts and information, that the licensee:

- no longer meets the requirements contemplated in section 8 of the FAIS Act;[69]
- did not, when applying for the licence, make a full disclosure of all relevant information to the Registrar, or furnished false or misleading information;
- has failed to comply with any other provision of this Act;[70] or
- is liable for payment of a levy under section 15A of the Financial Services Board Act, an amount or penalty under section 33(2) of the FAIS Act, a penalty under section 41(2) and (3) of the FAIS Act or an administrative sanction under section

69. Section 9(1)(a) of the FAIS Act.
70. Section 9(1)(b) of the FAIS Act.

6D(2) of the Financial Institutions (Protection of Funds) Act,[71] and has failed to pay the said levy, amount or administrative sanction and any interest in respect thereof.[72]

60. However, before suspending or withdrawing any licence, the Registrar may consult with any regulatory authority and must inform the licensee of the intention to suspend or withdraw. The Registrar must inform the licensee of the intention to suspend or withdraw and the grounds therefore and the Registrar should provide the licensee with a reasonable opportunity to make a submission in response to the anticipated suspension. In addition, the Registrar must also inform the licensee of the intended period of the suspension and any terms attached to the suspension. These terms may include a prohibition on concluding any new business by the licensee and as far as unfinished business is concerned, measures as the Registrar may determine which are aimed at the protection of the interests of clients of the affected licensee as well as terms aimed at the lifting of the suspension.[73]

61. The next step is for the Registrar to consider any response received from the licensee. A decision may only be made after the consideration of a response. If the licence is in fact suspended or withdrawn, there is a duty on the Registrar to make known the reasons for the suspension or withdrawal by publishing a notice in the Government Gazette.[74]

62. Section 9(3) of the Act provides for the provisional suspension or withdrawal of a licence where the Registrar 'is satisfied on reasonable grounds that substantial prejudice to clients or the general public may occur'. After a suspension, the Registrar must inform the licensee of the grounds for the suspension and also provide the licensee with a reasonable opportunity to respond thereto. This affords the licensee with an opportunity to furnish reasons for the lifting of the provisional suspension or withdrawal or the changing of the period and terms thereof. As with an ordinary suspension or withdrawal, the Registrar 'must give notice of the provisional suspension or withdrawal in the *Government Gazette*' and if necessary, by means of 'any other appropriate public media'.[75] The Registrar's next step is to consider the licensee's response as meant by section 9(3)(a). Depending on the response, the Registrar may elect to either lift the provisional suspension or render the suspension or withdrawal final. The licensee is informed of the decision and it is published in the *Government Gazette* and if necessary, by means of 'any other appropriate public media'.[76] Section 9(5) reiterates that the licensee concerned is for the purposes of the FAIS Act considered to be a person who is not authorized to act as an FSP during a provisional or final suspension. Furthermore, a person whose licence has been withdrawn under this section is debarred for a period specified by the Registrar from applying for a new licence.[77] However, section 9(6)(b) states that the Registrar may vary this period on good cause shown.

71. Act 28 of 2001.
72. Section 9(1)(d) of the FAIS Act.
73. Sections 9(2)(a)(i) and (ii) of the FAIS Act; Millard & Hattingh, 206.
74. Section 9(2)(c) and (d) of the FAIS Act; Millard & Hattingh, 206.
75. Section 9(3)(b) of the FAIS Act.
76. Section 9(4)(b) of the FAIS Act.
77. Section 9(6)(a) of the FAIS Act.

63. The FAIS Act has always been very clear on the Registrar's involvement in the process of surrender of an estate or winding-up of a company (FSP). Voluntary surrender or winding-up should be distinguished from compulsory sequestration in the case of an individual or compulsory liquidation in the case of a company or a close corporation.

64. For individuals or so-called natural persons who operate as an FSP, voluntary surrender is the process in terms of which a debtor himself or his representative applies to court for the surrender of his estate. A court will only accept the surrender of a natural person's (debtor's) estate if the estate is indeed insolvent, the debtor possesses sufficient property to defray the costs of sequestration from the free residue, and sequestration will be to the advantage of the creditors. The last requirement is stringent. The debtor must provide detailed information on his financial position and prove that there *will* be advantage to the creditors. The court must be satisfied that a debtor is bona fide and does not intend abusing the process in order to avoid his liabilities. In practice, a debtor needs to serve a copy of the court application on the Registrar. The Registrar then needs to ensure that the debtor has met all his liabilities to clients in terms of transactions the debtor had entered into which fall under the FAIS Act. Where a debtor failed to serve his application for voluntary surrender with the Registrar, or the application was served but then declared contrary to the FAIS Act, the result is that the voluntary surrender has no legal force.[78]

65. The FAIS Act also makes provision for a special resolution relating to the winding-up of a company who operates as an FSP. In terms of the 1973 Act (Old Companies Act, Act 61 of 1973) a voluntary winding-up could take place at the initiative of either the creditors or the members of the company.[79] The members could only engage in the voluntary winding-up of a company if the company was liquidated for a reason other than its insolvency. In the case of a voluntary winding-up by the creditors, the directors of the company had to provide a statement of the affairs of the company. This was submitted to the general meeting of the company convened for the purposes of passing the resolution for the winding-up. In addition to what the statute already required, the company also had to involve the Registrar in the proceedings in order to make sure that the Registrar was satisfied that no client (policyholder) would be prejudiced. Failing this, no special resolution would have any effect.

66. Similarly, a close corporation could not be wound up voluntarily by its members or creditors without adhering to section 38 of the FAIS Act. This section provided in the final instance for the voluntary closure of a business. It is submitted that this fourth category refers to any business form that is not a one-man proprietorship, a partnership, a company or a close corporation. The message in the section was clear, namely that the Registrar had the power to intervene in any voluntary sequestration, winding-up or closure of a business where clients were likely to be prejudiced. Section 38, as it stands, singles out voluntary procedures, as opposed to the compulsory

78. Section 3(1) of the Insolvency Act 24 of 1936; *Ex parte Greeff* 1940 (2) PH C80 (K); *Ex parte Deemter* 1962 (2) SA 228 (OK); *Ex parte Harmse* 2005(1) SA at 323 (N); *Ex parte Van Heerden* 1923 CPD at 279; *Mindel v. Shaer* 1937 TPD at 378; *Ex parte Collins* 1927 WLD at 172; *Hillhouse v. Stott*; *Freban Investments (Pty) Ltd v. Itzkin; and Botha v. Botha* 1990 (4) SA 580 (W).

79. F.H.I. Cassim (ed.) *Contemporary Company Law* (Juta 2012).

surrender of an individual's estate and the liquidation of companies and close corporations by the court. Because it was not only voluntary procedures that were open to abuse it was necessary to extend the powers of the Registrar to enable him to play a more pro-active role in sequestrations and liquidations in the interests of policyholders.[80]

67. The new section 38B entitled 'Application by registrar for sequestration or liquidation' of the FAIS Act now provides as follows:

(1) If the registrar, after an on-site visit in terms of section 4(5) or an inspection in terms of the Inspection of Financial Institutions Act, 1998 (Act No. 80 of 1998), considers that the interests of the clients of a financial services provider or of members of the public so require, the registrar may apply to the Court for the sequestration or liquidation of that provider, whether or not the provider is solvent, in accordance with—

(a) the Insolvency Act, 1936 (Act No. 24 of 1936);
(b) the Companies Act;
(c) the Close Corporations Act, 1984 (Act No. 69 of 1984); or
(d) the law under which that provider is incorporated.

(2) In deciding an application contemplated in subsection (1), the Court—

(a) may take into account whether sequestration or liquidation of the financial services provider concerned is reasonably necessary—
(i) in order to protect the interests of the clients of the provider; and
(ii) for the integrity and stability of the financial sector;
(b) may make an order concerning the manner in which claims may be proved by clients of the financial services provider concerned; and
(c) shall appoint as trustee or liquidator a person nominated by the registrar.

68. It is submitted that the power of the Registrar to become involved in the sequestration or liquidation of an FSP not only has the potential of safeguarding the interests of policyholders but also of warning FSPs not to abuse sequestration or liquidation proceedings in order to avoid being liable to creditors of FSPs.

69. Section 38C adds yet another remedy to the Registrar's existing enforcement measures. The proposed section 38C reads as follows:

(1) The registrar may, in order to ensure compliance with or to prevent a contravention of this Act, issue a directive to any person or persons to whom the provisions of this Act apply.
(2) A directive issued in terms of subsection (1) may –

(a) apply generally; or
(b) be limited in its application to a particular person or category of persons.

80. Millard & Hattingh, 58, 207.

(3) A directive issued in terms of subsection (1) takes effect on the date determined by the registrar in the directive.
(4) In the event of a departure from section 3(2) or 4(1), (2) or (3) of the Promotion of Administrative Justice Act (Act No. 3 of 2000), the directive must include a statement to that effect and the reasons for such departure.
(5) The registrar must, where a directive is issued to ensure the protection of the public in general, publish the directive in the *Gazette* and any other media that the registrar deems appropriate.[81]

70. To allow the Registrar to issue a directive is to some extent very invasive. It is however suggested that such directives may only be issued in order to protect the public in general and not for vindictive or any other unlawful reasons. As with any other decision, the Registrar must apply his mind and act bona fide in using his powers in terms of the proposed section 38C.

71. Section 8(10) stipulates that where a provider is a corporate or unincorporated body, a trust or a partnership, the provider must at all times be satisfied that every director, member, trustee or partner of the provider, who is not a key individual in the provider's business, complies with the requirements in respect of personal character qualities of honesty and integrity as contemplated in section 8(1)(a). In addition, a provider has a duty to inform the Registrar of the appointment of a new director, member, trustee or partner and also furnish the Registrar 'with such information on the matter as the Registrar may reasonably require'.

72. Section 8(1)(b) stipulates that if the Registrar is satisfied that a director, member, trustee or partner does not comply with the requirements as set out in section 8(1)(a), the Registrar may suspend or withdraw the licence of the provider in accordance with the provisions of section 9. The requirements in section 8(1)(a) are simply personal character qualities of honesty and integrity. Therefore, should a director, member, trustee or partner have a criminal record that involves conviction on charges of fraud, theft or other crimes that involve an element of dishonesty, it may jeopardize the whole operation to such an extent that a licence can be suspended or withdrawn.[82]

73. Section 14A empowers the Registrar to debar a person, including a representative, at any time and for a specific period from rendering financial services. The Registrar may use this section in two instances, namely when the person to be debarred does not meet or no longer meets personal character qualities of honesty and integrity or where a person has contravened or failed to comply with any provisions of the FAIS Act.[83] According to section 14A(2), the provisions of section 9(2) regarding the suspension of a licence, applies with the necessary changes to the debarment of a person in terms of section 14A(1). Furthermore, an authorized FSP must within a period of five days after being informed by the Registrar of the debarment of a representative or key individual, remove the name of that representative or key individual from the register. The Registrar may also publish a notice of such a debarment and

81. Millard & Hattingh, 58.
82. Millard & Hattingh, 36, 96, 211.
83. Millard & Hattingh, 109.

the reasons therefore as well as the lifting thereof in the *Government Gazette* or by means of any other appropriate public media.[84]

74. An example of debarment is found in the Enforcement Committee case of *The Registrar of Financial Services Providers v. Clifford Mey.*[85] In April 2008, an institution named Joy Finance (Pty) Ltd (Joy Finance) was duly authorized by the Registrar of Financial Services Providers (the Registrar) to render financial services in accordance with sections 1 and 8 of the FAIS Act. The key individual was Mr Anthony Lubbe. On 15 April 2008 the Registrar withdrew Joy Finance's licence to act as a FSP and Joy Finance was debarred from applying for another licence for five years. Joy Finance then entered into a 'strategic alliance' with Impact Corporate Brokers CC (Impact), an authorized FSP. This agreement entailed the transfer of Joy Finance's clients to Impact. In October 2008, the respondent was appointed as a representative of impact and mandated to render financial services on behalf of Impact to clients, including the former Joy Finance clients. On 1 August 2011 the Registrar debarred Lubbe from rendering financial services following his conviction on two charges of fraud. These two convictions of the Boksburg Regional Court were overturned by the South Gauteng High Court. In the meanwhile, between August 2011 and April 2014, while the respondent was a representative of Impact, he conducted financial services business with Joy Finance and Lubbe while he was aware of the fact that neither Lubbe nor Joy Finance were authorized to render financial services to clients. The respondent's conduct constitutes a contravention of section 7(3) of the FAIS Act and section 2 of the General Code of Conduct for Authorized Financial Services Providers and Representatives (GCC). The respondent admitted this contravention and paid a penalty of ZAR 800,000. Because a conviction of fraud by a criminal court would have affected Lubbe's honesty and integrity, the Registrar was entitled to debar Lubbe. Even where these convictions were overturned by the High Court, the fact remains that the respondent conducted business with a debarred person.

75. Section 33 empowers the Registrar to approach the courts in the event of a person having contravened or having failed to comply with any provision of the Act or where a person is likely to contravene or not to comply with the FAIS Act. However, before the Registrar goes to such an extreme, he will first use his powers in terms of section 4 of the FAIS Act or Regulation 19. Section 4 gives the Registrar a wide range of powers. For instance, section 4(4) stipulates as follows:

> If there is reason to believe that a person is contravening or failing to comply with, or has contravened or failed to comply with, a provision of this Act, the Registrar may—
>
> (a) By notice direct that person—

84. Millard & Hattingh, 211.
85. Case No. 16/2014.

(i) To furnish the Registrar within a specified period with any specified information or documents in the possession or under the control of that person and which relate to the subject-matter of such contravention or failure;

(ii) To appear before the Registrar at a specified time and place for the purpose of discussing such matter with the Registrar; or

(iii) To make arrangements for the discharge of all or any part of that person's obligations in terms of this Act;

(b) If satisfied that in the case concerned significant prejudice or damage to clients has occurred or may occur, apply to a Court for an order restraining such person from continuing business or dealing with the funds or other property held by such person on behalf of clients or other persons, pending the institution by the Registrar of an application or action contemplated in section 33 (1) and (2), or the exercising by the Registrar of such other legal remedy as may be available to the Registrar;

(c) If prejudice or damage may have occurred to a client, refer the matter, together with any information or documentation in the Registrar's possession, to the Office to be dealt with as a complaint by the client concerned.

76. Section 4(5) authorizes the Registrar to conduct on-site visits to investigate compliance with the FAIS Act. Both sections 4(4) and 4(5) provide the Registrar with an enforcement tool that, if used properly, is effective in order to ensure compliance, with the result that it is only in exceptional cases that it would be necessary for the Registrar to use the civil remedies as contemplated in section 33.

77. Regulation 19 deals with the powers of the Registrar to call for information. It stipulates that 'any authorized FSP and any particular nominee company or independent nominee referred to in Chapter V must furnish the Registrar with such information regarding the relevant shareholders, directors, trustees and senior employees, or regarding their operations, as the Registrar may from time to time in writing reasonably require from any of them'.

78. Where the Registrar has exhausted all his internal remedies and this did not have the desired effect, section 33 comes into operation. The type of relief sought will first and foremost be a court order restraining such person from committing such act or omission or from committing it in future. In addition, the Registrar can request the court to 'take such remedial steps as the Court deems necessary to rectify the consequences of the act or omission, including consequences which prejudiced or may prejudice any client'. In terms of procedural law, the remedy that will restrain a person from doing something is a prohibitory interdict. Generally, in order to succeed with such an interdict, an applicant must prove that there is an act by the respondent or a failure to act positively, that this act or failure is wrongful and that there is no other remedy available to the applicant. When asking the court to order the respondent to take remedial steps, this may include an order to compel the respondent to pay back money that had been taken from clients. Section 33 may only be used if the Registrar is convinced that non-compliance has occurred and such conviction is based on the available facts and information.

79. Another remedy is found in section 6(1) of the Financial Institutions (Protection of Funds) Act. This section is phrased in wider terms, and it stipulates the following:

> Powers of Registrar
>
> (1) The Registrar may institute proceedings in the High Court having jurisdiction in order to—

(a) Discharge any duty or responsibility imposed on the Registrar in terms of any law;
(b) Compel any institution to comply with any law or to cease contravening a law;
(c) Compel any institution to comply with a lawful request, directive or instruction made, issued or given by the Registrar under a law; or
(d) Obtain a declaratory order on any point of law relating to any law or to the business of an institution.

80. This particular Act also provides for prior investigations by the Registrar as well as the publication of statements indicating non-compliance by the persons under investigation. This means that the Registrar has the power to act immediately if there is reason to believe that an insurer is conducting business in a way that is harmful to policyholders.

81. Section 34 of the FAIS Act empowers the Registrar to declare a particular business practice undesirable either for all authorized FSPs, a category of such providers or a specific provider. The FAIS Act does not define 'undesirable practices' but it contains a number of principles that should guide the Registrar in declaring a specific business practice undesirable. In the first instance, the Registrar should make a declaration if the practice concerned, directly or indirectly, has or is likely to have the effect of harming the relations between authorized FSPs or any category of such providers, or any such provider, and policyholders or the general public, unreasonably prejudicing any policyholder; deceiving any policyholder; or unfairly affecting any policyholder.[86]

82. A circumvention of a code of conduct is an example of a business practice that will be undesirable or irregular. The procedure for making such a declaration may be summarized as follows:

- The Registrar must by notice in the *Gazette* publish an intention to make the declaration and reasons therefore must be given;

86. Section 34(1), (2)(a)(i)–(iv) and (b).

- In the notice, interested persons should be invited to make written representations to the Registrar within twenty-one days after the date of publication of the notice;
- On or after the date of publication of the notice, the authorized FSPs may not carry on the business practice concerned;
- Should an authorized FSP carry on business in contravention of the notice, the Registrar may direct such provider to rectify to the satisfaction of the Registrar anything which was caused by or arose out of the carrying on of the business practice concerned; and where the Registrar directs an authorized services provider to rectify anything, it should be done within sixty days after the issuing of the directive.[87]

83. Section 36 of the FAIS Act states in no uncertain terms that any person who commits any act listed in sections 36(a)–(d) is guilty of an offence and is on conviction liable to a fine of a maximum of ZAR 1,000,000 or to imprisonment for a period not more than ten years or to both a fine and imprisonment. First, these acts include a contravention or failure to comply with the following provisions, namely:

- That no provider shall do business unless he is not properly authorized to do so.
- That a licensee must display a certified copy of the licence in a prominent and durable manner within every business premises of the licensee, ensure that a reference to the fact that such a licence is held is contained in all business documentation, advertisements and other promotional material and ensure that the licence is at all times immediately or within a reasonable time available for production to any person requesting proof of licensed status under authority of a law or for the purpose of entering into a business relationship with the licensee.
- That a provider who is a corporate or unincorporated body, a trust or a partnership must at all times be satisfied that every director, member, trustee or partner of the provider, who is not a key individual in the provider's business, complies with the requirements in respect of personal character qualities of honesty and integrity.
- That representatives will comply with the qualifications criteria as set out in section 13(1) and that authorized FSPs will comply with section 13(2).
- That an authorized FSP must ensure that any representative of the provider who no longer complies with the requirements referred to in section 13(2)(a) or has contravened or failed to comply with any provision of the FAIS Act, is prohibited by such provider from rendering any new financial service. Effectively, this means that the FSP must withdraw any authority to act on behalf of the provider, and that the representative's name, and the names of the key individuals of the representative, are removed from the register referred to in section 13(3).
- That a compliance officer or, in the absence of such officer, the authorized FSP concerned, must submit reports to the Registrar in the prescribed way for the different categories of compliance officers, after consultation with the Advisory Committee;
- That authorized FSPs will maintain certain records.
- That an authorized FSP must cause annual statements to be audited and reported by an external auditor approved by the Registrar.

87. Millard & Hattingh, 59, 205, 215.

- That the auditor of an authorized FSP must report to and inform the Registrar in writing of any irregularity or suspected irregularity in the conduct or the affairs of the authorized Financial Services Provider concerned of which the auditor became aware in performing functions as auditor and which, in the opinion of the auditor, is material.
- That an authorized FSP concerned may not, on or after the date of the publication of a notice declaring a particular business practice undesirable, carry on the business practice concerned.
- That an authorized FSP who is directed to rectify anything pertaining to the carrying on of an undesirable business practice in contravention of a notice must rectify to the satisfaction of the Registrar anything which was caused by or arose out of the carrying on of the particular undesirable business practice within sixty days after such direction is issued.
- That any person deliberately makes a misleading, false or deceptive statement in any application in terms of this Act.
- That any person provides an appointed auditor or compliance officer information which is false or misleading or conceals any material fact in the execution of duties imposed by the FAIS Act.
- That any person in any way declares, pretends, gives out, maintains or professes to be a person who is authorized to render financial services to clients on the basis that he is appointed or mandated as a representative by an authorized Financial Services Provider in terms of the FAIS Act where this is in fact not the case.[88]

84. According to the FSB's website:

> [T]he enforcement Committee is an administrative body established to adjudicate on all alleged contraventions of legislation, regulations, codes of conduct, etc. administered by the Financial Services Board. The Committee may impose unlimited penalties, compensation orders and cost orders. Such orders are enforceable as if it was a judgment of the Supreme Court of South Africa.[89]

85. Since 1 November 2008, the jurisdiction of the Enforcement Committee extends to all the industries that fall under the FSB's regulatory umbrella, the FSB Enforcement Committee was established on by an amendment of the Financial Institutions (Protection of Funds) Act. In short, all enforcement action is the task of the enforcement committee. This committee is an administrative body established to adjudicate on all alleged contraventions of legislation, regulations, codes of conduct, etc. administered by the FSB. The Committee may impose unlimited penalties, compensation orders and cost orders. Such orders are enforceable as if it was a judgment of the High Court of South Africa. Section 10A of the Financial Services Board Act determines that the enforcement committee 'must consist of sufficient persons with appropriate knowledge and experience so as to enable the committee to perform the functions entrusted to it by this Act or any other law' and 'must include advocates or

---

88. Millard & Hattingh, 215–217; J. Moolman, C. Pillai, N.N. Bam & J. Appasamy, *Financial Advisory and Intermediary Services Guide* 201, 247–248, 272–273 (LexisNexis 2010).
89. FSB, www.fsb.co.za, 5 Dec. 2017.

attorneys with at least ten years' experience'. In addition, the committee may include a judge. The enforcement committee must be chaired by an advocate, attorney or a judge. The chairperson is appointed by the board and a deputy chairperson or chairpersons may also be appointed.

86. The proceedings of the committee against a respondent do not exclude the possibility of a civil action. Provided that the aggrieved party can prove the elements of his action, it is also possible to obtain a judgment against the respondent in a civil case.[90]

87. The Appeal Board is constituted in terms of section 26 of the FSB Act. The Board was re-established under the Financial Laws General Amendment Act.[91] Section 26A and 26B of this particular Act now deals with the Appeal Board, its panels and appeal proceedings. The Minister of Finance decides on the amount of members that should serve on the Appeal Board. The chairperson of the Appeal Board must be an advocate or an attorney with at least ten years' experience or a retired judge. Other members must have expert knowledge of the financial services industry. As far as its legal status is concerned, the Appeal Board is an independent tribunal comprising members who are not employees of the FSB and also do not participate in the financial services industry. Members serve for a term of three years and can be re-elected.

88. According to the FSB's website, the following persons may appeal to the Board, namely:

- Any person who feels aggrieved by a decision of the FSB's executive officer.
- Any person who feels aggrieved by a determination of the FAIS Ombud made in terms of section 28 of the FAIS Act.
- Any person who feels aggrieved by a decision of an exchange, central securities depository and claims officer as contemplated by the Securities Services Act.
- Any other person who feels aggrieved by a decision made under a law which provides for an appeal against that decision to the Appeal Board.[92]

89. The actual lodging of an appeal involves lodging a notice with the secretary of the Board within thirty days of the person becoming aware of, or ought to have become aware of, the decision. The regulations promulgated in terms of section 26B(19) of the Financial Services Board Act must be read with the Appeal Board's guidelines on proceedings.

90. It is not always clear where the dividing line lies between administrative decisions and judicial decisions. For an explanation of the meaning of administrative decisions, one should start with legislative definitions. Section 33 of the Constitution provides as follows:

(1) Everyone has the right to administrative action that is lawful, reasonable and procedurally fair.
(2) Everyone whose rights have been adversely affected by administrative action has the right to be given written reasons.

---

90. Millard & Hattingh, 212.
91. Act 45 of 2013.
92. FSB, www.fsb.co.za, 5 Dec. 2017.

(3) National legislation must be enacted to give effect to these rights, and must:

(a) provide for the review of administrative action by a court or, where appropriate, an independent and impartial tribunal;
(b) impose a duty on the state to give effect to the rights in subsections (1) and (2); and
(c) promote an efficient administration.

91. What exactly is meant by 'administrative action'? For purposes of the Constitution, it is the exercise of public power by all organs of state except the following, namely the legislatures (national, provincial, local) when exercising their legislative functions; the judiciary, when exercising judicial functions, the President when exercising the constitutional powers, and the cabinet and provincial cabinets.[93]

92. The subsequent Promotion of Administrative Justice Act[94] (PAJA) elaborates on the constitutional definition. It defines 'administrative action' as follows:

'Administrative action' means any decision taken, or any failure to take a decision, by–

(a) An organ of state, when –

(i) Exercising a power in terms of the Constitution or a provincial constitution; or

(ii) Exercising a public power or performing a public function in terms of any legislation; or

(b) A natural or juristic person, other than an organ of state, when exercising a public power or performing a public function in terms of an empowering provision, which adversely affects the rights of any person and which has a direct, external legal effect.

93. In short, an action will qualify as administrative action under PAJA if it is:

- a decision;
- of an administrative nature;
- made under an empowering provision;
- by an organ of state or a private person when exercising a public power;
- that adversely affects rights;
- that has direct external legal effect; and

93. De Waal & Curry, 651; 705–706.
94. Act 3 of 2000.

– that is not specifically excluded.

94. When the FSB revokes the licence of an FSP, it falls squarely within the meaning of 'administrative action'. The structures that are currently in place within the FSB provides adequately for just administrative action. It is evident from the discussion in this chapter that the general trend in terms of the financial legislation that falls under the FSB is to regulate in such a way that consumers are protected, but also with a view to the rights of providers and representatives to earn a living and to be commercially active. Of course, the Appeal Board acts as the ultimate institution for anyone who seeks justice and the rule that states that an application for review to the High Court is possible, re-enforces the disgruntled complainant's right to have access to courts as is intended by section 34 of the Constitution.

95. The case discussed in paragraph 72 above, *The Registrar of Financial Services Providers v. Clifford Mey* (Case No. 16/2014) is an example of an enforcement committee case.

96. The Registrar may at any time amend or withdraw the conditions and restrictions imposed on a licence. Such an amendment or withdrawal can be on the Registrar's own initiative or upon request of the Financial Services Provider. More specifically, section 9 empowers the Registrar to suspend or withdraw any licence at any time if the Registrar is satisfied, on the basis of available facts and information, that the licensee no longer meets the requirements contemplated in section 8 of the FAIS Act (section 9(1)(a)) or that the licence, when applying for the licence, failed to make a full disclosure of all relevant information to the Registrar, or furnished false or misleading information (section 9(1)(b) of the FAIS Act). Further grounds for suspension or withdrawal include where the licensee has failed to comply with any other provision of the FAIS Act or if the licensee is liable for payment of a levy, a penalty or an administrative sanction and he or she has failed to pay the said levy, amount or administrative sanction and any interest in respect thereof. The conviction on two counts of fraud would have prompted the registrar to withdraw Mr Lubbe's licence on the grounds that he was no longer fit and proper to act as a Financial Services Provider. The extensive fit and proper requirements deal with those individual characteristics of honesty and integrity, competency, operational ability and financial soundness. Here, a conviction of fraud by a criminal court would have affected Mr Lubbe's honesty and integrity and would have prompted the registrar to withdraw his licence. Even where these convictions were overturned by the High Court, the fact remains that the respondent conducted business with a person who did not hold a valid licence at the time.

IV. Private International Law

97. Foreign law is not always relevant because a company must be registered and incorporated in terms of the Company Law of South Africa before such company can conduct insurance business in the country. In principle, it is thus only in matters concerning marine insurance that a dispute pertaining to the jurisdiction of a South African court could become relevant. If there is no conflict of laws, a South African high court will exercise its admiralty jurisdiction. A recent case that serves as an example is *Viking Inshore Fishing (Pty) Ltd v. Mutual and Federal Insurance Company Ltd.*[95]

98. The laws that govern the insurance contract are usually determined by agreement between the parties to the insurance contract, or by the general rules that apply to a conflict of laws in respect of contracts. According to the principles of South African private international law, matters of procedure are governed by the domestic law of the country in which the relevant proceedings are instituted (the *lex fori*). On the other hand, matters of substantive law are governed by the law that applies to the underlying transaction or occurrence (the *lex causae*).

99. The only statutory provision that exists on the jurisdiction on matters pertaining to insurance can be found in section 59(1) of the STIA. It provides that any claim against a Lloyd's underwriter under a South African short-term insurance policy will be cognizable by any competent South African court.

South Africa is not party to any treaty regarding the reciprocal enforcement of foreign commercial court judgments, as opposed to foreign arbitral awards, as the issue is adequately dealt with by South African statutory and common law. The Enforcement of Foreign Civil Judgments Act 32 of 1988 which is not based on reciprocity is uniformly applied in the Republic.

100. Foreign judgments cannot always be enforced in South Africa. Foreign money judgments are frequently enforced in South Africa yet foreign judgments relating to property situated in South Africa will not be enforced because the foreign court would not have jurisdiction over immoveable property situated in South Africa. A foreign judgment relating to moveable property will be recognized in South Africa if the moveable property was within the foreign court's jurisdiction at the commencement of the action, when determining the basis of the foreign court's jurisdiction. Foreign judgments ordering specific performance are enforceable in South Africa if effect can be given to them in South Africa. Similarly, foreign permanent injunctions are enforceable in South Africa if the act sought to be restrained is due to take place or is taking place in South Africa or where the person sought to be restrained is present in South Africa. South African courts will enforce a foreign judgment if certain requirements, based largely on the Roman-Dutch common law, are met. The court in *Jones v. Krok* 1995(1) SA 677(A) set out the requirements as follows: (a) the foreign court must have had international competence as determined by South African law; (b) the judgment must be final and conclusive and must not have become superannuated; (c) the enforcement of the judgment must not be contrary to South African public policy (which includes the rules of natural justice); (d) the judgment must not have been obtained by fraudulent means; (e) the judgment must not involve the enforcement of a penal or revenue law of the foreign state; and finally that (f) enforcement must not be precluded by the Protection of Businesses Act 99 of 1978. The foreign court must have had international competence as determined in terms of South African law.[96]

101. In determining the jurisdiction of a foreign court, the judgment of the Appeal Court in *Richman v. Benn-Tovim* 2007(2) SA 237 (SCA) confirmed that a

95. Case No. AC 22/07 of 17 Oct. 2014 (WC).
96. R. Wakefield, *Werksmans Attorneys in Enforcement of Foreign Judgments in 28 Jurisdictions Worldwide* (Mark Moedritzer and Kay C Whittaker eds, Law Business Research Ltd 2012).

foreign court would have international competence only on two grounds, namely the residence of the defendant in the jurisdiction of the foreign court or his or her submission to its jurisdiction. To vest jurisdiction by residence in South African law requires a degree of permanence, and a South African court will examine at all relevant facts and circumstances to determine that degree. A corporation would be deemed to be resident in the foreign court's jurisdiction if it has established a place of business there. This is the case where an insurer complies with the requirements and authorized to do insurance business in this country. Submission to the foreign court's jurisdiction can also be by way of agreement or by conduct. A South African court will not re-examine the merits of the case leading to the foreign judgment in the enforcement thereof, notwithstanding conflict with any local judgment or a judgment in any other country.

V. Jurisdiction

102. The primary function of the courts is to administer justice and not to create rules of law. In a common law country however, courts are confronted with an issue that is not provided for by either the legislator or the common law. In such a case the courts may, through the judge's decision, create new rules of law.

103. The structure and jurisdiction of South African courts in accordance with the Constitution is the following in order of highest precedence: (a) The Constitutional Court; (b) The Supreme Court of Appeal; (c) The High Courts; (d) The Magistrates' Courts; and (e) Other courts specially instituted by Parliamentary legislation. The Constitutional Court, Supreme Court of Appeal and High Courts are colloquially referred to as the 'higher courts', whereas the Magistrates' Courts constitute the 'lower courts'.

104. The Constitutional Court has the highest authority yet only pertaining to constitutional matters in South Africa. The seat of this court is in Johannesburg, Gauteng. The Supreme Court of Appeal is the highest court for all other matters. This court is not a court of first instance and is purely a Court of Appeal. As it is not a court of first instance, a plaintiff must first approach one of the other courts for a decision before he can appeal to the Supreme Court of Appeal (previously known as the Appellate Division or Appeal Court). This court has its seat in Bloemfontein and has jurisdiction over all matters in the country taken on appeal.

105. Jurisdiction of the High Courts is determined by the Supreme Court Act of 1959. The High Courts can adjudicate on both criminal and civil matters. The fourteen seats of the High Court of South Africa are situated in Bisho (Eastern Cape High Court Bisho), Bloemfontein (Free State High Court), Cape Town (Western Cape High Court), Durban (Kwazulu-Natal High Court Durban), Grahamstown (Eastern Cape High Court Grahamstown), Johannesburg (South Gauteng High Court), Kimberley (Northern Cape High Court), Mafikeng (North-west High Court), Mthatha (Eastern Cape High Court Mthatha), Pietermaritzburg (Kwa-Zulu Natal High Court Pietermaritzburg), Port Elizabeth (Eastern Cape High Court Port Elizabeth), Pretoria (Northern Gauteng High Court), Thohoyandou (Limpopo High Court) and in Polokwane (the Polokwane Circuit Court of the North Gauteng High Court).[97]

97. http://www.judiciary.org.za, 8 Dec. 2017.

106. In a civil case a person institutes action against another by way of application or action. If the applicant or plaintiff proves his case on a balance of probabilities the court may grant any claim, application, interdict or declaratory order that may be sought.

107. The whole of South Africa is divided into magisterial districts and regions that are served by the respective magistrates' courts. A district magistrate's court serves a specific district and a regional magistrate's court serves a specific region. A regional court covers a broader area of jurisdiction than a district court. The civil jurisdiction of these courts is limited to a maximum amount of ZAR 100,000 for a district court and ZAR 300,000 for a regional court. The parties may in general institute action for higher amounts if they consent to the court's jurisdiction.

108. In criminal matters a district court may adjudicate on any crime except murder, high treason and rape. This court's criminal jurisdiction is limited to a maximum fine of ZAR 60,000 and/or a maximum term of imprisonment of three years. A regional court can try any matter except high treason (which may only be tried by higher courts), and its jurisdiction is limited to a maximum fine of ZAR 300,000 and/or a term of imprisonment of fifteen years.

109. There are a number of other specialized courts created by statute, such as Special Court for the Adjudication of Tax Appeals, Equality Courts and the Water Tribunal. Some of these courts have the status of a High Court (such as the Tax Court) and some have the status of a lower court. An example of a special lower court is the Small Claims Courts, where civil claims not exceeding the amount of ZAR 15,000 may be heard on behalf of natural persons only. Legal representation is not allowed in the Small Claims Courts.[98]

110. Appeals from the lower and other courts are heard in the relevant provincial division of the High Court. A judgment by a single judge in a High Court matter may also be taken on appeal to a so-called full bench of the same High Court. The matter is then heard by three judges in the same High Court. From the High Court a party may then appeal to the Supreme Court of Appeal. The Constitutional Court is the final court of appeal on all matters that the court consents to hear if it is in the interests of justice, and not only on constitutional matters.[99]

111. Pertaining to marine insurance, the law and practice of admiralty in South Africa is regulated by the Admiralty Jurisdiction Regulation Act of 1983 as amended with effect from 1 July 1992 ('the Admiralty Act'). Only the High Court of South Africa is able to exercise admiralty jurisdiction. The definition of a maritime claim in the Admiralty Act effectively covers all causes of action relating to ships and the carriage of cargo. The definition is wide enough to cover matters which are ancillary to shipping matters such as related insurance claims as it refers to 'Any other matter which by virtue of its nature or subject matter is a marine or maritime matter, the meaning of the expression marine or maritime matter not being limited by reason of the matters set forth in the preceding paragraphs … .' Pursuant to the Admiralty Act, with certain exceptions, every provincial, local and circuit local division of the High Court has jurisdiction to hear and determine any maritime claim irrespective of the place where it arose, of the place of registration of the ship concerned or of the residence,

98. Government Gazette. Latest: G 37450 RG 10153 GN 185, 18 Mar. 2014.
99. Chapter 7 of the Superior Courts Act 10 of 2013.

domicile or nationality of its owner. The area of jurisdiction of any High Court includes the portion of the territorial waters of South Africa adjacent to the coastline of its area of jurisdiction. The territorial waters are those within 12 nautical miles of the coastline. It is only in respect of a limited category of claims that an inland division of the High Court (i.e., one which is not contiguous to the sea) will be able to exercise admiralty jurisdiction. These claims are restricted basically to agreements concluded within the area of jurisdiction of the inland division (e.g., for the sale of a ship, a charter party or when procuring a policy of marine insurance).

112. Because the doctrine of precedent (or stare decisis) is applied in South Africa, certain courts create a precedent through their decisions that has to be followed by other courts. This doctrine has the effect that as soon as a legal principle is laid down by a court, judges of the same court; and those in courts of a lower order who are subordinate to that court have to follow this precedent.

113. A decision will only create a precedent if it was laid down as the *ratio decidendi*, or reason, for the specific decision. Where the court merely gives its opinion or makes a passing remark, this is called an obiter dictum, and does not create a precedent. The effect of the doctrine is that the Supreme Court of Appeal is only bound by its own decisions and those handed down by the Constitutional Court on constitutional matters. These courts may deviate from a previous decision if they are convinced that it was wrongly decided. High Courts are bound by decisions of the Supreme Court of Appeal and by their own decisions unless they are convinced that their own previous decision was wrong. A single judge is bound to a decision of two or more judges (a full-bench decision) of his own division. Lower courts are bound to the decisions of the higher courts, but not to their own decisions.

114. Reportable decisions of the higher courts are published monthly in the law reports to facilitate access to the decisions. In these reports, a decision is referred to in the following manner; the reference to the case of *Barkhuizen v. Napier*[100] reflects the following: the name of the plaintiff, applicant or appellant; the name of the defendant; the year in which the decision is reported; the volume for the year; the fact that it is a South African decision 'SA'; the page number in the law report (if published in hard copy); and finally the identification of the court that handed down the judgment.

§4. Dispute Settlement and Arbitration

115. Regardless of whether a prospective policyholder deals with the insurance company directly or whether he uses the services of an advisor or intermediary, there are plenty of opportunities of misunderstandings that may lead to litigation. For many clients problems only arise at claim stage. Litigation is expensive and that is why policyholders and beneficiaries may want to pursue alternative dispute resolution procedures. This is the reason insurers have developed voluntary ombudsmen in the long-term and short-term insurance industries. This provides claimants with the option of finding a solution outside the formal court system. In the insurance industry these ombudsmen are regulated and funded by the industry. Before these alternative dispute

100. 2007 5 SA 323(CC).

resolution mechanisms are discussed, the claims procedure will be discussed very briefly.[101]

116. In short-term insurance, the basic obligations of an insurer is to indemnify an insured against a loss proximately caused by the risks insured against. A claim vests in the insured when there is a valid contract of insurance; any suspensive conditions must have been fulfilled; the risk insured against should have materialized; the insured must have suffered a loss; and the loss must have been proximately caused by the risk insured against. The insured must prove that there was an insurable interest prior to the materialization of the risk and that the interest had been damaged. In addition, the insured must prove the extent of the damage or impairment and that the loss falls within the ambit of the contract of insurance.[102] In *Tarring Corporation CC v. New National Assurance Company Limited*[103] the policy contained a clause that stated that the loss was excluded in terms of exclusion 17, which states that: 'The insurers shall not be liable for loss or damage due to absconsion.' The crisp legal question was whether the plaintiff had breached the policy conditions by not taking reasonable precautions to prevent the theft of the machine, and whether such breach entitled the defendant to repudiate the claim. On the facts of the particular case the court was satisfied that the policyholder did not in fact abandon the machine but did take the necessary precautions, with the result that the insurer had to pay for the loss of the machine due to theft.

117. For long-term insurance, the basic obligations of a long-term insurer is to pay the sum insured on the occurrence of an event such as death which is a once-off occurrence or the payment of periodic amounts in the instance of a disability event such as the loss of the insured's eyesight. A claim vests in the insured if there is a valid contract of insurance, if any suspensive conditions have been fulfilled, if the risk insured against have materialized, if the insured have suffered a loss and if the loss was proximately caused by the risk insured against and such loss refers to non-patrimonial loss. Certain forms of long-term insurance are not 'risk-only' products and are use as savings vehicles. In those instances, a claim vests upon the maturity of the policy.[104]

118. The moment a policyholder or other interested party alleges that a claim is due and payable, claims procedures are set into motion. Where a claim is not settled, a disgruntled party may use a number of routes to enforce his rights. As a matter of background: in South Africa there is primarily a distinction between statutory ombudsman schemes and voluntary ombudsman schemes. A statutory ombudsman scheme is a scheme explicitly authorized by a statute. Often the statute will set out the powers of the Ombudsman, procedures to be followed and jurisdiction. A voluntary ombudsman scheme on the other hand is initialized by stakeholders in a particular industry who not only fund the scheme but also agree amongst themselves to be bound by the decisions of the Ombudsman.[105] The discussion that follows deals with the Financial

101. Millard, 129.
102. Reinecke et al., 215–216; *Nafte v. Atlas Assurance Co Ltd* 1924 WLD 239.
103. [2016] ZAGPPHC 823, 9 Sept. 2016.
104. Reinecke et al., 231.
105. Millard, 141–142.

Advisory and Intermediary Services Ombud (FAIS Ombud), the Ombudsman for Short-term Insurance and the Ombudsman for Long-term Insurance.

119. Section 20 of the FAIS Act establishes the Office of the Ombud for Financial Services Providers. Section 20(3) sets out the powers of the Ombud:

> The objective of the Ombud is to consider and dispose of complaints in a procedurally fair, informal, economical and expeditious manner and by reference to what is equitable in all the circumstances, with due regard to –
>
> (a) the contractual arrangement or other legal relationship between the complainant and any other party to the complaint; and
>
> (b) the provisions of this Act.

120. A client who has a complaint pertaining to the conduct of an insurance intermediary can however not simply approach the FAIS Ombud. Part XI of the General Code of Conduct: 'Internal complaint resolution system and procedures' stipulates that a client should first utilize a service provider's internal dispute resolution system.

121. Part XI of the GCC explains that 'resolution', or 'internal resolution', 'means the process of the resolving of a complaint through and in accordance with the internal complaint resolution system and procedures of the provider'. Also, 'provider' means an authorized FSP, and includes a representative. If a representative receives a complaint, the complaint should be dealt with by employing the complaints procedures of the FSP, as the FSP is responsible for its representatives. When a provider receives a complaint, the complaint should be dealt with by employing the provider's complaint resolution system.[106]

122. A provider must be transparent and fairness when dealing with a client's complaints. In addition, the most important obligations are contained in section 19 of the GCC which provides as follows:

> Specific obligations
>
> (1) Subject to the other provisions of this Part, the internal complaint resolution system and procedures of a provider excluding a representative must contain arrangements which-

(a) must-

> (i) reduce the details of the internal complaint resolution system and procedures of the provider, including all subsequent updating or upgrading thereof, to writing;

106. Sections 1(1) and 16(1) of the General Code of Conduct for Authorized Financial Services Providers and Representatives published in BN 80 in Government Gazette 25299 of 8 Aug. 2003, as amended.

(ii) provide that access to the procedures is at all times available to clients at any relevant office or branch of the provider, or by electronic medium, and that such availability is appropriately made known by public press or electronic announcements or separate business communications to existing clients;

(iii) include in the details envisaged in subparagraph (i), a reference to the duties of the provider and the rights of a client set out in Rule 6(a) and (b) of the Rules;

(iv) include in such details a clear summary of the provisions of the Act, which will apply whenever the client, after dismissal of a complaint by the provider, wishes to pursue further proceedings before the Ombud; and

(v) include in such details the name, address and other contact particulars of the Ombud;

(b) must stipulate that complaints must, if possible, be submitted in writing and must contain all relevant information, and that copies of all relevant documentation must be attached thereto;

(c) must provide that the receipt of complaints is promptly acknowledged in writing to the client, with communication particulars of contact staff to be involved in the resolution of the complaint, and are properly internally recorded by the relevant staff for purposes of compliance with section 18(b) and (d) of the Act;

(d) must make provision that after the receipt and recording of a particular complaint, the complaint will as soon as practically possible be forwarded to the relevant staff appointed to consider its resolution, and that-

(i) the complaint receives proper consideration;

(ii) appropriate management controls are available to exercise effective control and supervision of the consideration process;

(iii) the client is informed of the results of the consideration within the time referred to in Rule 6(b) of the Rules: Provided that if the outcome is not favourable to the client, full written reasons must be furnished to the client within the time referred to in Rule 6(b) of the Rules, and the client must be advised that the complaint may within six months be pursued with the Ombud whose name, address and other contact particulars must simultaneously be provided to the client.

(2) In any case where a complaint is resolved in favour of a client, the provider must ensure that a full and appropriate level of redress is offered to the client without any delay.

123. The purpose of a compulsory internal dispute resolution system is to force a client to first present his case to the Financial Services Provider. It affords the provider the opportunity to settle the dispute or to provide the client with reasons for a decision. If the client is still not satisfied he may approach the Ombud. As was already alluded to, the FAIS Ombud derives its authority to adjudicate from the FAIS Act and more specifically the Rules on Proceedings of the Office of the Ombud for Financial Services Providers, 2003 (Ombud Rules) promulgated by virtue of section 26. Rule 4 of the Ombud Rules, 'Type of complaint justifiable by Ombud' makes clear that:

For a complaint to be submitted to the Office –

(i) the complaint must fall within the ambit of the Act and these Rules;

(ii) the person against whom the complaint is made must be subject to the provisions of the Act (hereafter referred to as 'the respondent');

(iii) the act or omission complained of must have occurred at a time when these Rules were in force; and

(iv) the respondent must have failed to address the complaint satisfactorily within six weeks of its receipt.

124. A complaint should pertain to a matter provided for by the FAIS Act. For instance, where a long-term insurer is of the opinion that a claim by a beneficiary had become prescribed, the dispute may be adjudicated by the Ombudsman for Long-term Insurance as the matter deals with an aspect which falls squarely within the realm of the LTIA. However, where a broker advised a complainant that the product he has purchased covers disability and it transpires that this is not the case, the advice and possibly intermediary service rendered by the broker fall squarely within the statutory definitions of 'advice' and 'intermediary service' as set out in the FAIS Act. Furthermore, it pertains to a 'financial product' as defined by section 1(1)(g) of the Act because long-term insurance products are financial products.[107]

125. The scope of application of the FAIS Act should therefore be the primary point of departure in determining whether the FAIS Ombud may indeed adjudicate. A client should also consider whether the respondent is an FSP or a representative and whether any exclusions are perhaps applicable to the transaction between the complainant and the respondent. If both the complaint and the respondent's actions fall within the

107. Millard, 145–157.

ambit of the FAIS Act, it also needs to be established that the 'act or omission complained of must have occurred at a time when these Rules were in force'. If a dispute had arisen before 30 September 2004, it is not possible for the FAIS Ombud to adjudicate the matter. Remember, Rule 4(a)(iv) also implies that a complainant is obliged to first address his complaint to the respondent and it is only where the respondent had failed to address the complaint satisfactorily within six weeks that the FAIS Ombud has jurisdiction to hear the complaint.[108]

126. The rules provide for other matters pertaining to jurisdiction, such as that a complainant may seek any form of relief against the respondent. This is wider than an order to pay an amount of money. Where a complainant does claim a monetary award it 'must relate to the redress of financial prejudice or damage suffered or likely to be suffered by the complainant'. A monetary claim should not exceed ZAR 800,000 unless the parties have agreed in writing to exceed the limit.[109]

127. Although the FAIS Ombud has comprehensive powers and can in some respects be equated to a civil court, section 40 of the FAIS Act affords a client the choice between the FAIS Ombud or an ordinary civil court.[110] Section 40 reads as follows:

> Saving of rights –
>
> No provision of this Act, and no act performed under or in terms of any such provision, may be construed as affecting any right of a client, or other affected person, to seek appropriate legal redress in terms of common law or any other statutory law, and whether relating to civil or criminal matters, in respect of the rendering of any financial service by an authorised financial services provider, or representative of such provider, or any act of a person who is not an authorised financial services provider or a representative of such a provider.

128. There is nothing that forces the FAIS Ombud to adjudicate disputes. Section 27(3)(b)(i) that provides that 'the Ombud must decline to investigate any complaint if, before the date of official receipt of the complaint, proceedings have been instituted by the complainant in any Court in respect of a matter which would constitute the subject of the investigation'. Furthermore, section 27(3)(b)(ii) stipulates that 'where any proceedings contemplated in subparagraph (i) are instituted during any investigation by the Ombud, such investigation must not be proceeded with'.

129. An exclusion of the Ombud's jurisdiction is contained in section 4(f) of the Ombud Rules which states:

> The complaint must not relate to the investment performance of a financial product which is the subject of the complaint, unless such performance was guaranteed expressly or implicitly or such performance appears to the Ombud to be so deficient as to raise a prima facie presumption of misrepresentation,

108. Millard & Hattingh, Ch. 8.
109. Millard & Hattingh, 185.
110. F. Van Zyl, *Financial Advisory and Intermediary Services Manual* 1–24 (2000).

negligence or maladministration on the part of the person against whom the complaint is brought, or that person's representative.

130. As far as adjudication is concerned, section 27(5) of the FAIS Act stipulates that the Ombud:

(a) [M]ay, in investigating or determining an officially received complaint, follow and implement any procedure (including mediation) which the Ombud deems appropriate, and may allow any party the right of legal representation;
(b) must, in the first instance, explore any reasonable prospect of resolving a complaint by a conciliated settlement acceptable to all parties;
(c) may, in order to resolve a complaint speedily by conciliation, make a recommendation to the parties, requiring them to confirm whether or not they accept the recommendation and, where the recommendation is not accepted by a party, requiring that party to give reasons for not accepting it: Provided that where the parties accept the recommendation, such recommendation has the effect of a final determination by the Ombud, contemplated in section 28(1);
(d) may, in a manner that the Ombud deems appropriate, delineate the functions of investigation and determination between various functionaries of the Office; and
(e) may, on terms specified by the Ombud, mandate any person or tribunal to perform any of the functions referred to in paragraph (d).

131. If either party rejects a recommendation, the Ombud provides the parties with a final determination. The Ombud may also issue a determination without a recommendation. The Ombud has extensive powers and a determination may include the dismissal of the complaint or the upholding of the complaint. Where a complaint is upheld, it can be done either wholly or partially. It is also possible to issue a direction 'that the authorised financial services provider, representative or other party concerned takes such steps in relation to the complaint as the Ombud deems appropriate and just'. Finally, the Ombud may make any other order which a Court may make. A final determination may also include a cost order.[111]

132. The FAIS Act makes provision for appeals and any party to a dispute against whom the Ombud has made a determination, may apply in writing, within one month of the date of the determination, for leave to appeal against the determination. The application must set out the reasons for seeking leave to appeal. In considering the application, the Ombud should heed the stipulations of section 28(5)(b) of the FAIS Act which include the complexity of the matter, or the reasonable likelihood that the Board of Appeal will reach a different conclusion. In addition, the Ombud 'may request and consider submissions by any other party to the complaint concerning the merits of the application'. The Ombud may refuse or allow the appeal.

133. The Ombudsman for Long-term Insurance was established in 1985 as a form of self-regulation by some long-term insurers. The Ombudsman developed its own rules and procedures and in 1997 the members of the scheme decided that the Ombudsman's rulings would no longer be mere recommendations but would be binding

111. Millard & Hattingh, 196; ss 28 (1)(a), 28(1)(b)(i)–(iii) of the FAIS Act.

on them. This scheme is now recognized by the Financial Services Ombud Schemes Act.[112]

134. An important difference between determinations of a voluntary scheme such as the Ombudsman for Long-term Insurance and the FAIS Ombud is that while determinations are binding on members of the scheme (insurance companies) they are not binding on complainants. This means that complainants who are dissatisfied with a determination are free to take the matter to court. One of the biggest advantages of the scheme is that it is more accessible to complainants than courts and there are no cost implications.

135. The Ombudsman's scheme operates as a voluntary association not for gain. A set of rules deal with operational aspects, including jurisdiction. In terms of Rule 2.1 the Ombudsman considers the following matters, namely complaints by a policyholder, his successor in title, a beneficiary, a life insured, a premium payer or any person who represents them; complaints against a subscribing member; and complaints concerning or arising from the marketing, conclusion, interpretation, implementation or termination of any long-term insurance contract.

136. The following complaints will not be considered, namely a complaint that is subject to past, pending or contemplated legal proceedings; a complaint which had previously been determined by the Ombudsman and a complaint in terms of which three years or more had lapsed from the date the complainant was or should have been aware that he or she could complain.[113] In addition, the Ombudsman will also decline to consider complains if there is no reasonable prospect of success, if it is pursued in a dishonest, frivolous, vexatious or abusive manner, it can be better dealt with by a court of law, if it is mostly about the insurer's investment decisions and if the complainant has not and will probably not suffer financial loss or material inconvenience.[114]

137. It is possible for an unsuccessful party to appeal against the Ombudsman's decision. The prior consent of the Ombudsman is required and if consent is granted, the appellant has to pay a deposit as determined by the Ombudsman and this deposit is used to defray the costs. This application for leave to appeal must be made within one month of the date of the determination. Should leave to appeal be granted, the Ombudsman proposes a tribunal to hear the matter and both sides should agree on the constitution of the tribunal. If the parties are not able to settle, the appeal tribunal makes an order. This order is binding upon the insurer regardless of whether he wins or loses. However, where the complainant was the appellant and lost, the order is binding but where the insurer was the appellant and won, the other party may still institute proceedings in a court of law or any other forum.[115]

138. The Ombudsman for Short-term Insurance was established in 1989. This scheme complies with the basic requirements listed in the Financial Services Ombud Schemes Act. This section 21 company answers to a board of directors who represent the industry and consumer representatives. This voluntary scheme is comparable to

112. Nienaber & Reinecke, 38.
113. Nienaber & Reinecke, 52–55.
114. Nienaber & Reinecke, 55.
115. Nienaber & Reinecke, 39, 65–66.

the Ombudsman for Long-term Insurance in the sense that the initiative came from the industry and the aim of the scheme is to act as a mediator.[116]

139. The Ombudsman for Short-term Insurance assists consumers with the following complaints:[117]

Personal Lines Short-Term Insurance	*Commercial Lines Short-Term Insurance*
Claimants are private individuals. Disputes pertaining to: – Motor insurance – Home owner's insurance – Household contents insurance – Cell phone insurance – Travel insurance – Disability insurance – Credit protection insurance	Claimants including sole proprietorships, juristic persons, trusts or partnerships with a turnover over the past years less than ZAR 25 million. Disputes pertaining to: – Fire and related risks – Glass – Theft – Motor vehicle insurance – Travel insurance – Sickness and accident insurance – SASRIA claims in as far as it relates to any of these matters

140. Complaints by on behalf of policyholders are entertained only if the complainant had sought to resolve the matter with the insurer first. In addition, the Ombudsman will not hear a matter where the complainant had already instituted legal action in a court of law. The Ombudsman only makes a ruling after all the material facts had been agreed or established.[118]

141. Ombudman's ruling is referred to as 'a written directive issued by the Ombudsman which is binding on the insurer and which is based either on law or equity'. The Ombudsman for Short-term insurance, although an independent organization, functions along the same lines as the Ombudsman for Long-term Insurance in that directives are not precedents and are only binding on insurers. A complainant who is unhappy with a written directive may also pursue the matter further in a court of law.[119]

142. The case of *Kgabo Posch Molokomme v. Wayne Duval & Quanway Insurance Brokers CC* serves as an example of a FAIS Ombud case.[120] *In casu*, the complainant, Kgabo Posch Molokomme, alleges that the first respondent, Wayne Duval, failed to render financial services with care and diligence as prescribed in section 2 of the GCC in terms of the FAIS Act.

143. The complainant alleges that he was involved in an accident on 2 March 2008 as he was driving towards Pretoria from Johannesburg. He hit the pavement because his view was obstructed by another vehicle and this caused substantial damage to his vehicle. The complainant proceeded to lodge a claim with the respondent but

116. Nienaber & Reinecke, 39.
117. Millard, 154.
118. Nienaber & Reinecke, 39.
119. Nienaber & Reinecke, 39.
120. Case No. FAIS 5534/07-08GP 2.

he then learnt that he was no longer insured with Constantia Insurance Company Limited (Constantia).The respondent investigated the matter and when his calls to the respondent produced no results, he realized that he was in fact not insured. The respondent could not explain this to the complainant and the latter discovered that the respondent had in fact unilaterally and unlawfully cancelled his policy with Constantia in November 2007. It also transpired that the respondent's clients were transferred to another insurer, Renasa Insurance Limited (Renasa). The respondent did not explain why the complainant's insurance contract was not transferred to Renasa together with those of all the other clients. Because the complainant was not insured, he was not able to pay the repairs to his vehicle and the storage fees.

144. The Ombud's investigation revealed that the complainant procured short-term insurance cover for his vehicle with the help of the first respondent. The complainant procured the insurance on 24 November 2006, which is the day upon which he bought his vehicle, a 2 litre white Ford Focus. Constantia were the insurers and Watermark Risk Management Services (Pty) Ltd (Watermark), the underwriting managers. Evidently the policy's renewal date was 24 November 2007 and the monthly premiums were ZAR 696.95. After the accident, the complainant called respondent's offices to report the event. The complainant allegedly followed up on Monday, 4 March with a further call and a facsimile. A secretary from respondent's offices telephonically confirmed that she had received the complainant's facsimile and promised that respondent would make contact with the complainant. As promised, the respondent called the complainant and informed him that his insurance premiums had been outstanding since November 2007. The complainant replied that he could not believe this, as he always had sufficient cash in his bank account to pay his debit orders. The complainant proved this by faxing his banking statements to the respondent. The parties then agreed that the complainant would pay the sum of ZAR 3,000 into the second respondent's bank account to pay four months' arrear premiums.

145. Following this transaction, the complainant phoned Renasa for an update. Unfortunately, the institution's Colin Scott conformed that he was not aware of such an arrangement for arrear premiums. It was then that the complainant realized that the first respondent had been lying to him. On 16 March 2008, the complainant went to respondent's offices where he was informed that he had no insurance whatsoever and that the amount of ZAR 3,000 he had paid to respondent did not in fact reinstate his insurance policy. The respondent undertook to act as insurer, obtain quotations, repair the complainant's vehicle and pay for the storage. The complainant refused to accept respondent's offer and insisted that respondent should also pay for the cost of hiring a vehicle because vehicle hire was in fact included in the Constantia policy. The respondent undertook to pay for all of this but he never acted in terms of his undertaking towards the complainant and this prompted the complainant to lodge a complaint.

146. It appears that on the renewal date of the complainant's policy, the respondent unilaterally cancelled the complainant's policy with Constantia and moved all his clients' insurance arrangements to Renasa. Although brokers frequently do this in what is called 'moving the book', these new and alternative arrangements are not necessarily suitable to the needs of all the clients. The respondent's refusal to assist the client has prompted the complainant to claim the amount he would have received from the insurers, had it not been for the respondent's unilateral cancellation of his policy with

Constantia and in addition, he seeks compensation in the amount of ZAR 22,000, being storage fees, and the further ZAR 3,000 that was paid for premiums in arrears.

147. The respondents failed to resolve the complaint with the complainant and also refused to cooperate with the Ombud, despite having asked to file their response in terms of the section 27(4) notice that was sent to them in terms of the FAIS Act. Subsequent correspondence was also ignored, and this indicated to the Ombud that the respondent had no intention to resolve the complaint.

148. The Ombud had to establish whether respondents failed to act honestly, fairly, with due skill, care and diligence, and in the interests of the client and the financial services industry. In addition, if the respondents' conduct fell short of the provisions of section 2 of the GCC, the Ombud had to establish whether the conduct caused the complainant's loss. The Ombud viewed the respondents' refusal to deal with the complaint as contemptuous. They concluded that the respondents did not have a mandate from the complainant to cancel the policy and at no time did they seek to his mandate. The cancellation could therefore not have been in the complainant's interests. In fact, the respondents seemed unaware of the fact that the complainant's policy was not successfully transferred from Constantia to the new insurer. The Ombud states that:

> [I]t would be a waste of time to canvass the various sections of the Code that were violated by respondent's conduct. Respondent, clearly, was neither concerned with the Code nor his client's rights when he cancelled complainant's insurance. A further assault on the rights of the client is that of denying them the right to choose whether they want to deal with a particular insurer. Clients like complainant learn after the fact they are now insured with a new insurer without them having had any say in the matter and are expected to continue with the payment of premiums and adhere to the terms and conditions of the new insurer violation as though they were party to the negotiation of such terms. Such conduct cannot be allowed. Brokers like respondent continue to feel emboldened to act in this fashion because, very often, there is no resistance from clients. They are simply not aware that they have been violated.

149. The Ombud addresses the issue of non-payment by stating that the first respondent's attempt to blame the complainant for not paying premiums is 'disingenuous'. The Ombud accepts the complainant's averments that he has always made sufficient provision for the payment of his premiums. This leads the Ombud to conclude that had it not been for respondent's unlawful act of cancelling the complainant's policy, the 'complainant in all likelihood, would have been insured at the time of the accident'. The Ombud rules that the respondent is liable to pay to the complainant an amount of ZAR 22,000 for storage, ZAR 3,000 for the 'arrear premiums', and a further ZAR 49,700, which amount represents the cost for repairing the damage to the vehicle.

150. Rulings by the FAIS Ombud and any division of the High Court constitute precedents, which means that the FAIS Ombud and the court are bound by previous decisions when in future it has to determine a similar matter. Precedents by the courts are so important that it is a source of the South African law. However, the determinations of the Ombudsman for Long-term Insurance do not constitute precedents because of its equity jurisdiction. This means that although there is consistency in the way cases are treated, the main consideration is fairness between the parties. This makes sense. Unfortunately the FAIS Ombud is a system which is also based on fairness but decisions do constitute precedents.

151. It is submitted that where justice is the main consideration determinations should constitute precedents such as the case with high court decisions. However, what is fair between A and B is not necessarily fair between A and C. The FAIS Ombud's system is seriously flawed on that aspect and the Ombudsman for Long-term Insurance is therefore considered to be a better system.[121]

§5. Consumer Protection (in General and with Regard to Insurance)

152. The Consumer Protection Act is the main source of statutory consumer protection law in South Africa. Other acts include the National Credit Act (NCA) and Companies Act. Insurance products and services have been exempted from the scope of the CPA from 28 February 2014 by the Financial Services Laws General Amendment Act.[122] The absence of relevant statutory provisions do not in any way diminish the common-law duty not to make misrepresentations. Case law will furthermore inform and provide clarity and legal certainty as to the nature and extent of the insurer's information duty.

153. It should be noted that, although the CPA does not apply to insurance, general consumer protection principles as well as the PPR in terms of the LTIA and the STIA require contracts to be in plain language. An aspect that complicates matter in South Africa somewhat is that the country has eleven official languages. As this is a relatively newer dispensation (post 1994), and on a practical level, it is not ascertainable to expect all documentation to be issues or available in all official languages. As English is the most prevalent language in general business and trade, most insurance documentation, statutes and the like are in English, which makes them accessible to the international community. A deviation will most probably only occur where an insured insists on being served with documents and communications in another of the official languages. Clearly demands of this nature will place a heavy burden on insurers if they have to ensure that documentation is available in all languages. It can be accepted that translation will be done on an ad hoc basis only when required.

154. A failure to provide insurance contract documentation in the insured's language of choice may be a form of discrimination, with its ensuing consequences. It may furthermore be contrary to public policy. The evaluation of the requirement of public policy and discrimination is discussed extensively in this contribution below.

---

121. Nienaber & Reinecke, 55; J. Otto, 'The South African Legal System and its History', in *Commercial Law* para. 1 (Nagel et al. eds, 2015).

122. Act 45 of 2013.

§6. Compulsory Insurance

155. In terms of the Constitution persons have a freedom to trade, and forcing an insurer to provide specific insurance cover could infringe upon this specific constitutional right.[123] As the South African position is that mandatory insurance beyond the scope of government or specified industry funds does not require insureds to obtain cover from *specified* insurers, and therefore has little impact on competition between insurers. For specified industry funds, see, for example, the insurance that is procured from the Medical Protection Society Ltd under the auspices of the South African Medical Association for medical practitioners liability cover. Availability and affordability of insurance within the market determines from which insurer the cover will be obtained.

156. Opinion is divided on whether the advantages and benefits offered by mandatory insurance outweigh its disadvantages. Mandatory insurance has the potential of providing a solution to insurance claims issues, but that it can only be effective where the operators who are required to obtain the cover actually do so. It is here where the capacity to enforce statutory measures becomes problematic in South Africa. Government funds are focused on development and not necessarily on enforcement. Enforcement is simplified in cases where statutes provide for the possibility of revoking or refusing to reissue operating licences to ensure compliance.

157. Relating specifically to operations and technologies that affect the environment, mandatory insurance is required within the nuclear industry, the oil and petroleum industries, for the liabilities of waste disposal contractors, operators of waste disposal facilities, transporters of waste, and for underground or aboveground storage tanks. Most of these schemes are in accordance with international laws ratified or acceded to by the South African government.

158. Professional bodies, such as the Health Professions Council of South Africa,[124] and The Law Society of South Africa[125] require their members to procure professional liability insurance cover before they may practice.

159. Insurance contributions must be made by employers for the benefit of their employees in terms of the Compensation for Occupational Injuries and Diseases Act 130 of 1993 (COIDA), and for unemployment in terms of the Unemployment Insurance Act[126] and Unemployment Insurance Contributions Act.[127]

160. Pension fund contributions are currently not mandatory. At the moment proposals serve before Parliamentary committees for the introduction of mandatory health care insurance, and a mandatory National Pension Fund. Both are in their initial phases and realistic expectations place their introduction beyond 2016.

---

123. Section 22 of the Constitution on the freedom to trade; s. 36 on the limitation of a constitutional right.
124. *See* http://hpcsa.co.za.
125. *See* http://www.lssa.org.za.
126. Act 30 of 1966.
127. Act 4 of 2002.

161. Insurance must be procured for the carriage of persons or the transport of goods. Operators are required to procure insurance cover in terms of national and provincial legislation.[128]

162. Most forms of mandatory insurance are imposed by private agreements between persons who stand in a specific relationship. Examples include where a consumer is required to obtain insurance cover, of asset insurance, to the benefit of his credit grantor (e.g., where life insurance on the life of a debtor is required by a his bank); where a lessor of property requires a lessee to procure property or liability insurance; where a client my require insurance as security from independent contractors such as designers, builders, engineers and so forth, to cover their liabilities towards their client in specific projects; and where a tour operator may require tourists to procure life and personal accident cover.

163. Although insurance is not mandatory by operation of statute or regulation, the risk of incurring liabilities towards the state, for example, for clean-up costs, and potential liability towards third parties force persons to obtain insurance cover. Facility pollution liability serves as an example.

128. National Land Transport Act 5 of 2009, specifically ss 61(2) 69, 72, 81(bb); the mandatory insurance to be taken out in terms of this statute is in addition to the cover provided for road accidents in terms of the RAF Act 56 of 1996. No premiums are levied for purposes of this fund. A petroleum levy funds the RAF and claims are managed by the State.

Part 1. The Insurance Company

Chapter 1. The Insurance Company: Its Form

164. In most cases, the insurer as a juristic person is represented by an agent or the insurance is procured via a broker who may or may not also be a representative of the insurer or the prospective insured. The capacity of this type of intermediary will depend on his mandate or instruction and the facts and the circumstances in each situation.[129] As most insurers are companies the Companies Act 71 of 2008 (2008 Act) which came into operation on 31 March 2011 also applies. A company is a juristic person incorporated in terms of the 2008 Act; or a juristic person that, immediately before the effective date of the 2008 Act, was registered in terms of the Companies Act 61 of 1973 (1973 Act), or the Close Corporations Act 69 of 1984, if it has subsequently been converted in terms of Schedule 2 of the 2008 Act; or a company that was in existence and recognized as an 'existing company' in terms of the 1973 Act; or a company which was registered in terms of the 1973 Act and has subsequently been re-registered in terms of the 2008 Act.[130]

165. A key individual is any natural person who is, either solely or in conjunction with other similar persons, responsible for managing or overseeing the activities of an entity, trust or partnership in respect of the delivery of any financial service. If the entity only has one natural person as member, director, shareholder or trustee, then that person is described as the key individual in accordance with the FAIS Act. The key individual is responsible for managing or overseeing the activities of the FSP and that individual must comply with the Fit and Proper requirements as published in the Determination of Fit and Proper Requirements for Financial Services Providers, 2003.

166. If an FSP intends to render financial services, the key individual or individuals responsible for managing or overseeing the various financial services must, in accordance with section 13(4) of the FAIS Act, must be recorded in a register which must contain every or key individual's name and business address. The register must be submitted to the Registrar for reference or inspection purposes when required.

167. An FSP has to apply to the Registrar for approval of a key individual. The onus is on the applicant (when it is a partnership, a trust or a corporate or unincorporated body) to satisfy the Registrar that a key individual meets these fit and proper requirements in respect of honesty and integrity, as well as competence and operational abilities.

129. S.R. Van Jaarsveld, 'Agency', in *Commercial Law*, Part 3, 157 (C.J. Nagel ed.).
130. E.P. Joubert, 'Company Law' in *Business Law*, Part 13, 349 (C.J. Nagel ed., LexisNexis 2012).

§1. Mutual Insurance, Premium Insurance, Other

168. In South Africa mutual insurance is not recognized any more. All insurances are premium insurance. Insurance business may only be conducted by a company that is duly registered and incorporated by the Companies Act. See paragraph 164 above for a definition of 'company'.

§2. Public or Private Nature

169. There is no distinction between public and private companies for purposes of insurance business, although the definitions of these differ. A profit company is a private company if it is not a state-owned company; and its memorandum of incorporation both prohibits the offer of any of its securities to the public and restricts the transferability of its securities.[131]

170. The only difference between a private company and a public company is that the securities of a public company may be freely offered to the public.[132] What is more important is that all insurance companies must comply with all the requirements that are set out by sections 7–14 of the LTIA and sections 7–14 of the STIA respectively, notably sections 7–14.

§3. Factual Data

171. The LTIA and the STIA stipulate which aspects such as annual returns should be reported during various stages of the financial year. Different obligations in this regard exist for different types of insurance companies and insurance business.

172. Section 41 of the FAIS Act deals with fees and penalties. Section 41(2)(a) determines that a person who fails to furnish the Registrar with a return, information or a document provided for in the Act within the specified period, is liable to a penalty of not more than ZAR 1,000 (or any greater amount prescribed) 'for every day during which the failure continues'. The Registrar may waive the penalty on good cause shown.

173. In practice, the Registrar imposes the penalty by written notice after the person had been given a reasonable opportunity to be heard. The notice takes effect on a date specified in the notice, which may be a date prior to the date in the notice. Where a person fails to pay within the specified period, interest must be paid on the outstanding debt at the determined rate in respect of debts due to the state. The FSB has *locus standi* to recover any outstanding debts and here, the Board utilizes the same debt-collection procedure that will be employed by any other creditor in a civil court with jurisdiction. Regardless of what needs to be submitted, it must be submitted to the Registrar of Insurance at the FSB.

---

131. Section 1 of the Companies Act read with s. 8(2)(b).
132. F.H.I. Cassim (ed.), *Contemporary Company Law* 78.

Chapter 2. Access to Business and Authorization: Requirements and Procedures

174. As from 30 September 2004, any person not exempted from the FAIS Act who renders financial services must be duly authorized in terms of section 7(1) of the FAIS Act. The Act provides that the Registrar must ensure that a provider and the key individuals of a provider meet the criteria as set out by the Fit and Proper Requirements.

175. The Registrar has divided the FSPs into several categories and subcategories. These categories are the following:

- Category I – FSPs that give advice and render intermediary services not defined in other categories of FSPs.
- Category II – FSPs, defined as 'discretionary FSPs', who manage clients' investments on a discretionary basis.
- Category IIA – FSPs defined as 'Hedge Fund FSPs'.
- Category III – FSPs, defined as 'administrative FSPs', who administer clients' financial products by means of bulking investments.
- Category IV – FSPs, defined as 'assistance business FSPs', who render administrative intermediary services in relation to assistance policies.

By grouping together the various types of FSPs in categories, the Registrar ensures that a particular FSP is licensed according to the financial services offered by such FSP.

176. An applicant applying for a licence must submit an application form, the prescribed supporting documentation and the application fee as stipulated by section 8(1) of the FAIS Act and Board Notice 60 of 2009. The FSB then evaluates the application to ensure that the new insurer meets the Fit and Proper Requirements.

177. During the application process, the Registrar may require the new insurer to provide additional information. The Registrar has the power to either grant the application with specific restrictions and conditions or to refuse the application. When a licence is refused, the reason(s) for refusal must be provided and the applicant has the option of appealing against the decision of the Registrar in accordance with section 8(6) of the FAIS Act.

178. The 'Fit and Proper Requirements' for FSPs contains the requirements a provider must comply with relating to honesty and integrity, competency, operational ability and financial soundness. In order to determine whether a prospective insurer is honest and competent, the Registrar will consider the business structure of an FSP. In principle, an FSP may be any legal entity but an insurer must be a registered company. An FSP who is a company must have a key individual and the registrar will evaluate the key individual to see whether he or she personally complies with the Fit and Proper Requirements.[133]

133. Millard & Hattingh, 36–38.

Chapter 3. Supervision

§1. Solvency Control

179. As early as 2009 the FSB and the South African insurance industry embarked on the SAM project, with a view to establishing a risk-based supervisory regime for the prudential regulation of both long-term and short-term insurers in South Africa.

180. The South African FSB is an active member of the International Association of Insurance Supervisors (IAIS). The objectives of the IAIS are to promote effective and globally consistent supervision of the insurance industry in order to develop and maintain fair, safe and stable insurance markets for the benefit and protection of policyholders; and to contribute to global financial stability.[134] The IAIS' Insurance Core Principles (ICPs) provide a globally accepted framework for the supervision of the insurance sector. The SAM framework must therefore be aligned to the ICPs, as well as emerging supervisory requirements that form part of the IAIS' draft Common Framework for Supervision of Internationally Active Insurance Groups ('ComFrame').

181. With due consideration of global trends in insurance supervision, and particularly Solvency II developments in Europe and the ICPs as set by the IAIS, SAM governance structures started to develop a solvency framework that would comply with the criteria for Solvency II third-country equivalence, as well as accommodate the unique requirements of the South African insurance industry

182. Part of the mandate given to the various SAM task groups and working groups was that the various SAM discussion documents and position papers must consider and be consistent with the ICPs, appropriately applied to the South African context. In addition to ComFrame, the IAIS has separately begun to explore whether to pursue a global capital standard for insurers, including the feasibility and practical challenges of implementing such a standard. As part of this process, the FSB has been tasked by the IAIS to assist in a stocktake of the needs, expectations and existing efforts of emerging market and developing countries with respect to the modernization of their insurance solvency regimes. The lessons from ComFrame and the stocktake of emerging solvency regimes in other jurisdictions will feed into the FSB's final decisions on the SAM framework. Significant progress has been made in this regard with more than 100 documents representing the SAM governance structure's view on various components of the SAM framework in various stages of production. The FSB is introducing certain changes to the initial SAM timelines in response to stakeholder input and to ensure a rigorous approach to the implementation of the SAM framework.

183. In addition to the stakeholder request for greater clarity on the details of the steps required for SAM implementation, the FSB is also of the view that a prudent timetable should be followed to ensure that both insurers and the supervisor achieve a smooth transition to the new framework. The parallel run refers to the process whereby insurance companies will be required to calculate and provide information on the proposed SAM basis in addition to the current requirements and statutory returns

134. *See* www.fsb.co.za.

prescribed under the LTIA and the STIA (Insurance legislation). This two-phased parallel run will mean that even though insurers need to be in a position to comply with most of the requirements of the SAM framework by 2015, full implementation of the SAM framework is expected to only be effective at the earliest from 1 January 2016 onwards.

184. The FSB is engaging with the National Treasury and the SARS to develop an appropriate tax regime to be applied under SAM. The FSB agrees with the view that a fair tax basis is a prerequisite for the successful implementation of SAM, and is committed towards playing a key role in its development. An insightful research document entitled '*The impact of the implementation of the Solvency II Directive principles on the taxation of insurers in jurisdictions comparable to South Africa*' was produced by the SAM Tax Task Group. It provides useful and informative research on the tax base applied by various jurisdictions around the world that are currently adopting regimes similar to the Solvency II Directive. [135]

185. Pertaining to reinsurance matters, the FSB has initiated a project to assist in the development of reinsurance regulations in South Africa. The focus of the research is to scan and evaluate relevant international reinsurance regulatory framework issues in other jurisdictions, and international best practice in this regard. It also includes a public policy assessment, including examination of national interest issues with respect to the local reinsurance industry in the context of the National Treasury's Gateway to Africa initiative. The final results of this study have not been available upon date of this publication.

186. To give effect to these aims, notice was given by the South African National Treasury *Publication of Explanatory Summary of the Insurance Laws Amendment Bill* Notice 563 of 2013 (GG 36513) to amend legislation not only for increased supervision and for solvency purposes, but also to enhance participation in the global insurance market.

187. In summary, the primary objective of the Bill is to ensure a sound and well-regulated insurance sector and to promote financial stability by: (a) strengthening the regulatory requirements in respect of governance, risk management and internal controls for all insurers; (b) enhancing the FSB's ability to appropriately supervise insurance groups; and (c) effecting technical amendments to clarify the intent and purpose of certain provisions and to address gaps in the current legislative framework.

188. A full review of the primary insurance legislation in South Africa, namely the LTIA and the STIA is currently underway. In addition to a major restructuring of legislative provisions, it also aims to give effect to the SAM framework for the South African insurance sector. New legislation is not expected before the end of 2016.

§2. Supervision of Tariffs and Insurance Conditions

189. The FSB prescribes all tariffs and insurance conditions and these are spread over the LTIA, the STIA and the FAIS Act. As far as administrative fees are concerned, section 41 of the FAIS Act deals with fees and penalties. Section 41(2)(a) determines that a person who fails to furnish the Registrar with a return, information or a document

135. This document is available on the FSB's website at www.fsb.co.za.

provided for in the Act within the specified period, is liable to a penalty of not more than ZAR 1,000 (or any greater amount prescribed) 'for every day during which the failure continues'. The Registrar may waive the penalty on good cause shown.

190. As far as administrative fees and commission of brokers are concerned, the legislative framework is very strict. Section 7(1)(a)(vi) of the GCC stipulates that a provider other than a direct marketer must stipulate:

> the nature, extent and frequency of any incentive, remuneration, consideration, commission, fee or brokerages ('valuable consideration'), which will or may become payable to the provider, directly or indirectly, by any product supplier or any person other than the client, or for which the provider may become eligible, as a result of rendering of the financial service, as well as the identity of the product supplier or other person providing or offering the valuable consideration: Provided that where the maximum amount or rate of such valuable consideration is prescribed by any law, the provider may (subject to clause 3(1)(a)(vii)) elect to disclose either the actual amount applicable or such prescribed maximum amount or rate.

In addition, section 49 of the LTIA entitled: 'Limitation of remuneration to intermediaries' stipulates as follows:

> No consideration shall be offered or provided by a long-term insurer or a person on behalf of the long-term insurer or accepted by any independent intermediary for rendering services as intermediary as referred to in the regulations, other than commission or remuneration contemplated in the regulations and otherwise than in accordance with the regulations.

Section 48 of the STIA contains a similar provision.

191. As far as insurance conditions are concerned, the PPR's terms of the LTIA and the STIA generally regulate aspects such as time bar clauses. For instance, Rule 7.4 in terms of these rules contains stipulations on the periods within which a policyholder should institute a claim and stipulates the time period within which a policyholder may approach a court in the instance where a claim was repudiated. However, because South Africa's insurance law is uncodified, it is not possible to find all rules and restrictions on insurance terms and conditions in one statute or code. An example of how a court has to apply the general rules pertaining to litigation to insurance claims is found in *Glencarol (Pty) Ltd v. Eemerald Risk Transfer Ltd.*[136] In this case, the insurance company filed an exception to Glencarol's claim for it being 'vague and embarrassing' and therefore excipiable. The bone of contention was in fact whether the insurance company had or had not repudiated the claim by email. The insurer stated that an email sent from their office following a claim by the insurer did not constitute a repudiation and that it therefore renders the summons and particulars of claim vague. The policyholder was of the opinion that there was nothing vague about the summons as the email in question did in fact constitute a repudiation which did give rise to a claim between the policyholder and the insurance company. This case illustrates that

136. GPJHC 27 Oct. 2015 Case no. 246 (unreported).

both material and procedural law has an influence on the rights and duties between insurers and policyholders and the way in which claims are adjudicated.

Chapter 4. Technical Reserves and Investments

192. Sections 29–36 of the LTIA and sections 28–35 of the STIA deal with the insurance company's obligations to maintain a financially sound condition, assets, kinds of assets and the spread thereof, deeming provisions concerning assets, liabilities, prohibitions concerning assets and certain liabilities, the consequences of failure to maintain a financially sound condition and rules pertaining to returns that have to be submitted to the Registrars of long-term insurance and short-term insurance respectively. It is submitted that these rules are aimed at preserving the solvency of insurance companies and that there is strict supervision by the FSB of these requirements.

Chapter 5. Accountancy

193. The Companies Act of 2008 has brought about changes to the standard-setting process that has required the continued existence of South African Statements of Generally Accepted Accounting Practice ('SA GAAP') to be re-evaluated.

194. The Companies Act imposed an obligation on the Minister of Trade & Industry (Minister) to establish a body known as the Financial Reporting Standards Council (FRSC). The FRSC is the legally constituted standard-setter and its function is to advise the Minister on matters relating to financial reporting standards. The FRSC was formed in late 2011. As a consequence of the establishment of the FRSC, the fundamental motivation for the former Accounting Practices Board's ('APB') existence has fallen away. The former Accounting Practices Board ('APB') was formed in 1973 to consider what should be generally accepted accounting practice and issue SA GAAP. In 2003, the APB decided to harmonize SA GAAP with International Financial Reporting Standards ('IFRS'). Since then, after due process, the APB has issued the IFRS standards as SA GAAP without amendment.

195. The Companies Regulations, 2011 prescribe the reporting frameworks based on each individual company's public interest score. The Regulations permit the use of either IFRS, IFRS for Small and Medium Enterprises (SMEs) or SA GAAP in specific instances. However, in order to reduce the burden of issuing each IFRS standard as SA GAAP, it has been decided to withdraw SA GAAP. Accordingly, SA GAAP will no longer apply in respect of financial years that commenced on or after 1 December 2012. As a result of these decisions, companies with a public interest score below 350 that are currently applying SA GAAP need to start preparing for their conversion to IFRS or IFRS for SMEs. First-time Adoption of International Financial Reporting Standards must be applied when converting to IFRS. Adjustments may arise on transition to IFRS given differences in transitional provisions. Alternatively, a company may change to IFRS for SMEs provided all the scope requirements of the standard are met and the transition provisions followed.

196. Developing and maintaining financial reporting standards that lead to proficient performance in the public sector is critical to good corporate governance in national, provincial and local government. The Accounting Standards Board (ASB) is the national public entity charged with this important responsibility in South Africa. The ASB must ensure that standards are formulated that are readily understandable and which can be effectively integrated in the norms and practices of all public entities in the country. These standard setters set high value in consulting as widely as possible and facilitating feedback on new and revised Standards that are still in draft form. The ASB seeks optimum opportunities to consult with stakeholders on the most appropriate financial reporting in the public sector. The ASB does not formulate accounting opinions or give accounting advice on specific transactions and events that a public entity may require. The International Accounting Standards Board (IASB) is expected to release the exposure draft for IFRS 4: Phase II during 2015 on the accounting standard on the measurement of insurance contracts. As the IASB and Financial Accounting Standards Board (FASB) are still in the process of an overhaul of the insurance accounting standard no final information was available when going to print.

Chapter 6. Taxation of the Company

197. The SARS administers a number of tax Acts, in terms of which money (taxes, duties and levies) is collected and paid into the National Revenue Fund.[137] SARS also collects money on behalf of other departments under their legislation, which is then also paid into the National Revenue Fund. Income tax is the government's main source of income and is levied in terms of the Income Tax Act 58 of 1962.

198. Companies are taxed on an annually prescribed fixed rate (28% for the 2016 year of assessment). Small business corporations (those with an annual turnover in 2016 of less than ZAR 14 million, for example) benefit from a graduated tax rate on their taxable income. Small business corporations can also write off certain investment expenditure in the year in which it is incurred.

199. Capital Gains Tax (CGT) was introduced in October 2001. It forms part of the income tax system and includes in taxable income capital gains made on the disposal of assets.

200. Value added tax (VAT) is levied at a standard rate of 14% on all goods and services subject to certain exemptions, exceptions, deductions and adjustments provided for in the Value-Added Tax Act 89 of 1991. VAT is levied on the supply of all goods and services rendered by registered vendors throughout the business cycle. It is the government's second biggest source of income. VAT is also levied on the importation of certain goods and services into South Africa. It is levied at the standard rate of 14%, but provision for exemptions and zero-rating of certain goods or services exists.

201. Pertaining to the taxation of insurance companies, the ordinary rules for the taxation of a company applies. Some of the following aspects are specifically regulated.

202. Short-term insurers are allowed to deduct expenditure incurred in respect of their business of insurance, premiums on reinsurance and the actual amount of liability incurred for any claims, less any claims recovered. In addition, allowances subject to the discretion of the Commissioner, for unexpired risks, claims intimated but not paid and claims not intimated nor paid, are allowed. Such allowances claimed as a deduction in a tax year must be included as income in the succeeding tax year.[138]

203. The taxation of long-term insurance companies is based on the trustee principle and the recognition that insurers hold and administer certain of their assets on behalf of various categories of policyholders, while the balance of the assets represents the shareholders' interests.[139] These companies are liable for income tax according to a four-fund approach – Income Tax Act section 29A.[140] The application of this approach requires that long-term insurers allocate their assets to separate funds representative of the various policyholders. Each fund, as listed below, is taxed separately as if it is a separate taxpayer in accordance with the applicable taxation

137. www.sars.gov.za.
138. Income Tax Act s. 28; also http://www.sars.gov.za/About/HowTax; and http://www.treasury.gov.za/documents.
139. Income Tax Act s. 29A; also http://www.sars.gov.za/About/HowTax; and http://www.treasury.gov.za/documents.
140. *See* in general, http://www.treasury.gov.za.

principles. In terms of the four funds approach, all long-term insurance business written by a long-term insurer must be separated into three policyholder funds and a corporate fund. These are as follows: (a) The Individual Policyholder Fund (IPF) for policies owned by individuals; (b) The Company Policyholder Fund (CPF) for policies owned by corporate entities; (c) The Untaxed Policyholder Fund (UPF) for policies owned by untaxed entities and annuity contracts. It consists of policies owned by retirement funds and other tax exempt entities and annuity contracts currently paying annuities; and (d) Corporate Fund that consists of all the assets held by the insurer and all the liabilities owed by the insurer not falling in the above-mentioned policyholder funds.

204. With regard to the first three policyholders funds (i.e., IPF, CPF and UPF), the insurer is required to allocate assets, income, expenditure and liabilities relating to each fund and the taxable income of each fund is determined separately in accordance with the applicable taxation principles. With regard to the policyholder funds, the insurer acts as a 'trustee' to collect tax from the pool of policyholders and to pay it to SARS 'on behalf' of the policyholders.

205. With the corporate fund, the intention of the legislature is to tax the insurer (corporate fund) in respect of 'profits earned' from running the insurance business. The liabilities of each policyholder fund are required to be actuarially valued at the end of each year of assessment and to the extent that assets in a policyholder fund exceed the liabilities the surplus must be transferred to the corporate fund where it is taxed at the corporate income tax rate. The surpluses transferred represent part of the profit earned by the 'shareholder' fund of the long-term insurer.

206. A risk policy is defined as a policy issued by an insurer during the insurer's year of assessment in terms of which any benefits payable under a policy is dependent on any future event the happening of which is uncertain or in terms of which any amount payable under the policy is only payable by reason of death; or any reinsurance policy in respect of such a policy. A policy with both investment and risk elements will be a risk policy if any of the policy benefits under the policy are risk benefits, even if it represents only a small portion of the total policy benefits. Currently disability policies, health policies, term life insurance and credit life insurance are all policies where the benefits under the policy depend on any future event the happening of which is uncertain. Funeral cover and life cover are policies under which an amount is payable by reason of death. Assets to cover liabilities of policies where any of the total policy benefits are risk benefits are to be allocated to the corporate fund. Only assets having a market value equal to the value of liabilities determined in relation to policies that are not risk policies shall be placed in the policyholder funds for purposes of taxation.

Part II. The Insurance Contract: General

Chapter 1. Generalities

207. Although insurance contracts are sui generis and of a specialized nature, the general principles of contract law still apply. The South African common law of contract regarding the creation of a legal obligation by conclusion of a valid and binding contract; aspects pertaining to the content of the contract; breach of contract and remedies, cession of contractual rights and the prescription of claims all enjoy application. In certain instances, it may be argued that there is a case for creating insurance-specific rules for preventing miscarriages of justice. In *Muller v. Sanlam Life Insurance Limited* [2016] ZASCA 149 the crisp facts of the case were briefly that Muller, applied for reinstatement of his appeal on the roll and for condonation of his failure to comply with the rules of the court. His claim against the respondent was for payment of the benefits under four life insurance policies all in respect of Muller's former wife. The Mullers divorced several years before her death in 2006 in an alleged hijacking incident. The applicant alleged that they had divorced for business reasons. The policies had been taken out in 2005 and 2006 respectively. Muller was the owner of two of the policies and the beneficiary in respect of the other two, which were owned by Mrs Muller. Muller instituted an application in the Western Cape High Court for ZAR 8.876 million. This particular application was brought almost five years after the death of the insured and Sanlam raised several defences, including that Muller had had a hand in the death of his former wife, and that the claim had prescribed. The parties then agreed that the defence of prescription should be heard first. The way in which Sanlam handled the matter was unsatisfactory and the claim was never rejected outright. Several enquiries as to the status of the claim were answered by stating that Santam was still investigating the matter. Following one such enquiry, Muller was informed that his claim had become prescribed and that prompted the action in question. The court agreed with the insurer and ruled against Muller. The court ruled that the PPR that were amended in 2010 did not apply to the case in question and had that be the case, Sanlam's plea of prescription would not have succeeded. This unfortunate case illustrates why insurance contracts often need to provide for rules that is distinguishable from the general rules of contract in order to bring a about the fairer treatment of consumers.

208. Our courts have recognized that 'it is a contract between an insurer (or assurer) and an insured (or assured), whereby the insurer undertakes in return for payment of a price or premium, to deliver to the insured a sum of money or its equivalent on the occurrence of a specified uncertain event in which the insured has some interest'. This definition has been criticized by authors as it does not recognize the distinction between indemnity and non-indemnity insurance, as it does not accommodate the latter. In response Nienaber and Reinecke propose the following definition: An insurance contract can be defined as 'a contract to compensate the insured for a patrimonial loss proximately caused by the uncertain event insured against, or as a contract to satisfy the insured for a non-patrimonial loss consequent upon the occurrence of the uncertain event insured against'. For purposes of this discussion the terminology 'insurer' and 'insured' is preferred above the 'assurer' and 'assured'.[141]

209. South Africa recognizes the fundamental distinction between indemnity insurance where the object of insurance is patrimonial (i.e., property; business; loss or liability towards another person) on the one hand, and on the other capital or non-indemnity insurance (i.e., loss or impairment of life or limb) where the object is non-patrimonial. This compartmentalization is not absolute as some policies straddle both.[142]

210. In view of the fundamental distinction, legislation follows it by dividing insurance into short-term and long-term insurance (known in some other countries as general and life insurance).

211. The following are the features recognized for insurance: (a) an undertaking by an insurer to assume the risk of harm or loss; (b) by providing a promised benefit of compensation as satisfaction or indemnity; (c) upon the occurrence of an insured event which is uncertain as to its occurrence or timing; (d) for an interest by the policyholder deemed worthy of protection; (e) against payment of a premium calculated according to the nature and extent of the risk.[143]

141. Nienaber & Reinecke, para. 18; Reinecke et al., 1.17; *Lake v. Reinsurance Corp Ltd* 1967 (3) SA 124 (W).
142. Nienaber & Reinecke, s. A para. 13.
143. Nienaber & Reinecke, s. A para. 21.

Chapter 2. Insurable Risk

212. A loss is always closely linked to an interest the insured has in an object or in a non-patrimonial element such as his health or his life. The question is therefore whether insurable interest is an essential element of an insurance contract. Internationally it is mostly concluded that where insurable interest is lacking, the parties are agreeing to nothing other than a wager. Kuschke argues as follows:

> An insurable interest is not an essential element for the conclusion of an insurance contract. The intentions of the parties will indicate whether their contract is one of insurance or a wager. The object or subject matter of insurance is that an insurable interest must exist only at the time of materialization of the risk insured against. It is not a requirement for the existence of the insurance policy itself.[144]

213. Nienaber and Reinecke on the other hand advocate that it is an open issue whether the interest should exist at the time of conclusion of the contract or in future. They argue that the policyholder must at least 'have an interest deemed to be worthy of protection, in the object that, or in the person who, will be adversely affected if the insured event should occur. Absent such interest, the contract fails.'[145]

214. In most instances the existence of the insurable interest only becomes an issue when a defined risk materializes and an insured seeks compensation. If there is no insurable interest at the time of claim, the insured never incurred a loss and clearly cannot call upon the insurer to pay. The presence of property loss or harm in the context of first-party insurance cover, or legal liability incurred for causing loss or damage to another indicate the presence of an insurable interest and would trigger insurance cover. Ascertainable interests as well as future interests could serve as insurable interests for purpose of insurance cover, and must exist at the time when the cover is triggered. An insured who does allege loss where there is none, may be deemed to have acted fraudulently. In addition, because both cover and risk imply that there should be an insurable interest, it is not necessary to list insurable interest as a separate element of the insurance contract for purposes of its conclusion.[146]

215. 'Risk' can be described as 'the possibility of the occurrence of an uncertain event leading to an undesirable consequence, such as damage or harm, whether patrimonial or not, to which the insured himself, his property or any of his broader interests are exposed'. It also entails the possibility and probability of an undesirable change in circumstances of the insured. It is a basic rule of insurance law that insurance is to cover fortuities and not certainties. A loss is not fortuitous if it is, for example, the result of the natural behaviour of the subject matter insured, or a result of the intentional act of the insured, or due to ordinary wear-and-tear, natural deterioration or internal deficiencies of the subject matter that would eventually cause damage in any case.[147]

---

144. Prozesky-Kuschke, *Introduction in Commercial Law* Part 2 (Nagel ed.).
145. Nienaber & Reinecke, 9.
146. Nienaber & Reinecke, Ch. 1, 7–11.
147. Reinecke et al., Ch. 13.

216. Insurance contracts are usually based on the assumption that the risk has not yet materialized and is not a certainty, as already discussed above. Risk that is altered or increased during the insurance period is clearly excluded from the original cover. Because the possibilities of damage or prejudice, especially consequential losses are infinite, the scope thereof is limited contractually in most policies. These limitations specify and quantify the risks that are passed onto the insurer.[148]

217. On the other hand, the availability of insurance is directly influenced by the probability that a certain type of loss or liability may be incurred. It goes without saying that the insurer and the insured must agree on the nature and scope of the risk that should pass from the insured to the insurer. Reinecke et al. state that the whole purpose of insurance is for the insured to be 'relieved' of the risk of a loss or the impairment of an interest.[149] In indemnity insurance, the risk is usually determined by reference to an event that causes the loss, rather than the loss itself. Yet disability insurance, refers to the consequences of an event or accident that caused the disability, rather than the event itself. In capital insurance the same principle applies. In whole life insurance, the risk insured against is death and even though the occurrence of the death event is not uncertain, it still qualifies as an insurable risk as it is in fact the time when death occurs that remains uncertain.

218. In this context, 'all risk cover' refers to risks and not to certainties and in policies with such clauses the risks do not have to be specified. The use of the term 'all risk' insurance is misleading as it appears to the average policyholder that the policy covers all loss, however caused, and that the nature of the casualty causing the loss is immaterial. In the market policies usually include extensive standard exclusion clauses that are adapted from time to time where an insurer has a right to change the cover in its own discretion. The policyholder has to prove that the loss was proximately caused by an insured peril, and that he suffered the loss. The burden of proof then rests with the insurer to show that the loss arose from an excluded cause and is therefore not covered under the policy, or that another defence exists that denies his liability such as prescription of the claim. It is important to note that any clause that restricts an insurer's liability under an 'all-risks' policy must, however, be interpreted restrictively.[150]

219. The duty of an insurer to perform in terms of the contract arises when the risk materializes. It is the insured's duty to prove that the risk agreed upon has materialized and that the claim falls within the description of the risk. The insured does this by notifying his insurer in the manner prescribed. Usually this consists of completing a claim form issued by his insurer. The completed claim form together with any supporting documentation is returned to the insurer who will then be able to assess the authenticity of the claim. The insurer must in the first instance undertake to perform in terms of the contract, by paying an amount of money, replacing goods or delivering services to the insured. The payment of a premium is a characteristic of insurance. It is a contractual duty, yet may also be seen as a suspensive positive condition, or a resolutive negative condition on which the insurer's duty to perform

148. *Lourens v. Colonial Mutual Life Assurance Society Ltd* 1986 (3) SA 373 (A) 384.
149. Reinecke et al., 2.
150. Reinecke et al., 207, 241; *see also Auto Protection Insurance Co Ltd v. Hanmer-Strudwick* 1964 (1) SA 349 (A) 354.

depends. Section 51 of the LTIA regulates this issue for the long-term insurance industry, by stating expressly that where the Act applies payment of the premium is a suspensive condition.[151]

220. Cover refers to the extent of the insurer's liability to accept the loss the insured would have suffered had he not been insured. The loss or damage in both situations must have been brought about by the specified event insured against. Cover is provided for a specific number of insured events and for each of these deductibles, self-insured retentions and limitations of claim usually apply. Property policies generally contain lower limits of indemnity when compared to liability policies. Standard property policies provide that the insured property must be damaged during the period of cover. It is possible to buy-back cover that provides retroactive cover. In general, the insurer is liable to deliver direct compensation in the form of a reinstatement, or indirect compensation in the form of money. This will be the case for first-party insurance such as property insurance. In the context of liability insurance, the insurer's performance usually consists of the payment of monetary damages that were owed to a third party.[152]

221. Where the policy is one of non-indemnity or capital insurance, the contractually agreed amount becomes payable, and holds no relevance to actual loss suffered. The purpose of the insurance is not to compensate the insured but provides him with consolation for the loss of a non-patrimonial interest. A capital insurer can also be obliged to pay an amount of money or render a service such as the providing a funeral or burial upon the occurrence of an uncertain future event. It is possible to agree on various aspects to limitations on insurance cover, exclude specific risks from cover (e.g., suicide) and also to specify the duration of cover. In some cases there are statutory limitations on the amounts payable.[153]

222. In indemnity insurance, the indemnity insurer is obliged to pay the insured or to render a service in order to compensate the insured for loss of or damage to a patrimonial interest. In these cases the amount of the claim payable will be equal to the loss suffered or in some cases even less. This will be where the insured is under-insured, and the cover provided is lower than the actual loss. The principle of average will in this case apply and the claim will be reduced.[154]

223. Insurers are constantly evaluating their policies to minimize their exposure to risks. They might exclude specific risks from cover during the period of cover. Standard exclusions from property policies can include, for example, fraudulent conduct or intentional realization of the risk by the policyholder. Claims for damage caused to the property by an 'inherent vice' or 'latent defect' that is not discoverable upon reasonable inspection is often excluded under the policy. An 'inherent vice' refers to the situation where the internal composition of the property or some aspect thereof causes its damage or destruction. Damage caused by normal wear, tear and deterioration is as a general rule excluded from cover. A typical property policy exclusion clause concerns loss caused by 'the enforcement of any law or ordinance' that regulates the construction, use, repair or removal of the property.

---

151. Millard, 88–89; *Visser v. 1 Life Direct Insurance Lim*ited (1005/13) [2014] ZASCA 193 (28 Nov. 2014).
152. Reinecke et al., 10, 27–28, 40.
153. Reinecke et al., 77, Nienaber & Reinecke, Ch. 11.
154. Reinecke et al., 62–67.

224. An important constitutional issue is the one of discrimination in the insurance industry where refusal to insure a specific risk or the unequal treatment of prospective policyholders pertaining to their cover cannot always be justified legally or for technical insurance reasons. Discrimination remains an important issue in the South African context. The relevance and importance of the theme of discrimination is obvious, the more so as it continues to play an ever-increasing role in this age of consumerism.

225. Insurance companies are in fact in the business of discrimination when they segregate insureds into different risk groups or pools based on their risk profiles. Stereotyping is used to predict insurance risks and those who pose a higher risk pay higher premiums than others for the same insurance cover. Whether this discrimination is fair or not, depends on constitutional norms. Grounds of discrimination include race, gender, sex, pregnancy, marital status, ethnic or social origin, colour, sexual orientation, age, disability, religion, conscience, belief, culture, language and birth.[155] Section 9 of the Constitution clearly states that '[n]o person, including the state, may unfairly discriminate against any other person'. Public and private actors are bound by the principle of equality and therefore also by the principle of non-discrimination.

226. Section 8 of the Constitution provides that:

(1) Every person shall have the right to equality before the law and to equal protection of the law.
(2) No person shall be unfairly discriminated against, directly or indirectly, and, without derogating from the generality of this provision, on one or more of the following grounds in particular: race, gender, sex, ethnic or social origin, colour, sexual orientation, age, disability, religion, conscience, belief, culture or language.
(3) This section shall not preclude measures designed to achieve the adequate protection and advancement of persons or groups or categories of persons disadvantaged by unfair discrimination, in order to enable their full and equal enjoyment of all rights and freedoms.
(4) Prima facie proof of discrimination on any of the grounds specified in subsection (2) shall be presumed to be sufficient proof of unfair discrimination as contemplated in that subsection, until the contrary is established.

227. Equality and discrimination are the focal points of the Promotion of Equality and Prevention of Unfair Discrimination Act[156] (Equality Act) that gives effect to the Constitution. It binds the state and all persons, described as including juristic, non-juristic and even a group or category of persons. The Act specifically lists race, gender, sex, pregnancy, marital status, ethnic or social origin, colour, sexual orientation, age, disability, religion, conscience, belief, culture, language and birth as 'prohibited grounds' for discrimination. This is not a *numerus clausus* as it furthermore contains criteria that courts may apply to determine which other characteristics are prohibited grounds. It prohibits discrimination which is described in section 1(1)(viii) as 'any act

155. C. Albertyn & B. Goldblatt, 'The Bill of Rights: Equality', in *Constitutional Law of South Africa* Part 2 Ch. 31 (S. Woolman & M. Bishop, eds.); P. Bracher, *Gender Premiums and Discrimination* in NRSA Insurance law September 2011 (updated at www.nortonrosefullbright.com) (last consulted on 10 Feb. 2015).
156. Act 4 of 2000.

or omission, including a policy, law, rule, practice, condition or situation which directly or indirectly: (a) imposes burdens, obligations or disadvantages on; or (b) withholds benefits, opportunity or advantages from any person on one or more of the prohibited grounds'.

228. Clearly inequality could affect the validity of a contract or contractual clause, as it may be contrary to public policy to enforce a clause agreed to while labouring under the inequality. It must be kept in mind that the right to equality in fact does not prohibit discrimination but rather unfair discrimination. *See President of the Republic of South Africa and Another v. Hugo*[157] that '[w]e need, therefore, to develop a concept of unfair discrimination which recognizes that although a society which affords each human being equal treatment on the basis of equal worth and freedom is our goal, we cannot achieve that goal by insisting upon identical treatment in all circumstances before that goal is achieved'. Discrimination is, in terms of the Constitution section 8(4) from the outset assumed or deemed to be unfair unless it is established to be fair in accordance with specific statutory criteria. When determining whether discrimination is fair or not, one should evaluate the outcomes or impact of the discriminatory treatment on the victim, and also weigh the importance of the limitation with the proportionality of the infringement. Even though South Africa enacted extensive legislation to prohibit most forms of discrimination, it allows for affirmative action to be taken to redress past unfair discrimination.

229. Section 6 of the Equality Act prohibits unfair discrimination in general. The following discriminating factors are identified in paragraph 5 of the Schedule to the Act under insurance services: (a) unfairly refusing on one or more of the prohibited grounds to provide or to make available an insurance policy to any person; (b) unfair discrimination in the provision of benefits, facilities and services related to insurance; and (c) unfairly disadvantaging a person or persons, including unfairly and unreasonably refusing to grant services, to persons solely on the basis of HIV/Aids status. Paragraph 6 of the Act refers specifically to grounds of discrimination regarding exclusion from membership or refusal of benefits from pension funds.[158]

230. Care must be taken in insurance risk profiling in order not to discriminate unfairly by merely using stereotypes in classifying risk groups. Use must be made of precise risk-tailored classifications to attempts to group together equal-risk insureds. The degree of risk is inevitably determined on the basis of a specific group's common or general characteristics which are material to the risk. Some insureds placed in a group do not necessarily share the average characteristics of that group with the result that the rate discriminates against them.

231. It is emphasized that discrimination in insurance is not prohibited outright and that it can be justified as a form of personalization of the insurance product. One must recognize that it is impossible not to take person-related factors into consideration when assessing insurance risks, and that individual characteristics must be considered without being classified outright as discriminatory per se. It allows insurers to maintain financially sound underwriting policies, to bring competitive offers to the market and enables insurers to charge different premiums for the different risk profiles. By doing

---

157. 1997 (4) SA 1 (SCA) 41.

158. A.G. Nienaber & D. Van der Nest, *An Exploration of the Impact of a Claimant's HIV/AIDS Status on a Personal Injury Claim*, 2 *TSAR* 290 (2002).

this, it also offers the benefit that it acts as a deterrent as it can persuade insureds to reduce their risks.

232. It is a common understanding that not all types of discrimination should be tolerated. The issue is how to identify acceptable grounds for differentiation and the limits for legitimate economic discrimination. To maintain equity among insured persons, each policyholder should be charged a rate proportional to the actual risk he transfers to the insurer. If one person is allowed to pay less than his or her share to prevent discrimination, it will necessitate an overcharge against other persons, again creating inequality and reverse discrimination.

233. The right not to be discriminated against is enshrined in international and regional agreements and instruments that are legally binding. South Africa has enacted specific anti-discrimination laws and acknowledges a list of factors in their own constitutions or other laws, and also confirms, adopts or ratifies the international principles found in these instruments. The primary documents which south Africa respects and enforces includes The Universal Declaration on Human Rights, adopted by the United Nations General Assembly in 1948, and the International Covenant on Economic, Social and Cultural Rights (ICESCR) as the primary international legal source of economic, social and cultural rights. This is supplemented by the Optional Protocol to the International Covenant on Economic, Social and Cultural Rights as established in accordance with the Vienna Declaration and Programme of Action. The Convention on the Rights of the Child and the Convention on the Elimination of All Forms of Discrimination against Women recognizes and protects many of the economic, social and cultural rights recognized in the ICESCR relevant to children and women. Furthermore, the Convention on the Elimination of All Forms of Racial Discrimination prohibits discrimination on the basis of racial or ethnic origin pertaining to a number of economic, social and cultural rights. The Convention on the Rights of Persons with Disabilities prohibits all discrimination on the basis of disability. Regionally the African Charter on Human and Peoples' Rights aims to protect a range of economic, social and cultural rights within the African human rights systems.

234. In South Africa insurance discrimination in the form of economic and statistical discrimination appears to be the norm. Economic discrimination, specifically price discrimination causes insurers to charge minorities higher rates, and deal discrimination disqualifies some minorities to access the same extent or nature of cover. With statistical discrimination stereotyping is based on the average behaviour of a specific risk group. This causes the unfair discrimination of atypical individuals from the disadvantaged group.

235. The most prolific factors in the country that constitute discriminatory conduct include age, gender, disability, pregnancy and maternity, sexual orientation, education risk-related occupation and area of residence or geographical location (persons who, for example, reside in areas where crime rates are higher could pay more for home insurance). The latter has been perceived as a type of discrimination based on race, as segregation of persons in residential areas is still a national reality.[159]

236. Statistical discrimination is mostly tolerated where, for example, older people are charged more for life insurance, people with a medical history more for

159. A. Kok, *The Promotion of Equality and Unfair Discrimination Act: Why the Controversy?*, 294(5) *TSAR* 294 (2001).

health insurance and men charged more in the calculation of motor insurance premiums. This may be criticized on the basis that it violates the primary insurance principle that risk must be calculated by taking all the relevant information into account, and that one cannot treat all persons and all risks equally.

237. Techniques that cause discrimination most often include pricing or premium adjustments and limitations of benefits or cover. Insurers must be allowed to complete realistic risk assessments as bespoke cover for each individual is not a feasible option. They should always respect principles of transparency, anti-discrimination, proportionality and good customer policy such as TCF. The TCF principles specifically the FSB's 'Treating Customers Fairly Framework': Annexure B on fairness in service or product delivery are being introduced in South Africa. These will apply for instance where a customer may not have been treated fairly, for example, if sold a product such as a policy on which they subsequently may be unable to claim. Clearly discrimination should be avoided unless it is justified by a legitimate aim, and means of achieving it are appropriate and necessary, with a reasonable proportion between the differentiated treatment and the aim pursued.

238. A universal cause for concern appears to be the so-called marginal cases where persons are merely temporarily lacking in the criteria required for proper risk differentiation. This would include individuals who have been diagnosed from suffering from, for example, epilepsy, dementia and schizophrenia in the past, yet who upon full recuperation, fail to procure sufficient cover in future due to their medical history. This has not yet been addressed by statutory or industry rules in South Africa.

239. Gender determines risk especially in motor insurance, life insurance; annuities; superannuation and private health insurance. It is likely that a transition towards unisex or gender neutral pricing will affect existing premiums or benefits for both genders, balancing out the market. Depending on the product, certain categories of consumers could experience either a price increase or decrease.[160]

240. The industry is assisted by the developing science of genetics or geneticism. In the past, South African insurers discriminated based on the factual family history disclosed to them by the insured (e.g., the tendency to develop breast cancer in the female line, or familial heart disease), or where an existing condition manifested from general medical tests (e.g., high cholesterol levels or high blood pressure). An increase in mandatory genetic testing by insurers will enable them to more accurately predict risks, which could both decrease and increase discrimination based on the genotype of a person rather than their individual merits.[161]

---

160. H. Combrinck, *Testing the Boundaries: Women's Equality in South Africa, in The Principle of Equality – A South African and Belgian Perspective* 230 (J. Vandelotte, J. Sarkin & Y. Haecks eds. Maklu 2001); B. Kuschke, *Gender Equality in Insurance: Association belge des Consommateurs Test-Achats ASBL, Vann van Vugt, Charles Basselier v. Conseil des ministers*, 3 De Jure 624 (2012); A. Kok, *Motor Vehicle Insurance, the Constitution and the Promotion of Equality and Prevention of Unfair Discrimination Act*, 18 SAJHR 59 (2002); *see also* the Women Empowerment and Gender Equality Bill (as introduced in the National Assembly (proposed s. 75)); explanatory summary of the Bill published in Government Gazette No. 37005 of 6 Nov. 2013.

161. B. Kuschke, *Access to Genetic Information and the Insurer's Duty of Genetic Data Protection*, 2 De Jure 305 (2007); A.G. Nienaber & D. Van der Nest, *Genetic Testing for the Purpose of Insurance Risk Assessment and the Constitutional Right to Privacy*, 67(3) THRHR 451 (2004).

241. The implementation of anti-discrimination rules falls within a variety of institutions or official bodies that regulate, enforce, control or decide on discrimination issues. Some are state or governmental, whereas others are industry related, such as the insurance Ombud. South African Equality courts include all magistrates' courts and the High Courts. The High Court of Appeal and the Constitutional Court have jurisdiction on issues pertaining to constitutional rights.

242. The South African Human Rights Commission is an independent national institution established to support constitutional democracy. It is committed to promote respect for, observance of and protection of human rights for everyone without fear or favour. The Commission was established and inaugurated on 2 October 1995 under the Human Rights Commission Act.[162] It is made up of Commissioners and a Secretariat. Commissioners provide strategic leadership and direct policy. They are appointed by the Parliament on a seven-year term and can be reappointed to an additional term.

243. The CGE is also an independent institution in South Africa that draws its mandate from the South African Constitution by way of the Commission for Gender Equality Act of 1996. The vision of the CGE is 'a society free from gender oppression and inequality'. Its mission is to 'advance, promote and protect gender equality in South Africa through undertaking research, public education, policy development, legislative initiatives, effective monitoring and litigation'.

244. Very little case law on discrimination specifically in the insurance industry has been reported, although many deal with discrimination in other contexts. Regarding gender, sex, marriage and maternity discrimination in insurance three judgments may be highlighted.

245. The earliest case to be heard when the final Constitution was enacted in 1996 was *Brink v. Kitshoff NO*[163] where the issue of discrimination against married women of certain benefits of life insurance policies was brought before the court. The court had to determine whether section 44 of the Insurance Act[164] was in conflict with the provisions of Chapter 3 of the Constitution of the Republic of South Africa Act (1993), in so far as it discriminates against married women by depriving them, in certain circumstances, of all or some of the benefits of life insurance policies ceded to them or made in their favour by their husbands. O'Reagan J stated in paragraph 50 of the judgment that: 'The purposes sought to be achieved by the provisions do not require a distinction to be drawn between married women and married men. The discrimination occasioned by the provisions cannot be said to be reasonable or justifiable.'

246. In *Satchwell v. President of the Republic of South Africa*[165] that dealt with discrimination of same-sex partners in claiming pension and retirement benefits, the court held that any differentiation on this basis was discriminatory. It may be noted that same-sex marriages were only legalized in South Africa in 2006, after this case was heard.

---

162. Act 54 of 1994.
163. 1996 (4) 197 (CC).
164. Act 27 of 1943.
165. 2002 (6) SA (CC) 1.

247. The case of *Robert and Others v. Minister of Social Development*[166] dealt with both age discrimination and gender discrimination. The court was required to address the differentiation between the ages of indigent men and women who qualified for social benefit grants. Women qualified for the grant from the age of 60, whereas men only qualified after having attained the age of 65. The discrimination was found not to be unfair as it attempted to redress past injustices against women in the country, yet was not decided on age alone.

248. In the judgment in *Minister of Finance v. Van Heerden*[167] it was held that differentiated employer contributions to a pension fund, based on a person's level of employment or employment position, was discriminatory in nature.

249. To evaluate whether the challenged differentiation constitutes unfair discrimination, one should consider whether the differentiation is based on one or more of the prohibited grounds, which is an attribute or a characteristic that can have the potential to impair the fundamental human dignity of persons as human beings or to affect them adversely in a comparable manner. Further development in jurisprudence on these issues can be expected as the awareness of the general population pertaining to discriminatory practices increases.

250. Insurers will have to note not only developments on a national level regarding discriminatory conduct in the private commercial sphere, but also international trends that affect the insurance industry at large, such as the one highlighted by the European Union (EU) ruling in the case of *Association belge des Consommateurs Test-Achats ASBL, Vann van Vugt, Charles Basselier v. Conseil des ministres* C-236/09 heard in the European Court of Justice, and the responses of EU countries subsequent to the judgment.

---

166. No. 32838/05 High Court (TPD) September 2007.
167. 2004 (6) SA 121 (CC).

Chapter 3. Formation of the Insurance Contract

§1. Validity Requirements

251. South Africa does not have a specific statute dedicated to insurance contract law. The LTIA, STIA and FAIS acts do not regulate the conclusion of insurance contracts, although they address some aspects thereof. FAIS, for example, deals extensively with the duties of financial advisors, for example, the duty of disclosure of information prior to the conclusion of the insurance contract.

252. In addition to these statutes the Electronic Communications and Transactions Act[168] also enjoys some application as it applies to contracts concluded via data messages as well as the protection of electronic data and other related matters.

253. A contract is an agreement made with the intention to be legally bound thereto. In essence what is required for the conclusion of a legally binding contract is consensus between legal subjects who have the capacity to do so, and which agreement is lawful, physically possible to perform and certain, and complies with any prescribed formalities, reached with the intention of creating a legal obligation with resulting rights and duties.[169]

254. The general requirements for the conclusion of any contract are therefore consensus, contractual capacity, legality, physical possibility and certainty and formalities, should they be required by statute or by the parties themselves. These also have to be met for the conclusion of insurance contracts, and are discussed in greater detail separately below.

255. Generally, contracts of insurance are concluded informally and need not be in writing to be valid, but the standard practice is to reduce insurance contracts to writing. Therefore, any document that expresses the terms of a contract of insurance is called a 'policy'.[170]

256. It should be mentioned that good faith is not a general requirement for the conclusion of valid contracts in South Africa.[171] In insurance contracts, the legal duty of good faith that the one party owes the other is concerned with the pre-contractual duty of the parties to disclose information to each other prior to the conclusion of the contract. This duty is discussed in greater detail under the section on misrepresentation below.

257. The notion that an insurance contract may be a contract of utmost good faith was rejected by our Appeal court in 1985 in the case of *Mutual & Federal Insurance Co Ltd v. Oudtshoorn Municipality*[172] as this concept was foreign to Roman-Dutch law and therefore did not form part of our common law. Furthermore, the

168. 25 of 2002.
169. B. Prozesky-Kuschke, *Law of Contract*, in *Commercial Law*, para. 3.82 (Nagel, C.J. et al. eds).
170. Prozesky-Kuschke, para. 24.55.
171. *Brisley v. Drotsky* 2002 (4) SA (SCA) 1.
172. 1985 (1) SA 419 (A).

presence of good faith is not acknowledged as an essential element of insurance contracts.[173]

258. Because the application of the Roman law defence *exceptio doli generalis* has been abolished in our law,[174] broad considerations of equity, good faith and fairness also cannot provide a general defence against contractual liability. The role of good faith in our law is therefore limited, in that it merely underlies the duty imposed on the parties to act in good faith towards one another during the negotiations preceding their eventual agreement. This relates only to their duty to disclose material facts. Some essential provisions are relevant in the context negotiating, concluding and eventually performing an insurance relationship. It is suggested that failure to disclose these terms or, if they are disclosed incorrectly may constitute a material intentional or negligent misrepresentation. This will render the contract voidable at the option of the innocent party. The essential terms viewed from the insurer's side include: (a) details of the cover to be provided (the nature and extent of cover of the product); (b) the name and legal status of the insurer; (c) the premium to be paid and payment details; (d) the effect of non-payment of the premium; and from the side of the insurer; (e) special terms and conditions, exclusions, waiting periods, loadings, penalties, excesses, restrictions or circumstances in which benefits will not be provided. From the side of the insured all facts that (a) increase the risk or (b) reduce the risk, form essential elements which require proper disclosure to the insurer.

259. Failure to comply with this duty, whether by positive conduct or by omission, whether intentionally or negligently, leads to a misrepresentation. This renders the contract not void but merely voidable at the election of the prejudiced party. Where the misrepresentation is blameworthy in that it is made intentionally or negligently, a claim for delictual damages may also arise.[175]

260. Furthermore, once the contract is concluded (for which good faith is not a separate requirement), the parties must, where, for example, a fiduciary relationship exists between them, perform their respective contractual duties in good faith towards each other. In failing to do so, they might run the risk of breaching the contract between them. The role of good faith in South African law may thus differ from that in other jurisdictions such as in English and Australia law.[176]

261. For the conclusion of a specific nominate contract of insurance, consensus must be reached on the required *essentialia.* These are dealt with in greater detail below.

§2. Formation of the Contract

262. Consensus in South African law is based primarily on the will theory that requires corresponding intentions or wills. Where the parties are not *ad idem* true consensus cannot exist, yet one party may believe that he has concluded a contract due to his reliance upon the other party's conduct. Our law therefore recognizes a

173. Reinecke et al., paras 2.20 and 8.20.
174. *Bank of Lisbon and South Africa Ltd v. De Ornelas* 1988 (3) SA 580 (A).
175. D. Hutchison et al., *The Law of Contract in South Africa* Ch. 4, 115 (Oxford U. Press 2013).
176. *Mutual & Federal Insurance Co Ltd v. Oudtshoorn Municipality* 431.

secondary basis for consensus, on the direct reliance theory. This theory entails that the reasonable reliance created by one party in the mind of another that consensus actually exists and is recognized as consensus for a binding contractual obligation.[177]

263. Consensus requires negotiations between the parties. In practice, the offer for insurance is usually made by the insured upon completion of a standard application form. The insured usually, in response to advertising or marketing done by the insurer, makes the first offer to the insurer by completing a proposal or application. After perusing the information the insurer may accept the prospective policyholder's offer, resulting in the required agreement.

264. This is not always the case, as it could be possible that the initial comprehensive offer is actually made by the insurer to the insured, awaiting the latter's approval or acceptance, or that the insurer makes a counter-offer in response to the insured's initial proposal. Whatever the structure is, will depend on the facts and circumstances of each case. In *Nkungwini v. Old Mutual*[178] there was a dispute on whether a valid contract of insurance came into existence. As there was no consensus between the parties on the essential terms of the agreement, there was no contract and the insurance company was obliged to pay back all the premiums they have collected from Mr Nkungwini.

265. What is required for binding consensus is that a firm, complete, clear and certain offer must be must be accepted unconditionally and unequivocally by the addressee of the offer, in a conscious response to the offer. The acceptance must also be in the form prescribed by the offeror should there be one.[179]

266. As stated above, the offer and acceptance do not have to be in writing to create a valid insurance contract. Contracts may be concluded informally such as by telephone, by means of electronic communications or via a website and automated systems. In these cases the Electronic Communications and Transactions Act applies. The Act in section 12 recognizes data messages that are accessible as 'writing'. Furthermore, in accordance with section 13(2) an electronic signature is recognized as a so-called wet signature.

267. The exact time and place of conclusion of the contract are important as it determines the moment from which rights and duties exist between the parties. This is often the moment from which cover is granted (unless the parties agree on a future commencement or implementation date), the currency of statutes that apply to the relationship between the parties, their contractual capacity and also what the governing law and jurisdiction for dispute resolution will be. The default theory that applies to most contracts is the information theory. It determines the time and place of conclusion to be the time and place when the offeror who made the final offer during negotiations is informed that his offer has been accepted.[180]

268. Two exceptions to this rule exist in South African law. The first is that where a contract is concluded by traditional post (both offer and acceptance exchanged via the postal system), the time and place where the acceptance is posted will be the time and place of conclusion. This is called the expedition theory. The offeror may

177. Hutchison et al., Chs 2 and 3; *Sonap Petroleum (SA) (Pty) Ltd v. Pappadogianis* 1992 (3) SA 234 (A).
178. [2017] ZAECMHC 10.
179. Hutchison et al., paras 2.2 and 2.3.
180. *Ficksburg Transport (Edms) Bpk v. Rautenbach* 1988 (1) SA 318 (A) 332; Hutchison et al., 57.

exclude this default position by a stipulation to that effect in his offer. He may prescribe a different medium of communication for the acceptance or state that their contract will only exist upon receipt of the acceptance or only once the content thereof has come to his attention. One could hold the opinion that this position is outdated due to the disuse of ordinary mail in favour of communication by electronic means, yet is still applies and its application should be noted.[181]

269. The Communications and Transactions Act[182] provides for an exception to both previous theories. A contract concluded via data message as defined in section 1 of the Act will be concluded at the time that the final acceptance enters the information system or server of the addressee thereof. This is known as the reception theory. The place of conclusion, however, is deemed to be the place where the offeror usually resides or where his place of business is situated.[183]

270. The contract, which is concluded between the parties, is usually embodied in a written policy document. The policy document may in some cases, for example, where the contract of insurance is concluded by telephone or via the internet, be issued by the insurer to the insured only after date of conclusion of the insurance contract. The application form completed by the insured is usually incorporated into the written contract by reference. Each renewal or reinstatement of a contract constitutes a new contract of insurance. The insured has no automatic right to renewal. Where the insurer sends a renewal notice to the insured at the end of an insurance term, this usually constitutes a new offer for insurance. Should the insured accept this offer for renewal, a new insurance contract comes into existence as soon as the term of the previous contract comes to an end. The acceptance can be made orally or through conduct, for example, where the insured continues to pay his premiums after termination of the original contract. The renewed contract is not an extension of the previous contract, but a totally new contract, which immediately replaces the previous contract.[184]

271. For a contract to be identified as a specific nominate contract, the parties must reach consensus on the *essentialia* or essential minimum elements for that specific type of contract. For conclusion of an insurance contract specifically, the parties must reach consensus on the essential elements at the least as mentioned above.

272. An element of uncertainty or contingency is most certainly essential for insurance. It is in this aspect that insurance can be confused with gambling or wagering, as both types of agreement depend on the occurrence of an uncertain future event. In both cases a benefit that becomes due upon the occurrence of the event. The risk in insurance is described as the possibility that a specific peril will cause loss, harm or prejudice.[185]

273. The doctrine of insurable interest is a foreign doctrine to South African law, an insurable interest is not an essential element for the conclusion of an insurance contract. The intentions of the parties will indicate whether their contract is one of insurance, or merely a wager. The object or subject matter of insurance is that an

181. *Cape Explosive Works Ltd v. South African Oil and Fat Industries*; *Cape Explosive Works Ltd v. Lever Brothers (South Africa) Ltd* 1921 CPD 244.
182. Act 25 of 2002.
183. Section 22(2) of the Act on the time of conclusion; s. 23(b)–(c) on the place of conclusion.
184. Nienaber & Reinecke, Ch. 9 at para. 16.
185. Reinecke et al., 1, 75, 79.

insurable interest must exist only at the time of materialization of the risk insured against. No claim can be made under an existing policy if an insurable interest is lacking when the risk materializes. It is not a requirement for the existence of the insurance policy itself. As was amplified in the case of *Refrigerated Trucking (Pty) Ltd v. Zive (Aegis Insurance Co Ltd, third party)*,[186] insurable interest is not defined strictly as in English law, but is merely employed as a yardstick for damage or loss. In South Africa, the difference theory is applied to determine whether a loss or damage occurred. The difference between the value of a person's patrimonial estate had the insured event not occurred, and the value of his estate once it has occurred, reflects his interest and represents the loss he suffered. This was addressed specifically regarding insurance in the case of *Dippenaar v. Shield Insurance Co Ltd*[187] and *Evins v. Shield Insurance Co Ltd.*[188]

274. A subjective approach is followed to establish whether loss has in fact occurred. An evaluation of the position of the parties in each situation is required, as confirmed in *ISEP Structural Engineering & Plating (Pty) Ltd v. Inland Exploration Co (Pty) Ltd.*[189] Even expectancies are recognized as part of a person's patrimony and therefore as insurable interests. Reinecke reiterates this viewpoint that '[n]othing should restrict an insurable interest to something less than loss or damage and neither is there any justification for extending insurable interest to something more than loss or damage'.[190]

275. The position on insurable interest in capital insurance is uncertain due to lack of legal precedent. As stated above, capital insurance law follows English law, even though Roman-Dutch law was reinstated as the common law for insurance in 1977. The opinion is held that an interest will be eligible for capital insurance cover if its loss or impairment would cause prejudice or immeasurable hardship such as pain, emotional distress, disfigurement, discomfort, loneliness, mental shock or inconvenience. Although it is an implied duty, some policies specifically state that the policyholder has the duty to mitigate his losses. A policyholder has to act proactively in order to prevent the risk from materializing, and must limit the extent of the harm once it occurs.

276. Once a loss has occurred, the claim has vested and the insurer's liability in terms of the policy has been determined, the loss must be quantified. Property policies mostly require the policyholder to give 'prompt' or 'immediate' notice to the insurer of the loss within specified time limits, which provides the insurer with the opportunity to investigate, determine or adjust a claim. The interpretation of whether the policyholder complied with this provision will clearly depend on the facts and circumstances, as well as the policy wording, of each case. For 'all risk' policies the policyholder typically carries the burden of proving that the damage to the insured property was caused by a proximate insured peril. The insurer then carries the burden to prove that the claim falls within a policy exclusion. In case of 'named-peril' policies

186. 1996 (2) SA 361 (T).
187. 1979 (2) SA 904(A).
188. 1980 (2) SA 814 (A). *See also* Hutchison et al., 329.
189. 1981 (4) SA 1 (A).
190. Reinecke et al., 330, 338.

the policyholder shoulders a heavier burden, as he has to prove that the damage resulted from one of the specifically named perils.[191]

277. Reference is often made that cover is limited to a 'direct loss' caused by the realization of the risk. The exact meaning of 'direct physical loss or damage' is often contested. It is often found to exclude a decrease in property value, pure economic loss and consequential or intangible loss. The word 'direct' in this context can be interpreted as meaning proximate or dominant. In order to avoid the problematic issue of compensation valuation and quantification, clauses in the policy document such as a reinstatement clause, a valued policy or a policy for new value may simplify matters.[192]

278. Generally speaking, various factors can influence consensus. A contract is void where a party can prove that he made a reasonable and material error, known as an *iustus error*. Factors that render the contract merely voidable include material misrepresentation, duress, undue influence and economic bribery.[193]

279. In accordance with the duty of good faith, a pre-contractual duty of disclosure rests on the insurance proposer to disclose material and relevant information to the insurer that affects the latter's decision to insure the risk or not. Providing sufficient information for risk determination is crucial for insurance business. Failure to do so will result in an actionable misrepresentation, provided that the misrepresentation was wrongful and material, yet will not void the contract *ipso facto*. Where the innocent party elects to void the contract based on any of these factors, he must give notice of his election to the other party and full restitution must be given.[194]

280. In addition to the contractual consequences, the innocent party may also institute a claim for delictual damages (known in other jurisdictions as damages claimable in tort). Damages may be recouped in this manner only where the misrepresentation was intentional or negligent.[195]

281. The requirements to succeed with a delictual claim in South African law that the plaintiff must prove the following on balance of probabilities: conduct (either positive conduct or an omission); wrongfulness (unless a ground of justification exists for the wrongdoing); fault (intent or negligence, whether it is in the latter case *culpa levis* or *culpa lata*); factual causation (determined by the *conditio sine qua non* test) and legal causation (usually determined by the application of aspects such as foresee ability, proximate cause and public policy); and finally damages. The injured party must suffer some form of patrimonial or non-patrimonial damage, harm or loss.[196]

282. As stated above, the presence of good faith is not a general requirement for the conclusion of valid contracts.[197] In insurance contracts, the legal duty of good faith is concerned with the pre-contractual duty of the parties to disclose information to each other prior to the conclusion of the contract. The duty is derived primarily from common law, and the statutory rights of access to information in accordance with

191. Reinecke et al., 330.
192. Reinecke et al., 32.
193. Hutchison et al., Chs 3 and 4.
194. Reinecke et al., 53, 132, 139–144.
195. Reinecke et al., 28, 134.
196. J. Neethling & J.M. Potgieter, *Neethling Potgieter Visser's Law of Delict* 4 (LexisNexis 2014).
197. *Brisley v. Drotsky* 2002 (4) SA 1 (SCA).

the provisions of the Constitution and the Promotion of Access to Information Act.[198] The constitutional right is embodied in section 32(1) of the Constitution that '[e]veryone has the right of access to (b) any information held by another person and that is required for the exercise or protection of any rights'. The Constitution provides for the horizontal application of the right of access to information held by another person to everyone when that information is required for the exercise or protection of any of the latter's rights. In accordance with this, the Promotion of Access to Information Act aims to give effect to the constitutional right of access to any information held by the State and any information that is held by another person and that is required for the exercise or protection of any rights; and to provide for matters connected therewith.

283. All parties to the contract must give the required contractual capacity to conclude a valid and binding contract. Persons married in community of property may only deal with their insurance policies, particularly regarding the cession or cancellation of such policies, after obtaining the required consent from their spouse according to the provisions of section 15 of the Matrimonial Property Act.[199] This is especially relevant where spouses deal with insurance policies or their rights thereunder. Consent without any formalities (consent may be given expressly or tacitly, verbally or through conduct) from the other spouse is required where the one spouse receives any payment to which the other spouse is entitled from the proceeds of any insurance policy or annuity in favour of the other spouse. The written consent of the other (non-acting) spouse must be obtained where shares, stocks, debentures, debenture bonds, insurance policies, mortgage bonds, fixed deposits or similar assets are alienated, ceded or pledged.[200] Some insurance contracts are incapable of being ceded. In *Propell Specialised Finance (Pty) Ltd v. Attorneys Insurance Indemnity Fund NPC and Others*[201] the court ruled that due to the sui generis nature of professional insurance such as was offered by the first defendant, a *pactum de non cedendo* could be read into the contract.

284. Where this is done in the normal course of business, occupation or trade of the acting spouse, consent need not be obtained. Consent may in certain cases be given after the transaction by way of *ex post facto* ratification. This is not possible in case of a contract of suretyship, or where registration in the Deeds Office is required (such as for the transfer of immovable property, in which case the signatures of both spouses are required at the time that the deeds are lodged), yet is the case where the spouse deals with insurance policies. One should keep in mind that policy provisions may prescribe formalities above and beyond these as provided for in the Act, that will affect the validity or effectiveness of the conduct of the insured parties.[202]

285. The consequences of a failure to obtain the required consent is that the conduct does bind the joint estate, yet allows the prejudiced spouse to claim from the share of the defaulting spouse who fails to obtain consent. If the third party, with or towards whom the juristic act was performed (e.g., with whom the contract was concluded), was not aware of the fact, or should not reasonably have been aware of the fact, that consent was never given, the joint estate remains bound to the contract.

198. Act 2 of 2000.
199. Act 88 of 1984.
200. Nienaber & Reinecke, 219, Reinecke et al., 229.
201. [2017] ZAWCHC 71, [2017] 3 Saa SA 1005 (WCC) (Unreported, 30 Jun. 2017).
202. Nienaber & Reinecke, 219.

Thus, upon dissolution of the marriage through divorce or death, the share of the joint estate to which the acting spouse is entitled, will be held liable for the damage caused to the estate by the act performed without consent.[203]

286. Juristic or legal persons include companies, close corporations, statutory entities and common law associations or societies. Trusts, partnerships and joint ventures are not *ipso facto* separate entities, yet are in limited situations recognized as individual entities with separate legal personality by statute. This is, for example, the case in terms of the NCA[204] and the CPA.[205] The capacity of a legal person depends on its founding documents or constitution, and on statute. Companies are regulated by the Companies Act, and a company doing business as an insurer by the LTIA, STIA and FAIS Act as discussed above.

287. Contracts must conform to the requirements of legality. The conclusion of the contract, its purpose and any performance due in terms of the agreement may not be contrary to statutory measures, public policy or good morals. Where a contract is illegal due to the operation of a statute, the consequences depend on the intention of the legislator. The sanction that is provided for by the legislation could be that the illegal contract is void, that the conduct of the party is a punishable offence for which monetary penalties or fines must be paid, or both. In some cases, the insurer who concludes illegal contracts failing to act in accordance with the common law or with statutory prescriptions, may be prohibited or limited in continuing its insurance business.[206]

288. The criteria of what is contrary to public policy and what not is vague and depends on the facts and circumstances of each particular situation. Where a contentious contractual provision is so unreasonable that it offends public policy, freedom to contract and the sanctity of contract should bear less weight and bow before public policy that requires the provision to be unenforceable. In the words of the judge in *Sasfin (Pty) Ltd v. Beukes*:[207] '[p]ublic policy should take into account the 'doing of simple justice between man and man'. The determination of public policy considerations is informed by constitutional values. The Supreme Court of Appeal in the case of *Barkhuizen v. Napier*[208] paragraph 13 cautioned that 'intruding on apparently voluntarily concluded arrangements is a step that Judges should countenance with care, particularly when it requires them to impose their individual conceptions of fairness and justice on parties' individual arrangements'. Public policy is deeply rooted in the Constitution and its underlying values. It can accommodate and limit the application of the principle of *pacta sunt servanda*. Public policy cannot be separated from the notions of fairness, justice and equity and reasonableness which are all open-ended. Constitutional values inform the interpretation of policy considerations in each individual case.[209]

289. As these principles apply especially to all contractual provisions containing limitations, exclusions and restraints, their impact should be noted by the insurance

203. Hutchison et al., Ch. 5.
204. Act 34 of 2005.
205. Act 68 of 2008.
206. Hutchison et al., Ch. 7.
207. 1989 (1) SA 1 (AD) 7.
208. 2007 5 SA 323(CC).
209. Hutchison et al., 35–38.

industry where these clauses are prolific and appear in most policy documents. Complications arise especially where an insured signs a standard-form document that contains clauses that he is unaware of or that are unexpected. As illiteracy is still a major problem in Africa, care must be taken by insurers especially to bring exemption and exclusion clauses to the attention of the insured. Many inexperienced and illiterate insurance consumers are exposed to contractual limitations they do not always understand.

290. Insurance contracts are adhesion or standard-form contracts *par excellence*. Whether it is in the public interest to allow enforcement of the terms contained in these contracts or not, can be challenging. In *Barkhuizen v. Napier* the court provided the following guidance in this regard:

> What is needed is neither a blanket acceptance of standard form terms, nor a blanket rejection, nor an ad hoc determination by each judge in accordance with his or her predilections as to what is fair nor not, but rather a principled approach based on objective criteria that are consistent with the principles of contract law and with sensitivity to the way in which economic power in public affairs should be appropriately regulated to ensure standards of fairness in an open and democratic society.[210]

291. In accordance with the principle of *ex turpi causa non oritur actio*, no contract can exist where legality is absent. Loosely translated, it means that no action may arise from an illegal contract. In terms of the *par delictum* rule, any performance already delivered by a party to an illegal contract, cannot be reclaimed by an enrichment action where both parties were aware of the illegality of their agreement. This rule may on principles of equity be relaxed by a court of law. A court may order the delivery of counter-performance in any proportion that it deems fit.[211]

292. The consequences in the absence of statutory legality requirements in the life insurance industry are in this regard are strictly regulated by section 60(1) of the LTIA. The Act provides that '[a] long-term policy, whether entered into before or after the commencement of this Act, shall not be void merely because a provision of a law, including a provisions of this Act, has been contravened or not complied with in connection with it'. This clearly provides the uninformed insured with some protection. Where an insured procures insurance from an insurer who is not entitled to enter into such a contract, section 60(2) provides that the insured may cancel the contract by giving written notice to that effect. The contract is not void *ab initio*, on the other hand, the election to cancel the contract does not vest only with the insured. The Registrar may also cancel the contract by issuing a notice to that effect in the *Government Gazette.* In both instances the insurer will be liable for breach of contract.[212]

293. Performance must be objectively possible and certain. Absence of certainty renders the contract void for vagueness. Certainty entails that performance, such as the payment of the premium, must be determined or at least determinable. In the latter

210. At para. 146.
211. *Klokow v. Sullivan* 2006 (1) SA 258 (SCA).
212. Nienaber & Reinecke, Ch. 2 at paras 9–14.

case, the law requires some form of certainty in the formula or method of determination, for example, valuation by third parties, market-related pricing and the like.[213]

294. The final requirement for the conclusion of a valid contract is that the agreement must conform to formalities prescribed by statue or by the parties themselves. Insurance contracts do not, as a general rule, have to be in writing to be valid and enforceable. No insurance legislation exists that addresses this as a validity requirement. Stamp duties have also been abolished for new policies in accordance with the Revenue Laws Amendment Act which was signed into law on 8 January 2009.[214] Older contracts concluded or documentation issued prior to this date and that carried stamp duty which was not paid, cannot serve as evidence in a court of law, until penalty duties have been paid.

295. It should be noted that, although the CPA does not apply to insurance, general consumer protection principles as well as the PPR in terms of the LTIA and the STIA require contracts to be in plain language. An aspect that complicates matter in South Africa somewhat is that the country has eleven official languages. As this is a relatively newer dispensation (post 1994), and on a practical level, it is not ascertainable to expect all documentation to be issues or available in all official languages. As English is the most prevalent language in general business and trade, most insurance documentation, statutes and the like are in English, which makes them accessible to the international community. A deviation will most probably only occur where an insured insists on being served with documents and communications in another of the official languages. Clearly demands of this nature will place a heavy burden on insurers if they have to ensure that documentation is available in all languages. It can be accepted that translation will be done on an ad hoc basis only when required.

296. A failure to provide insurance contract documentation in the insured's language of choice may be a form of discrimination, with its ensuing consequences. It may furthermore be contrary to public policy. The evaluation of the requirement of public policy has been discussed extensively above.

297. It is not possible to provide an exhaustive list of all the types of clauses that may form part of an insurance contract or policy document. It is instructive to identify some of the most common types of clauses and their function and effect in the insurance relationship. The contract will contain not only the provisions that the parties have by express agreement included in their agreement. The contract may also contain implied or tacit terms.

298. Some of the terms of an insurance contract may also be described as obligationary or non-obligationary. Obligationary terms refer to performance due and place a positive duty on a party to perform in a particular way. Failure in compliance amounts to breach of contract. Non-obligationary terms on the other hand do not create positive duties on any party to perform. Their function is to regulate the relationship between the parties in other ways. Standard terms and standard-form contracts or contracts of adhesion are typical in the insurance industry. These terms generally appear on insurance proposal form and the proposed insured accepts these terms by submitting the proposal to the insurer. The application does not form part of the insurance contract unless it is expressly included as part of the policy. This is usually

213. Hutchison et al., Ch. 6.

214. Act 60 of 2008.

done by way of a 'basis of contract' clause which declares as follows: (a) that the policyholder confirms that he has investigated his responses; (b) that he warrants that they are correct; (c) that the insurer issues the policy on the basis of these responses; and (d) that the proposal forms part of the insurance policy. Care must be taken to ensure that the policyholder is in fact aware that he is providing a warranty, and that it is not merely a representation of fact, due to the serious nature of the consequences of a breach of warranty.[215]

299. Whether the standard terms are in fact part of an insurance contract in a specific case remains a question of fact. The principles that apply in South African law in so-called ticket contracts become relevant. One must determine whether the potential insured saw the actual wording, and also whether he was aware that it referred to provisions that will apply to his contractual relationship with the insurer. Where the answer to both these questions is in the affirmative, the provisions are binding and form part of the insurance contract. Where this is not the case, one must enquire whether the insurer who issued the terms did everything reasonable to bring them to the attention of the potential insured. What will be reasonable in a specific situation will depend on the facts and circumstances of each case.[216]

300. A policy may confer the discretion upon the insurer to amend its own performance or that of the policyholder during the existence of the policy. A contractual provision that affords the insurer to adapt the cover or increase premiums can be onerous, although terms of this nature are standard practice in especially indemnity insurance policies. A potential insured should not agree to such a provision where it could be to his distinct disadvantage. Any such discretionary terms must be interpreted to mean that the discretion to unilaterally amend contractual provisions pertaining to the performances of the parties should be exercised in accordance with the judgment of a reasonable person. Where a disability policy provides for the payment of a benefit where the insured becomes disabled, a contractual provision may entitle the insurer to determine the nature and extent of the disability and in accordance determine the extent of policy benefits provided. Premiums may also be amended by the insurer according to eventualities and nature of the risk insured. Insurers regularly amend and increase the scope of exclusion clauses.[217]

301. A supposition or assumption is a contractual term which makes the contract dependent on the existence of a fact unknown to the parties. Where the fact assumed proves to be correct, the contract is valid. Where the assumption proves to be incorrect, the contractual obligation has no proper foundation and is held not to be valid. An example would be where the parties assume that a potential insured does not have cancer at the time that he procures the cover. Where it appears that he did have a pre-existing condition, it will affect the validity of the policy and he will not enjoy cover. In each instance the suppositions likely to appear on the application form that the prospective insured completes.[218]

302. Insurance contracts usually contain warranties, in terms of which the insured guarantees or warrants that a specific fact is correct or exists, or that he will

215. Hutchison et al., 117–120.
216. Hutchison et al., 239–240.
217. Nienaber & Reinecke, 143–147; Millard, 88.
218. Hutchison et al., 252.

conduct himself in a particular manner once the policy is in operation. A prospective insured usually completes an application for insurance form and supplies answers to set questions, and then affirms the truth of a statement of fact. This is an affirmative warranty. A promissory warranty has bearing on the future conduct or circumstances of the insured. Warranties are not only provided by the insured. An insurer may guarantee that it will pay a sum of money upon maturity of the policy or the occurrence of a specific event. Promissory warranties were ruled on in two recent cases, namely *Viking Inshore Fishing (Pty) Ltd v. Mutual & Federal Insurance Company Ltd*[219] and *Leading Prospects Trading 38 (Pty) Ltd v. Centrique Insurance Company and Tromp.*[220] In the former case the court *a quo* found in favour of the insurer on the basis of the policyholder's breach of a warranty and stated that the purpose of such a warranty in a contract is to impose certain duties on an insured, and breach of those duties amount to breach of contract. However on appeal the court cautions that the mere fact that there is a breach of a promissory warranty is not in itself a ground for repudiation. Rather, if such breach is inconsequential in relation to the loss, it should not be a ground for an insurer to repudiate the claim. In the latter case, the parties' contract stipulated that the insurer would be entitled to refuse compensation where the aircraft that was insured breached any of the Civil Aviation Regulations. These were incorporated by reference into the contract. The pilot did in fact breach these regulations by flying under 5,000 in circumstances where he was not allowed to do so. This constituted breach of a promissory warranty and therefore entitled the insurer to repudiate the claim.

303. In warranties of fact the insured only warrants facts which fall within his field of knowledge. He can only be held liable for the facts of which he had actual knowledge. An insured who innocently and in good faith makes a faulty warranty, remains liable for breach of warranty (breach of contract). He can protect himself by giving a warranty of knowledge. In a warranty of knowledge the insured warrants the presence or absence of a certain fact, irrespective of whether or not the fact falls within his field of knowledge. An insured can be held liable for breach of warranty (breach of contract), even if he in good faith warrants a fact that proves to be incorrect. He can protect himself by giving only warranties of knowledge. He could, for example, qualify all his replies by adding the words 'as far as I know' or 'to the best of my knowledge'.

304. In some cases the warranty given by the insured can amount to an estimate or the expression of an opinion. Where the estimate or opinion proves to be excessive, it can amount to a breach of warranty. This does not mean that an estimate or opinion must always be true or correct. Everyone is entitled to his own opinion. The insured simply guarantees that the statement given contains his honest opinion or estimation. A relative warranty is framed in general terms and does not specify in detail what the insured must do. The insured has to comply with the warranty to a substantial degree, according to the standards of the reasonable person, regarding what the reasonable person deems to be an adequate compliance.

---

219. *Viking Inshore Fishing (Pty) Ltd v. Mutual & Federal Insurance Company Limited* (Case No. 154/2014 WCHC, 17 Oct. 2014); *Viking Inshore Fishing (Pty) Ltd v. Mutual and Federal Insurance Co Ltd* [2016] 2 All SA 730 (SCA), 2016 (6) SA 335.

220. GPPHC, 8 Apr. 2015 (Case No. 302 unreported).

305. Breach of warranty is breach of contract, which means that if the insured fails to comply, he could incur contractual liability. This is irrespective of the absence of fault or the occurrence of force majeure events. The breach must however be material in nature. A negligible breach does not justify breach of contract and negotiated remedies. Insurers prefer to exclude or limit a claim due to the insured's breach of warranty, rather than claim specific performance, cancel the contract and/or claim damages.[221]

306. The Office of the Ombudsman for Long-term Insurance treats clauses in policies that provide for a forfeiture of premiums in the event of cancellation of the contract on the grounds of misrepresentation or breach of warranty as penalty clauses. Penalties remain subject to the provisions of the Conventional Penalties Act[222] that applies to all penalties. For penalty clauses in long-term insurance contracts, section 3 of the Conventional Penalties Act allows for penalties to be prima facie enforceable but that the amount of the penalty will be reduced to actual prejudice suffered. Millard cautions that although it is a long-standing practice to include penalty or forfeiture clauses in insurance contracts, it is advisable for insurers, intermediaries, representatives and advisors to draw their clients' attention to these clauses at the earliest possible opportunity. This will not only protect the insurer but also show that onerous clauses have been explained to clients and that the parties reached consensus on the forfeiture of premiums under certain circumstances.[223]

307. Exception and exclusion clauses appear in most contracts. It is possible to limit the risk or to exclude certain events from the risk covered by so-called exception clauses. The exclusion or limitation is often included under headings such as 'limitation', 'qualification', 'exclusion' or 'exception'. Where these exact words do not appear, the purpose and nature of another clause could indicate an exception not expressly identified as such in its title. Such a clause is not necessarily called an exception clause.

308. It is important to distinguish between a limitation and an exclusion. Although both have the effect of restricting the insurer's liability from the insured's point of view it is preferable for insurers to expressly bring exclusions and limitations to the attention of the insured. In addition, clients may be advised to procure special named-peril risk insurance where specific risks are excluded from the cover provided by general property or general liability policies. There are many examples of standard exclusions and limitations. For instance, policies may exclude war, civil disturbance and similar risks.[224]

309. Most insurance policies contain warranties. A warranty is seen as a strict contractual provision that confirms that certain representations are true or that specific undertakings will be performed. A warranty in South African law creates a normal contractual obligation. The continuation or validity of the contract does not depend on the performance under the warranty. Breach of warranty is breach of contract, irrespective of fault, and normal contractual remedies accrue. These include specific performance, cancellation and damages. The normal rules and principles that apply

221. Hutchison et al., Ch. 13.
222. Act 15 of 1962.
223. Millard, 92; Nienaber & Reinecke, 150.
224. Reinecke et al., 241–245.

to breaches of contract in general also apply where breach of an insurance contract occurs.[225]

§3. Disclosure

310. Both the insured and the insurer have to disclose relevant and material information during the pre-contractual negotiation phase. Important functions of insurance intermediaries in the disclosure of information are discussed in Part VII paragraphs 553–570 below.

311. The prospective insured with knowledge of all facts pertaining to the risk which is to be insured, is required to disclose all relevant material information within his actual or constructive knowledge. This enables the insurer to evaluate the proposal by the insured and decide to afford him cover or not. This duty is created by operation of law and not due to an existing legal obligation to that effect between the parties. The duty also applies to any renewal of an insurance contract, which is in fact the conclusion of an independent new insurance contract. The prospective insured must answer all questions put to him by the insurer, honestly and in good faith, and must out of his own volition disclose all other material information of which he has knowledge or should have had constructive knowledge, even though it has not been pertinently asked of him.

312. However, the insurer must disclosure all information of the product to the prospective policyholder to enable the latter to make an informed purchase decision. The prospective insured is entitled to disclosure of all information to the insured which is to the latter's benefit and could be used to the latter's advantage. The insurer should, for example, inform the insured of aspects that form part of the *naturalia* of insurance, such as the principle of average which applies in cases of under-insurance; limitations on a cession of the policy, and the like.

313. Failure to comply constitutes a misrepresentation that improperly induces consensus. This renders the insurance contract voidable at the election of the aggrieved party. Fault is not a requirement for voidability, yet materiality of the representation is.[226] Where statute regulates the nature and extent of information duties, failure to comply could also trigger statutory sanctions, as discussed in this contribution in paragraph 568 below.

225. Hutchison et al., para. 4.2.1; Millard, 91.

226. *Mutual & Federal Insurance Co Ltd v. Oudtshoorn Municipality* 1985 (1) SA 419 (A); *Anderson Shipping v. Guardian National Insurance* 1987 (3) SA 506 (A); *Qilingele v. SA Mutual Life Assurance Society Ltd* 1993 (1) SA 69 (A); *De Waal NO v. Metropolitan Lewens Bpk* 1994 (1) SA 818 (O); *SA Eagle v. Norman Welthagen Investments (Pty) Ltd* 1994 (2) SA 122 (A); *Commercial Union Insurance Co of South Africa Ltd v. Lotter 1999* (2) SA 147 (SCA). *See also* regarding materiality of pre-contractual disclosures as opposed to continuous contractual disclosures in *Jerrier v. Outsurance Insurance Co Ltd* 2015 (5) SA 433 (KZP).

§4. Proof of the Contract

314. Roman-Dutch law does not prescribe formalities, in other words, there are no rules that state that parties must reduce their pre-contractual negotiations or their contract to writing. Legislation also does not require writing or any other formalities that need to be complied with in order for an insurance contract to be valid. The only stipulations regarding writing is section 48 of the LTIA which stipulates that an insurer must, within a certain time, provide a summary of certain particulars of the conclusion or variation of certain long-term policies to the insured. In addition, section 48(3) of the LTIA stipulates that an insured may request a free copy of his policy. Section 47(1) of the STIA stipulates that short-term insurers must, within a certain time, provide a policyholder with a copy of the document that embodies the contract. The insured is entitled to receive a copy of any short-term policy against payment of a fee. However, if the insurer does not provide a copy of the contract, this does not affect the validity of the contract.[227]

315. The party who relies on a contract has the burden of proving the conclusion, the validity and the terms of the contract and the standard of proof is the same for insurance contracts than for all other contracts, namely a balance of probabilities. The general principles for contracts, including insurance contracts, are that there are two stages in determining the terms of a contract. The first is to establish the actual words and other conduct relied on, and the other is to interpret them. In addition, the normal rules of the law of evidence govern the admissibility of evidence produced to prove the existence of a contract and its contents and the normal rules relating to the interpretation of a document govern its interpretation.[228]

§5. Insurance Policies

316. Generally, contracts of insurance need not be in writing to be valid, but the standard practice is to reduce insurance contracts to writing. Therefore, any document that expresses the terms of a contract of insurance is called a policy. The policy can consist of a single document or more than one document, for example, the application form as completed by the insured during the pre-contractual phase, together with a *pro forma* document issued by the insurer containing the standard contractual provisions, terms and conditions.

317. Legislation does not require writing or any other formalities that need to be complied with in order for an insurance contract to be valid. As was indicated above, the only stipulations regarding writing is section 48 of the LTIA which stipulates that an insurer must, within a certain time, provide a summary of certain particulars of the conclusion or variation of certain long-term policies to the insured. In addition, section 48(3) of the LTIA stipulates that an insured may request a free copy of his policy. Section 47(1) of the STIA stipulates that short-term insurers must, within a certain time, provide a policyholder with a copy of the document that embodies the contract.

227. Reinecke et al., South African Insurance Law 118.
228. Reinecke et al., South African Insurance Law 196.

The insured is entitled to receive a copy of any short-term policy against payment of a fee.

§6. INTERPRETATION

318. The ordinary rules of interpretation of contracts also apply to the interpretation of insurance contracts. These rules only apply when the wording of a contract is vague, uncertain and/or ambiguous.[229] The rules do not apply where the contract contains a provision which is strict or unfair.[230] The discussion below covers some of the most important rules of interpretation, and not all of them as interpretation of contracts are a science on their own. The interpretation of contracts follows a prescribed sequence and requires the interpreter apply the primary, thereafter the secondary and finally the tertiary rules of interpretation.

319. An aspect that deserves discussion before the rules of interpretation can be discussed is the application of the parol evidence rule that was received into our law from English law.[231] According to the parol evidence rule, where the contract states that it is the sole source of the agreement between the parties, no extrinsic evidence beyond the contract itself may be presented to prove the content of that contract. On the other hand, where there is an uncertainty or ambiguity in the wording of a contract, extrinsic evidence is allowed for the interpretation of the contract. The parol evidence rule does not apply where the question before the court is whether the parties intended to reduce their agreement into an exclusive memorial thereof. The rule will also not apply where an aggrieved party attempts to avoid contractual liability by alleging illegality, fraud, error, misrepresentation, duress or undue influence.[232]

320. A forced distinction between background and surrounding circumstances proved to be a hurdle. Background circumstances were said to be always admissible whereas surrounding circumstances generally were not, unless the agreement was ambiguous. The distinction was never clear. Surrounding circumstances were found to be evidenced by 'what passed between the parties during the negotiations that preceded the conclusion of the agreement'.[233] This includes, for example, the negotiations leading to the actual consensus, and includes previous correspondence exchanged by the parties. In *KPMG Chartered Accountants (SA) v. Securefin Ltd*,[234] Harms DP in the majority judgment from a unanimous bench found that the terms 'background' and 'surrounding circumstances' are vague and confusing, and that the artificial and forced distinction should be abandoned. This was, however, as an obiter dictum not

---

229. S.J. Cornelius, *Principles of the Interpretation of Contracts in South Africa* 23 (2016).
230. *Price v. IGI* 1983 (1) SA 311 (A); *Standard General Insurance v. Croucamp* 1959 (3) SA 162 (A).
231. C. Lewis, *Interpretation of Contracts*, in *Southern Cross: Civil Law and Common Law in South Africa* 195 at 197 (R. Zimmerman & D. Visser eds. 1996).
232. Hutchison et al., para. 11.5.1.
233. *Engelbrecht v. Senwes Ltd* 2007 (3) SA 29 (SCA) at para. [7]; *Delmas Milling Company Limited v. Du Plessis* 1955 (3) SA 447 (A); *Coopers & Lybrand v. Bryant* 1995 (3) SA 761 (A).
234. 2009 (4) SA 399 (SCA).

binding yet provides an overwhelming indication of a new trend which is expected to be followed by our courts in matters heard on this point in future cases.[235]

321. It is possible to circumvent the parol evidence rule, by alleging a tacit term in the contract. This requires leading extraneous evidence to indicate that the memorial contains a tacit term. A claim for rectification of the contract or a term thereof also requires presenting evidence that parties included an incorrect provision in their memorial, or omitted to include a term. Evidence then becomes admissible to prove that the document does not reflect the true intentions of the parties.[236]

Primary Rules of Interpretation

322. Where the wording of a contract remains unclear, a court is required to apply the classic rules of interpretation. No *numerus clauses* of rules exists, yet the most important rules that are applied regularly are addressed below.

323. A court will first address the problem by applying the primary rules of interpretation. The first of these is that the true intentions of the parties have to be determined. This is deemed to be the so-called golden rule for the interpretation of contracts. Thereafter words must be given their ordinary general grammatical meaning. Technical terms should be given their proven technical meaning. Where a word is defined in a contract that defined meaning should be applied consistently throughout the contract. It is crucial that every word must be given a meaning, unless it is evidently superfluous or meaningless. In the third place, the contract must be interpreted in a textual context, thus as a whole.[237]

324. If it is impossible to determine the parties' true meaning in this manner, or lead to absurd results or inconsistencies or expose a clear ambiguity, the secondary rules of interpretation have to be applied.[238] The most important rules include the following:

(a) The immediate language of the parties prevails. This of course presents problems in a country that has eleven official languages.[239] Written words enjoy preference over typed words, which in turn enjoy preference over printed wording. Electronic data messages enjoy statutory recognition as 'writing' for purposes of South African law, provided it is accessible.
(b) Wording or clauses must be interpreted according to the nature and purpose of the contract.

235. M. Wallis, *What's in a Word? Interpretation through the Eyes of Ordinary Readers*, 127 SALJ 673 (2010); Hutchison et al., 260–262.
236. Hutchison et al., para. 11.5.2; Cornelius, Ch. 6; *Robyn v. Guarantee Life Assurance Co Ltd* 1984 (4) SA 558 (A).
237. *Coopers & Lybrand v. Bryant* 1995 3 SA 761 (A) at 767.
238. *Lourens NO v. Colonial Mutual Life Assurance Society* 1986 (3) SA 373 (A); *Fulton v. Waksal Investments* 1986 (2) SA 363 (T).
239. Afrikaans, English, Ndebele, Northern Sotho, Sotho, Swazi, Tsonga, Tswana, Venda, Xhosa and Zulu.

(c) The conduct of the parties after conclusion of the contract could be taken into consideration to determine their intention regarding the problematic wording or clause.
(d) General words, used in conjunction with specific words, are limited in their meaning according to the meaning of the specific words (known as the *eiusdem generis* or *noscitur a sociis* rule).[240]
(e) Where the document refers to a particular thing, it is presumed that everything else that is not specifically mentioned is excluded (known as the *expressio unius est exclusio alterius* rule).
(f) The court should choose the meaning which would render the contract valid and enforceable, rather than that which would render it null and void (known as the *ut res magisvaleat quam pereat* rule). This creates a rebuttable presumption of validity. The interpretation should also aim for a contract to be legal rather than illegal, and to provide business efficacy to the agreement.[241]
(g) Where an exception and exemption clause, or any provision that limits indemnification (in the context of insurance especially of the insured by the insurer) is ambiguous, it has to be interpreted restrictively.[242]
(h) Where words used are doubtful, they must be interpreted to place the least possible burden on the debtor or *promissor* (also known as the *quod minimum* rule).
(i) The courts should choose the most fair or equitable interpretation of the clause or words in question.[243] In the spirit of consumerism, one may expect that the interpretation which favours the insured must be followed, although each case must be decided on its own merits.

325. It has been considered by authors Nienaber and Reinecke that good faith could serve as a secondary rule of interpretation. When a contract is ambiguous, the principle that all contracts are made in good faith is applied. This entails determining the intention of the parties on the basis that they negotiated with each other in good faith which could shed some light on the interpretation of the problematic wording. This may be justified by the judgment given in *Mutual and Federal Insurance Co Ltd v. Oudtshoorn Municipality* and in *South African Forestry Co Ltd v. York Timbers Ltd*;[244] as well as by recent statutory rules aimed at the insured's duty of disclosure and the insurer's information duties.

326. As a last resort, the tertiary rules may be applied. They aim to provide a fair outcome rather than establishing the actual or presumed intentions of the parties. The first of these rules is the *contra proferentem* rule, in terms of which the contract is interpreted against the favour of the party who drew up the contract, or who had it drawn up on his behalf.[245] This universally applied rule is most often applied by courts

240. Hutchison et al., 267.
241. *First National Bank v. Rosenblum* 2001 (4) SA 189 (SCA) 196.
242. *Drifters Adventure Tours CC v. Hircock* 2007 (2) SA 83 (SCA); *Durban's Water Wonderland (Pty) Ltd v. Botha* 1999 (1) SA 982 (SCA).
243. *South African Forestry Co Ltd v. York Timbers Ltd* 2005 (3) SA 323 (SCA) at 340I.
244. *South African Forestry Co Ltd v. York Timbers Ltd* at 340.
245. *Kliptown Clothing Industries (Pty) Ltd v. Marine and Trade Insurance Co of South Africa Ltd* 1961 (1) SA 103 (A).

for purposes of interpretation of standard-form or contracts of adhesion, and in most consumer contracts.[246] It only applies where there is an ambiguity or uncertainty, and not where the fairness of the provisions has to be determined.

327. Where rules of interpretation offer no solution, the ambiguous or uncertain clause or wording is deemed to be *pro non scripto* with the ensuing consequences. This includes that the entire contract or a portion thereof may be declared void for vagueness.[247]

328. Rectification may be effected where the contract document does not reflect the true intentions of the parties. Where the parties cannot amend their contract by agreement, the dissatisfied party may approach the courts for a rectification order. By proving the true intentions of the parties, the contract is then rectified by an order to bring it in line with these intentions. A contract that is null and void due to a failure to comply with prescribed formalities cannot be validated by a subsequent rectification.[248]

246. *Fedgen Insurance Ltd v. Leyds* 1995 (3) SA 33 (A) at 38.
247. *Namibian Minerals Corporation Ltd v. Benguela Concessions Ltd* 1997 (2) SA 548 (A) at 557, 563.
248. Hutchison et al., 109.

Chapter 4. Obligations of the Insured

§1. Description of Risk

329. Due to the prospective insured's intimate knowledge of all facts pertaining to the risk which is to be insured, he is required to disclose all relevant material information within his actual or constructive knowledge, to the insurer prior to conclusion of the insurance contract. This enables the insurer to accept the proposal by the insured and afford him cover or not. The positive duty requires the prospective insured to answer all questions put to him by the insurer, honestly and in good faith. The negative duty requires the insured to disclose all other material information of which he has knowledge or should have had constructive knowledge, even though it has not been pertinently asked of him. If the insured provides false information, does not answer a question at all or refrains from disclosing material information, the misrepresentation improperly induces consensus which renders the insurance contract voidable at the election of the aggrieved party. Fault is not a requirement for voidability, yet materiality of the representation is.[249]

330. Where the policyholder has to do a due diligence investigation and complete a proposal form based on a questionnaire, proving a misrepresentation is simple when one can refer to documentation at hand. One should keep in mind that the application for cover does not always form part of the insurance contract unless it is expressly by agreement incorporated as part of the policy.

331. The duty to disclose is clearly a pre-contractual duty. The information must be disclosed by the insurer and by the insured to enable the other to decide whether he is prepared to conclude a contract of insurance. This duty is created by operation of law and not due to an existing legal obligation to that effect between the parties. The duty also applies to any renewal of an insurance contract, which is in fact the conclusion of an independent new insurance contract.

332. However, a duty rests on an insurer to inform the prospective insured of information that affects the latter's purchase decision. The insurer's duty to inform for the sake of transparency was already recognized by Joubert JA in the case of *Mutual & Federal v. Oudtshoorn Municipality.*[250] It could also reasonably be expected of the insurer to disclose to the insured all information which could decrease or even exclude the risk. The insurer can be expected to disclose all information to the insured which is to the latter's benefit and could be used to the latter's advantage. The insurer should also inform the insured of aspects that form part of the *naturalia* of insurance, such as the principle of average which applies in cases of under-insurance; limitations on

249. *Mutual & Federal Insurance Co Ltd v. Oudtshoorn Municipality* 1985 (1) SA 419 (A); *Anderson Shipping v. Guardian National Insurance* 1987 (3) SA 506 (A); *Qilingele v. SA Mutual Life Assurance Society Ltd* 1993 (1) SA 69 (A); *De Waal NO v. Metropolitan Lewens Bpk* 1994 (1) SA 818 (O); *SA Eagle v. Norman Welthagen Investments (Pty) Ltd* 1994 (2) SA 122 (A); *Commercial Union Insurance Co of South Africa Ltd v. Lotter* 1999 (2) SA 147 (SCA).

250. 1985 (1) SA 419 (A) 432A.

a cession of the policy, and the like. The average insured does not necessarily know of or understand important aspects that affect his cover or claims. This means that it is often those fine details that are contained in the incidentalia of a contract that gives rise to complaints and litigation against insurers. One such example is found in the case of *Marc Rupert Hughes v. Mariette Jolene Slippens and Gen-Assist Insurance Brokers (Pty) Ltd.*[251]

333. The duty to inform is primarily derived from a common law duty not to make misrepresentations by commission or omission. The insurer's duty to speak is an *ex lege* duty due to the involuntary reliance of the prospective insured on information supplied by insurers in the market. A misrepresentation concerning information that goes to the root of the matter, and that induces the prospective insured to buy the insurance product, is recognized as an actionable misrepresentation. According to section 16 of the FAIS Act, codes of conduct in the insurance industry should adhere to certain principles. One of these is that a code of conduct must specifically contain provisions relating to the adequate disclosures by a FSP or a representative of material information relevant to the insurance relationship. The particular code must specify what would be considered relevant and material and may for instance include a disclosure of actual or potential own interests in relation to dealing with clients. This is especially the case where brokers and agents are concerned.[252]

334. The insurer's duty is furthermore derived from the statutory rights to information in accordance with the Constitution and the Promotion of Access to Information Act. It is furthermore supported by the detailed provisions on mandatory disclosures in the FAIS Act, the LTIA, the STIA and, finally, the PPR issued in accordance with these acts. Provisions to regulate advertisements of insurance products and pre-contractual disclosures by the insurer or insurance intermediary are prescribed by the GCC issued under the FAIS Act.

335. Insurance products and services have been exempted from the scope of the CPA from 28 February 2014 by the Financial Services Laws General Amendment Act.[253] The absence of relevant statutory provisions do not in any way diminish the common-law duty not to make misrepresentations. Case law will furthermore inform and provide clarity and legal certainty as to the nature and extent of the insurer's information duty.

336. Both the policyholder's duty to disclose and the insurer's duty to inform are usually by agreement expanded to a continuous duty which applies while the contract remains in force. Policies that expire after a specific term but are renewable require a disclosure duty upon every renewal.

337. Over time and in the absence of statutory regulation, the courts struggled to find a universal benchmark regarding the extent of the insured's duty to disclose information, specifically how to determine whether or not information is *material* and has to be disclosed. In 1993 in the case of *Qilingele v. SA Mutual Life Assurance Society Ltd*[254] the court held that it is merely a question of fact to make this determination. The question is whether the reasonable person would view the information as relative

251. Case No. FAIS 05470/13-14/GP (3).
252. Millard & Hattingh, 31, 58, 88–89, 119.
253. Act 45 of 2013.
254. 1993 (1) SA 69 (A).

to the assessment and quantification of the risk. The risk as determined without the specific information at hand, and the risk determined after disclosure of the specific information, should be compared. If any discrepancy exists, the information should have been disclosed.

338. In an attempt to provide more clarity, section 52(1)(b) of the LTIA was introduced which states specifically that:

> the representation or non-disclosure shall be regarded as material if a reasonable, prudent person would consider that the particular information constituting the representation or which was not disclosed, as the case may be, should have been correctly disclosed to the insurer so that the insurer could form its own view as to the effect of such information on the assessment of the relevant risk.

339. It still does not remove the uncertainty whether this is the reasonable person in the shoes of the underwriter or insurer, or the reasonable prospective insured. This section also deals only with the information that the insured must disclose to the insurer, and not the insurer's duty to inform. The latter is regulated under the provisions of the FAIS Act. Facts which need not be disclosed include those which are general knowledge or obvious and of which the insurer was, or should have been, aware; facts in respect of which the insurer has either expressly, or tacitly, waived his right of disclosure; facts which reduce or diminish, and do not increase, the risk; and facts covered by a warranty in the insurance contract itself.[255]

340. The failure to comply with a pre-contractual duty to disclose or to inform amounts to a misrepresentation. The misrepresentation can be made by disclosing false information or by omitting or withholding material information. This may be intentional, negligent or innocent. It is conduct that influences consensus, as a result of which the contract is voidable at the election of the party prejudiced by the misrepresentation. The voidability is irrespective of whether the misrepresentation is made innocently or with a degree of fault (intentionally or negligently). The contract remains valid and enforceable until the prejudiced party exercises his choice and elects to void the contract. If he chooses to set the contract aside, restitution has to take place. If the insurer is the prejudiced party, he must return all premiums already received to the insured.[256]

341. A prejudiced party who has the contract set aside because of misrepresentation cannot rely on any other contractual remedies such as claiming contractual damages (as a contract in terms of which he could do so, no longer exists). If the misrepresentation is made intentionally or negligently, the prejudiced party can also institute an additional action for damages based in delict, provided the requirements for a delict have been met. These include conduct, wrongfulness, fault, suffering of damages or loss, and factual and legal causation between the conduct and the damages or loss suffered.

---

255. Kuschke, *Specific Aspects of Insurance Contracts and Indemnity and Non-indemnity Insurance*, in *Commercial Law*, para. 25.14 (Nagel, C.J. et al. eds).

256. *De Waal NO v. Metropolitan Lewens Bpk* 1994 (1) SA 818 (O); also *Jerrier v. Outsurance Insurance Co Ltd* 2015 (5) SA 433 (KZP).

Disclosure of false or inaccurate information is prima facie wrongful and contrary to the public interest, unless it merely an opinion or estimation.[257]

342. These remedies of the insurer to act on the misrepresentation made and to void the contract or avoid responsibilities in terms of the contract are limited by section 59 of the LTIA and section 53 of the STIA. The insurer may only act on a misrepresentation made, whether warranted or not, which could possibly materially influence the assessment of the risk under the policy at the time of conclusion thereof.

343. Insurers try to solve this problem by couching the replies made by the prospective insureds in the form of contractual warranties or guarantees, and including them into the contract. These strict contractual undertakings or warranties given by the insured form the basis of the contract and are part of the insured's contractual duties. The insured's pre-contractual disclosures are therefore incorporated in the contract as continuous terms of the contract. A breach of warranty is a breach of contract.[258]

344. The insurer may, however, also be entitled to other contractual remedies to which the parties specifically agreed, such as a *lex commissoria* (right of rescission) or a penalty clause. The contract may also contain a forfeiture clause which is also classified as a penalty clause.[259] Such a clause allows the insurer to retain all premiums already paid as liquidated damages where the insured commits breach of warranty. In *Jordan v. New Zealand Insurance Co*[260] the Judge decided 'there can be no relative degrees of truth. The answer is either true or untrue.' It is the materiality of the untruth that requires evaluation.

§2. Payment of Premium

345. Both the LTIA and the STIA define a premium as 'the consideration given or to be given in return for an undertaking to provide policy benefits'. As discussed, the actual payment of the premium by the insured may be a suspensive or resolutive condition in the contract depending on its purpose and function. In *Lake v. Reinsurance Corporation Ltd*[261] the court held that although an insurance contract is valid even though the premium is not paid, the insured cannot require the insurer to perform where he himself had not performed his obligation to pay the premium.

346. This is also an analogy of the *exceptio non adimpleti contractus* or defence of reciprocity. Where contracts are reciprocal, such as insurance contracts, a party may not claim until he himself has performed. A plaintiff of a performance, who has not delivered his simultaneous or prior counter-performance, may be precluded from claiming performance from the defendant until he has performed. This defence may be relaxed and a reduced counter-performance payable. Yet this appears not always

257. Kuschke, in *Commercial Law*, para. 25.16 (Nagel ed.).
258. *Qilingele v. SA Mutual Life Assurance Society Ltd* 1993 (1) SA 69 (A); *SA Eagle v. Norman Welthagen Investments (Pty) Ltd* 1994 (2) SA 122 (A); *Clifford v. Commercial Union Insurance Co of South Africa Ltd* 1998 (4) SA 150 (SCA).
259. Section 1 of the Conventional Penalties Act.
260. 1968 (2) SA 238 (E).
261. 1967 (3) SA 124 (W).

to be the case in insurance where failure to pay a premium, for example, will void the entire insurance claim and not require the insurer to pay out the claim proportionately.[262]

347. Several statutory provisions are in force pertaining to premiums. In accordance with section 47 of the LTIA payment of the premium to an agent of the insurer is deemed to be a payment to the insurer himself. Section 51 expressly interprets payment of a premium as a suspensive condition. The insurer's duties are suspended until the premium is in fact paid or satisfactory arrangements have been made for payment. The consequences of a failure to pay premiums are also dealt with in section 52. Section 45 of the STIA regulates the collection of premiums by intermediaries, and section 46 requires that a receipt is issued for payments made in cash.

348. In addition to the provisions in the Acts, the PPR 4.3(j), 7.2 and 6.1(b) address a variety of issues pertaining to premium payments. Rule 4.3(j) stipulates that a direct marketer must, when rendering direct marketing to a policyholder, furnish the policyholder with a list of particulars at the earliest reasonable opportunity but prior to the conclusion of a relevant insurance transaction and one particulars that must be disclosed is whether the contract provides for the increase of premiums. Rule 7.2 deals with charges levied upon the discontinuation of fund policies. Rule 6.1 provides as follows:

> A policyholder may—
>
> (a) in any case where no benefit has yet been paid or claimed or an event insured against has not yet occurred; and
>
> (b) within a period of 30 days of receipt of the summary contemplated in section 48 of the Act, or from a reasonable date on which it can be deemed that the policyholder received the summary referred to above, cancel any insurance transaction, excluding any policy or variation which only lasts for 30 days or less, by written cancellation notice sent to the insurer. All premiums or moneys paid by the policyholder to the insurer up to the date of receipt of the cancellation notice or received at any date thereafter in respect of the cancelled or varied policy, shall be refunded to the policyholder, subject to the deduction of the cost of any risk cover actually enjoyed and any market loss where the market value of the investments made has decreased in the intervening period due to prevailing market conditions.

349. In view of the issues addressed above, non-payment of the premium is a business risk that most insurers face. To limit the risk, insurers resort to various techniques. Reinecke et al., explain that insurers may use different techniques in order to ensure that they do receive their premiums. The parties may expressly agree that the payment of a premium is a formality requirement and when it is not met, there can be no contract. The parties may rather agree that the insurer will compensate the insured but that this obligation will be conditional and subject to the materialization of the risk

262. Hutchison et al., 316.

as well as to the payment of the premium. It could also be agreed that no contract can exist between the parties until the premium is paid, yet this construction appears to indicate that no insurance contracts exists at all from the outset. Finally, the parties may expressly agree that if a premium is not paid, the contract will lapse in terms of a resolutive condition, and thus terminate automatically without the insurer's decision whether to terminate or not. Even though failure to pay the premium is a breach of contract by the insured, a claim for damages by the insurer is very seldom a remedy that an insurer will seek to enforce. The exemption from providing cover and paying out a claim is far more valuable to the insurer.[263]

350. In modern insurance the premium will always consist of payment of a sum of money. It is inconceivable to trade a commodity or goods in exchange for insurance cover. Should that be the case, which in the third world crop or agricultural microinsurance industry could be a possibility, the 'premium' would have to be converted to a monetary value. If acceptable to the insurer, it will at the end of the day still be payment that sounds in money. A risk reduction by the insured could lead to lower premiums and reduced deductibles, which serves as an incentive that clearly benefits the insurer.

351. A suspensive condition, known as a 'condition precedent' in other jurisdictions, has the effect that a valid contract is unenforceable until the fulfilment of the condition. The condition pertains to an uncertain future event. In short-term insurance it may be the theft of a car or a fire. The insured enjoys no cover, and the insurer does not have to pay a claim until the insured pays his premium. If a suspensive condition is never fulfilled, the contract comes to an end as it remains unenforceable and thus pointless. It is however possible for a specific obligation to lapse, but for other independent obligations to survive the non-fulfilment.[264]

352. The application of the doctrine of the fictional fulfilment of the condition that applies in South African law should be noted. Where a condition is potestative in that a party must cooperate or act in some way to enable fulfilment of the condition and he fails to do so, the doctrine will apply. In accordance with the doctrine the condition is deemed to have been fulfilled and the contract becomes unconditional and thus enforceable.[265]

353. Payment of the premium may also be interpreted as a resolutive condition, in that the duty to provide cover exists yet terminates if an insured does not pay the premium that is due. Other resolutive conditions may include that the contract terminates after a specific occurrence or event, for example, that a key-employee policy lapses once the specific employee terminates his employment. A contract may also be subject to a resolutive time period or term. This will be when the contract terminates upon a certain future event, such as the passing of time, or death. Cover is often issued only for a specific period and lapses once the time has passed. Although death is a certainty, it remains uncertain when the death event occurs.[266]

354. The agreement on payment of a monetary premium is therefore not an essential element of the contract. As the doctrine of valuable consideration does not

263. P.M. Nienaber, *On the Payment of Premiums and the Lapsing of Long-Term Insurance Policies*, 19 SA Merc LJ 1–13 (2007).
264. Hutchison et al., 249.
265. Hutchison et al., 251.
266. Hutchison et al., 251.

form part of South African law, the validity of the contract does not depend on the exchange of consideration. This is distinctly different from other jurisdictions, for example, the position in English law. In *Conradie v. Rossouw*,[267] the court already held that the doctrine of valuable consideration is foreign to the Roman-Dutch law and does not form part of our law. In the case of *Barkhuizen v. Napier*, the minority did remark that the insured did not receive any valuable consideration in return for paying his premiums, and that a time bar or suit limitation clause of ninety days should not be enforced against him, for this reason. It is submitted that in view of the position explained above, this argument cannot be supported.[268]

355. In terms of an *excess clause*, the insured has to bear a certain amount of the damages in respect of every successful claim instituted against the insurer. Excess fees increase where the insured institutes more than one claim within a specified time period, or if the insured moves into a higher risk group because of changed circumstances (e.g., where the health of the insured decreases, or he relocates to another riskier location). This acts as a deterrent to prevent unnecessary or minor claims which reduces the insurer's administrative burden and costs. Of course, subsequent premiums payable may also be increased by the insurer where an insured moves into a higher risk category, or where he institutes multiple claims within a certain period of time.[269]

356. Breach of contract occurs when a party fails to honour his or her contractual obligations, by not performing or accepting performance timeously, delivering improper performance, refusing to continue with the contractual undertaking or by rendering performance impossible (preventing performance).[270] Where the insured fails to honour his obligations, breach of contract may occur and ex lege remedies as well as negotiated remedies become available to the insurer. Where the insurer on the other hand fails to honour his obligations the same common law rules apply. The general position on breach of contract in South Africa, whether by the insured or the insurer, are discussed below.

357. A debtor is in default or *mora* if he does not perform timeously in terms of the contract. However, breach of contract is not constituted by the mere late delivery of performance or the fact that the debtor delays performance. The debtor must still be able to perform yet fails to deliver performance that is due and enforceable. Intent or negligence on his part is not required. In most contracts, a specific date or time for performance is stipulated. Some contracts merely provide for performance to be made at some future time or for a method or formula by which the time of performance can be determined. Where a specific time for performance is set or where the method to determine such time is agreed upon, the debtor is automatically *in mora ex re* if he does not perform at such time. No demand for performance by the creditor is necessary in order to place the debtor in *mora,* as the arrival of the time for performance is in itself seen as a demand for performance. Where the parties do not agree on a specific time for performance the debtor is not automatically in *mora* upon his failure to perform,

267. 1919 AD 279.
268. Hutchison et al., 6.
269. Reinecke et al., 398–399.
270. G.B. Bradfield, *Christie's The Law of Contract in South Africa* Ch. 13(7th ed., LexisNexis, 2016); Hutchison et al., Ch. 12; *South African Forestry Co Ltd v. York Timbers Ltd* 2005 (3) SA 323 (SCA).

unless the creditor demands performance from the debtor. If the latter subsequently fails to meet the demand, he will be in *mora ex persona*. The demand may be in writing or verbal, and the time set must be *reasonable* in the circumstances and will depend on the facts and circumstances of each case which were or should reasonably have been foreseen at the time of conclusion of the contract. The performance is due and enforceable if the duty is not subject to a suspensive condition or time period, and where the debtor has no defence against the creditors claim, for example, that the right to claim performance has prescribed, or where the defence of reciprocity or *exceptio non adimpleti contractus* allows the debtor to withhold performance until the creditor has offered counter-performance. The breach does not affect the existence of the contract yet perpetuates the legal obligation between the debtor and creditor. Remedies in law (specific performance, cancellation and/or a claim for damages) and additional negotiated remedies as discussed below afford the creditor relief.[271]

358. The creditor is in *mora creditoris* if he fails to accept proper performance by the debtor, or fails to cooperate in order to enable the debtor to perform. If the creditor through his lack of cooperation renders performance impossible, he is guilty of breach of contract in the form of prevention of performance. This form of breach is only possible where a creditor has a duty to cooperate with the debtor in order to enable the latter to make proper performance. As a general rule, a creditor is under no obligation to accept performance or to cooperate with the debtor if performance is not yet due or is unenforceable. Where delivery of the debtor's performance is subject to a suspensive condition or time period which is clearly to the benefit of the creditor, the creditor may refuse premature performance. If not, the debtor is entitled to deliver performance prematurely. The debtor must tender proper performance in terms of the contract. The creditor will not be in breach should he refuse to accept performance that is substantially defective, or where partial performance is tendered as full and final performance. As with *mora ex re* and *mora ex persona* under default of the debtor as mentioned in paragraph 357 above, a creditor does not have to cooperate where no date for performance has been agreed upon, until the debtor has notified him and demanded performance within a reasonable time. It appears that the creditor's failure to accept performance or to cooperate must be due to fault on his part. If, therefore, he is entitled to reject defective performance or if the delay is due to a force majeure there will be no breach of contract.

359. The creditor's *mora* does not free the debtor from his duty to perform in terms of the contract. *Mora creditoris* and *mora debitoris* cannot exist simultaneously in respect of the same contractual obligation. If the debtor rectifies his own delay by tendering performance and the creditor then falls in *mora creditoris*, the debtor is no longer in default and his *mora debitoris* is cancelled. The creditor can also bring an end to his own *mora* by making a new demand for performance upon the debtor, and by disclosing his willingness to receive the debtor's performance. A debtor is obliged to protect the object of performance with the care which the reasonable man would exercise. But if the creditor is in *mora*, this duty is diminished as the debtor is then only responsible for damage caused by his intentional or gross negligent conduct. As in the case of *mora debitoris,* the contractual obligation is perpetuated and the creditor

---

271. Bradfield, Ch. 14; Hutchison et al., 280–288; *Scoin Trading (Pty) Ltd v. Bernstein* 2011 (2) SA 118 (SCA).

also bears the risk that the performance may become impossible without fault on the part of any of the parties while he himself is in *mora.* In such event the creditor still has the duty to make performance to the debtor in terms of the contract, while the debtor is excused from making his performance which has become impossible. Where default by debtor does not release the sureties, a surety is released where the creditor commits a default by creditor pertaining to delivery of the secured debt. Remedies by operation of law allow the debtor to claim enforcement, cancelation or damages, or enforce other remedies as negotiated between the parties.[272]

360. Positive malperformance occurs where improper performance is delivered, and refers to the nature or quality of the performance agreed upon. A performance is actually delivered yet is incomplete or defective. Where a debtor must perform by refraining or omitting from doing something, and he acts in contravention to his undertaking, it is also a form of positive malperformance. The predominant view is that fault on the part of the debtor is not a requirement for this form of breach of contract, yet the issue has not been finally determined by our courts. Where a debtor commits breach in the form of positive malperformance, he may be prevented from claiming counter-performance due to the defence of reciprocity, the *exceptio non adimpleti contractus.* This is discussed under remedies below.[273]

361. A form of anticipatory breach of contract called repudiation occurs where a party to a contract, by his words or conduct, and without lawful justification, communicates in writing, verbally or by conduct, expressly or tacitly, to the other party his unequivocal intention to no longer be bound to his obligations in terms of the contract. The test to determine whether repudiation takes place is an objective one and requires determination in view of the facts and circumstances of the specific case, whether a reasonable person would have reached the conclusion that the debtor intends to repudiate his contractual duties. A mere delay does not constitute repudiation. The subjective intention of the debtor is irrelevant As repudiation is an anticipatory form of breach of contract, the debtor, for example, may make an express statement in advance that he will not perform on the date specified for performance, or that his performance will be defective or that he is not going to perform at all. Furthermore, he could deny the existence of the contract altogether, notify the creditor of his future inability to perform or that performance is objectively impossible to deliver (where it is not the case), cancel or terminate the contract without any proper reason to do so. The act of repudiation together with the intention to repudiate already constitutes a breach of contract. The acceptance of the innocent party is not required to complete the repudiation. The repudiating act in itself is already the completed breach of contract. Acceptance of repudiation is the actual cancellation of the contract due to the breach. The innocent party may elect not to accept the repudiation, in which case the contract remains in force yet other remedies for breach of contract may accrue.[274]

---

272. Bradfield, 616; Hutchison et al., 280–288; *Martin Harris & Seuns OVS (Edms) Bpk v. Qwa-Qwa Regeringsdiens* 2000 (3) SA 339 (SCA).

273. Hutchison et al., 294–296; Bradfield, 486–490; *Singh v. McCarthy Retail Ltd t/a McIntosh Motors* 2000 (4) SA 795 (SCA).

274. Bradfield, 610–613; Hutchison et al., 296–301; *Datacolor International (Pty) Ltd v. Intamarket (Pty) Ltd* 2001 (2) SA 284 (SCA); *South African Forestry Co Ltd v. York Timbers Ltd* 2005 (3) SA 323 (SCA).

362. Finally, breach of contract may be caused by prevention of performance, where either the debtor or the creditor of a performance renders it absolutely objectively impossible by *culpable conduct.* This must be distinguished from initial impossibility of performance where performance is objectively impossible at the time of conclusion of the contract. The requirement of physical possibility of performance, which is one of the requirements for the conclusion of a valid contract, is not met. Where performance is merely subjectively impossible, a contract does exist and the debtor will be in breach of contract. Subsequent impossibility of performance after conclusion of the contract, which is not due to the fault of any of the parties, as a general rule causes an existing legal obligation to terminate.

363. Where performance is prevented by one of the parties the contract is not automatically terminated. Where the debtor prevents his own performance from being delivered, the creditor may cancel the contract, reclaim any performance already made by him to the debtor and claim damages (if suffered); or uphold the contract, deliver his own counter-performance and claim damages as a substitute for performance Clearly the disappointed creditor cannot obtain an order for specific performance, as the object of performance no longer exists. A creditor who becomes aware of the fact that the debtor is soon going to render performance impossible, may obtain an interdict preventing the debtor from doing so. Where the creditor prevents the debtor from performing, the impossibility is not due to the debtor's fault, and the debtor is, therefore, freed from his contractual obligation to perform.

364. The debtor may choose to cancel the contract, return any performance already received to the creditor and claim damages (if suffered) or uphold the contract and claim counter-performance from the creditor, provided that he either tenders to the creditor any saving on his part occasioned by the fact that he as debtor is excused from making performance (which has been rendered impossible through the conduct of the creditor), or that the saving is set-off against that performance which the creditor has to deliver as counter-performance.[275]

365. Because a contract creates a legal obligation, the parties are by operation of law entitled to certain remedies. They may supplement or replace their remedies by the negotiation of additional remedies.

366. Remedies by operation of law to which a party is entitled include a claim for specific performance of the contract; or cancellation of the contract; and in both cases a claim for damages. A party may also choose not to enforce the contract or cancel it, but accept his position and sue only for pecuniary damages. A claim for specific performance in terms of the contract is the natural remedy of the injured party, as the purpose of this remedy is the fulfilment of the contract. Courts are not inclined to make such an order where its enforcement cannot be guaranteed, for example, where the delivery of personal services is required, it causes the party against whom the order is given undue hardship, limits his freedom and the like. Cancellation is seen as a drastic remedy, as it aims to nullify the original intention of the parties to be bound by their agreement. The law is reluctant to enforce this as a remedy, and, as a general rule, only allows the injured party to cancel if the breach of contract is of a material or substantial nature. The reason is that the parties intended to be in a specific position

275. Hutchison et al., 303–305; *ISEP Structural Engineering and Plating (Pty) Ltd v. Inland Exploration Co (Pty) Ltd* 1981 (4) SA 1 (A).

if the contract was performed properly, and that this goal is never achieved where the contract is cancelled. Damages can be claimed on its own or in combination with the other remedies discussed above. Bespoke remedies are mostly directed at avoiding the practical problems and strict legal requirements regarding the implementation of ex lege remedies. Some popular remedies include a penalty clause, forfeiture clause, *acceleration clause and cancellation clause (or lex commissoria).*[276]

367. The remedies directed at fulfillment of the contract include an interdict, and an enforcement order. Where a party to a contract wishes to prevent the other party from acting in conflict with his contractual obligations, the appropriate remedy is an interdict or urgent court order. The requirements which have to be met before a court will allow an interdict are that a clear right must exist, that is infringed upon or will be infringed upon; and that no other remedy must be available at that time to the prejudiced.[277]

368. The aim of a claim for specific performance is to force the defaulting party, by an order of court, to make performance in the very terms agreed upon by the parties. The courts will refuse to issue such an order where it is impossible for the court to exercise control over specific performance and over compliance with the order. It cannot issue an order where performance has become impossible. Where the order for specific performance affects the freedom of the individual, or creates undue hardship for the debtor or the public at large, or where it is evident that the debtor is unable to effectively deliver performance to fulfil the obligation, the court will refuse to issue the order. A court will also be reluctant to grant such an order to force a party to maintain a continuous close or personal relationship between himself and the other party, as for example, in a partnership or a contract of employment. A court will only use its discretion to refuse to make such an order if the order would bring about an unjust result or would be contrary to public or legal policy, depending on the merit, facts and circumstances of each case.[278]

369. An indirect way to enforce a contract is where a debtor of a performance in a reciprocal contract may resist an order for specific performance by raising the *exceptio non adimpleti contractus*. It can only apply where the parties have to perform simultaneously or where the one (the plaintiff) has to perform before the other (the defendant), for the defendant to rely on this defence. In principle, the *exceptio* gives the defendant the *right to withhold* the delivery of his own performance until he receives counter-performance (or at least tender thereof) by the plaintiff. Where the plaintiff's performance is divisible, the defendant can exercise his right to withhold the delivery of his own performance in respect of that portion of the plaintiff's performance that is still outstanding. If the plaintiff's performance is indivisible and he delivers a defective performance, the prejudiced defendant has a choice to cancel the contract if the malperformance was material and claim damages. He may also reject the delivered performance, enforce the contract and claim proper performance and damages. Where he rejects the performance and claims proper performance, he will be able to ward off any claim by the plaintiff for counter-performance with the *exceptio* until the plaintiff

276. Bradfield, 636; Hutchison et al., 309–314.
277. Bradfield, 629; Hutchison et al., 321; *Setlogelo v. Setlogelo* 1914 AD 221.
278. Bradfield, 619; Hutchison et al., 315–324; *Benson v. SA Mutual Life Assurance Society* 1986 (1) SA 776 (A).

has performed properly or has tendered such performance. Where the malperformance is not substantial enough to justify rejection thereof, or that the defendant chooses to retain the defective performance, the defendant has the benefit of the performance, but he is still able to ward off a claim by the plaintiff with the *exceptio* due to the fact that the plaintiff himself has not performed properly.[279]

370. The question is whether the plaintiff should be entitled to receive counter-performance for that portion of the indivisible performance that he himself has already made and that is being utilized by the recipient thereof, and if so, how the extent thereof is determined. The court in the case of *BK Tooling (Pty) Ltd v. Scope Precision Engineering (Pty) Ltd*[280] recognized that the court may in the interests of fairness exercise its judicial discretion and relax the strict enforcement of the principle of reciprocity and the concomitant right to withhold, and order the defendant to pay a reduced contract price. Such an order will only be given if the plaintiff can prove that the defendant is utilizing the defective or incomplete performance; that circumstances exist making it equitable for the court to exercise its discretion in favour of the plaintiff (where the defendant, for example, refuses to give the plaintiff the opportunity to repair or complete the defective performance); and what the extent of the reduced contract price is (which usually it entails the agreed contract price less the defendant's costs of remedying the defect or shortfall). It should be noted that where the defence fails, the claim for a reduced contract price is based a contractual claim and that it can be brought only when the defendant has not cancelled the contract. However, where the court allows the *exceptio*, thereby barring any possible contractual claim, the plaintiff only has a claim based on unjustified enrichment against the defendant. Where the defendant has cancelled the contract but retains and utilizes the defective performance, there is no contract in terms of which the plaintiff can bring an action, in which case the plaintiff can only recover compensation from the defendant on the basis of an unjustified enrichment claim.

371. The second *ex lege* remedy is cancellation, which is viewed as a drastic remedy. The law of contract does not allow parties to cancel their contracts at will in all circumstances where inconvenience or breach occurs. A party may only cancel the contract if he is entitled in law to do so. He is not compelled to do so, for he may rather choose to claim specific performance and/or damages. Parties may always cancel where they have agreed that it is a remedy by ways of inclusion of a cancellation clause in their contract. This remedy is available even if the breach is negligible or of a non-material nature. Insurance contracts usually contain a clause that enables the insurer to cancel the contract upon the policyholder's breach. In the absence of such a cancellation clause, the right to cancel depends upon the type of breach. These clauses often contain certain specifications and requirements (such as notices and demands) with which the innocent party has to comply before the right to cancel the contract accrues. Failure to meet these requirements could result in an unjustified cancellation of the contract, in which case the injured party could commit breach of contract in the form of repudiation.[281]

---

279. *BK Tooling (Pty) Ltd v. Scope Precision Engineering (Pty) Ltd* 1979 1 SA 391 (A); Bradfield, 486; Hutchison et al., 316–320.

280. 1979 (1) SA 391 (A).

281. Hutchison et al., 325–328; Bradfield, 610; *Sasfin (Pty) Ltd v. Beukes* 1989 (1) SA 1 (A).

372. Cancellation in the absence of a *lex commissoria* is only possible in the case where there is either *mora debitoris* or *mora creditoris* and where time for performance is of the essence. Where time is not of the essence, the creditor may acquire a right of cancellation by delivering a notice of rescission to the debtor. If the debtor is already in *mora ex re,* the creditor must demand performance within a reasonable time (depending on the facts and circumstances of each situation) and notify the debtor that he intends to cancel the contract if the debtor does not make performance within the given time Where the contract does not specify a date for performance, the creditor must first place the debtor in *mora ex persona* by means of a notice of demand. Strictly speaking, upon failure to comply, the creditor should then follow up this demand with a new demand in order to acquire a right to cancel. It is, however, possible to combine both these notices in one document, resulting in simultaneous notices of default and cancellation being given. Where the debtor then does not perform on time, the creditor acquires the right to cancel the contract.

373. Where breach occurs either by positive malperformance or repudiation, an injured party is only entitled to cancel the contract in the absence of a *lex commissoria* where the malperformance or repudiation is substantial. This will once more depend on the facts and circumstances of each case. The injured party may thus cancel the contract where the malperformance is of such a serious nature that he cannot reasonably be expected to keep the performance and be satisfied with a claim for damages. If breach does not justify cancellation, or where the injured party elects to retain the defective performance, he only has a claim for damages. It should be noted that in case of positive malperformance it is not possible to acquire a right to cancel though notice as discussed under *mora debitoris* and *mora creditoris* above. If a party repudiates a contract and indicates that he is not going to fulfil his contractual obligations at all, his repudiation is serious or material enough to entitle the injured party to cancel the contract. Where he indicates that he is only going to make a partial or defective performance, the facts and circumstances of each case have to be examined in order to determine whether the repudiation is substantial enough to allow cancellation of the contract. He does not have to follow any procedure to acquire the right to cancel, except that the repudiation must be material before it may be accepted and the contract be cancelled as a result thereof. Where any party to a contract prevents performance, specific performance and enforcement of the contract are obviously impossible. Where the performance is indivisible, the injured party's only option is to cancel the contract and claim damages. Where the performance is divisible, the contract may be partially cancelled and a claim for damages instituted.

374. It has already been said that a party is not compelled to cancel a contract merely because he has the right to do so. Upon breach, a party must exercise this right to cancel within a reasonable period of time, where after it might be deduced that he has decided not to enforce this right. However, the injured party may still bring evidence to show why he did not exercise his right within a reasonable period of time, which means that his right to cancel and resile from the contract is not necessarily extinguished by lapse of time. It is possible for a party to expressly or tacitly waive his right to cancel, by upholding the contract and claiming specific performance and damages, or by tendering performance in terms of the contract or by accepting late or defective performance. It is important to note that where a party has made restitution of the guilty party's performance impossible, the right to cancel is lost.

375. In South Africa no formalities are required for cancellation. A contract can be cancelled verbally, in writing or even tacitly. What is required is that the injured party must communicate his cancellation to the other party. Contracts often stipulate the procedure which the party who chooses to cancel the contract must take for the cancellation to be effective. As a rule, cancellation of a contract causes all contractual obligations to come to an end, and no party may claim performance from the other. Furthermore, each has to return to the other any performance already received by claiming and tendering restitution. Where parties have included survival and severance clauses, some obligations may survive the cancellation. As stated above, the right to cancel is forfeited where the party who wishes to cancel the contract makes restitution impossible. He may cancel only where the fact that restitution is impossible is not due to any fault on his part.[282]

376. The basis of our law is that damages rest where they fall. This means that one cannot claim from another person merely because one has suffered a loss. One may only claim where a recognized source of legal obligation exists, for example, in contract, delict, and *ex variis causarum iuris figuris*, which include claims based on unjustified enrichment, unauthorized agency (or *negotiorum gestio*), statute or where family relationships exist. A claim for damages can be combined with either a claim for specific performance or for cancellation of the contract, or instituted on its own.[283]

377. Traditionally the purpose of such a claim is to place the injured party in the position he would have been in had breach of contract not taken place. It is said that the party is entitled to his positive interest or interest in the performance of the contract. The amount payable as damages is calculated by comparing the position in which the prejudiced party finds himself upon breach of contract, with the position he would have been in, had the breach not occurred and the contract been fulfilled properly. Only suffering the loss is insufficient for a damages claim to succeed. Legal rules influence the recoverability of damages as well as the extent of the claim, which could make it difficult and sometimes even impossible for the injured party to succeed with such a claim. Recent developments recognized the possibility to claim negative interest, where by means of damages the injured party is placed in the position he would have been in, had the contract never been concluded. This is not the norm but possible where the calculation of positive interest is, for example, impossible.[284]

378. The plaintiff is not automatically entitled to damages merely because he has suffered a loss. He has to prove that a valid contract existed, that the contract was breached, that he did in fact suffer patrimonial damages, and that the breach is causally linked to the damages suffered. Only patrimonial losses can be recovered in an action based on breach of contract, and compensation for intangible losses cannot be claimed in contract compensation for moral and sentimental damages, inconvenience, including

282. *Extel Industrial (Pty) Ltd v. Crown Mills (Pty) Ltd* 1999 (2) SA 719 (SCA); *Datacolor International (Pty) Ltd v. Intamarket (Pty)* Ltd 2001 (2) SA 284 (SCA); Hutchison et al., 325–328.

283. *Holmdene Brickworks (Pty) Ltd v. Roberts Construction* Co Ltd 1977 (3) SA 670 (A).

284. Bradfield, 642–647; Hutchison et al., 329–340; *Lillicrap, Wassenaar and Partners v. Pilkington Brothers* 1985 (1) SA 475 (A); *Mainline Carriers v. Jaad Investments* CC 1998 (2) SA 468(C); *Thoroughbred Breeders' Association v. Price Waterhouse* 2001 (4) SA 551 (SCA).

pain and suffering, or the injured feelings of prejudiced party, are delictual damages and cannot be claimed because of breach of contract yet can be claimed in delict provided the necessary requirements are met.[285]

379. The plaintiff must prove the extent of the damages by quantifying the extent of the amount he is claiming. Damages must be proven and are never presumed. The time when damages have to be calculated is determined by the specific facts and circumstances of each case, but it is usually the date when performance was due and enforceable, or the date of breach of contract. The amount claimed does not require mathematical exactness, as the court will within its discretion on a reasonable estimation calculate and award damages, should the court be presented with sufficient evidence to allow it to do so. The courts follow a flexible approach, by adopting a market-price formula, by rejecting claims that are too speculative and by falling back on actual expenditure incurred. Where the exact amount of damages is unclear the courts also adopt the lowest measure of damages shown by evidence. As a last resort, a court will award a fair and reasonable sum under the circumstances. A court will not award nominal damages to a plaintiff merely to enable him to recover his litigation costs.[286]

380. The plaintiff must furthermore at all times mitigate his losses, which means that he must as far as possible within his ability through reasonable care reduce the extent of the loss, and prevent new damage or further losses from occurring. He is precluded from recovering damages which he could have prevented through reasonable care. If the defendant can prove that the plaintiff failed to take reasonable steps to ensure that further damages are prevented, the plaintiff will not be able to claim these damages from the defendant. It must be noted that the Apportionment of Damages Act 34 of 1956 does not apply to contractual claims, and only to claims in delict where there is contributory negligence attributable to both plaintiff and defendant.

381. A causal link between the breach of contract and the damages suffered must be proven. Factual causation is determined by applying the *conditio sine qua non* test, which means the damages must not have occurred if one takes the act that constitutes the breach of contract out of the equation. To prevent an endless chain of events and consequential damages, factual causation must be limited by a legal causation. The presence of legal causation is tested in view of policy considerations, such as foreseeability, reasonableness, proximate causes and the like.

382. General damages caused by the breach may always be claimed. These are damages that flow naturally and generally from the type of breach that has occurred, and include two types, namely *damnum emergens* (damages that are directly due to the breach of contract), and *lucrum cessans* (namely losses that are also directly due to breach of contract). The injured party must prove that the damages would have realized with absolute certainty had it not been for the breach of contract.[287]

383. Special or consequential damages are those that flow from the direct damages caused by the breach of contract and can only be claimed where the parties agreed, expressly or tacitly that these losses could be recouped. This is the position due to the application of the so-called convention principle. The agreement can be

---

285. *Dominion Earthworks v. MJ Greef Electrical Contractors* 1970 (1) SA 228 (A).

286. *Scott v. Poupard* 1971 (2) SA 373 (A).

287. *Holmdene Brickworks v. Roberts Construction* 1977 (3) SA 670 (A); *Administrator Natal v. Edouard* 1990 (3) SA 581 (A).

based on real or presumed consensus. Most academics agree that the previously applied contemplation principle should apply, which means that where the special damages were contemplated (foreseeable), they can be claimed. This is though not the current position on our law.[288]

384. Concurrency of claims is possible. Due to the operation of the once-and-for-all rule, it is possible to claim concurrently (in the alternative) on breach of contract or on delict, provided that the requirements for both claims are met. The principle that one may not be compensated for the same loss or damage twice clearly applies.[289]

385. Parties may agree on a specific interest rate for payment on outstanding amounts. The interest rates are then payable provided they comply with the rates prescribe and limited by statute from time to time. In the absence of agreement and where a court makes an order for payment together with interest, interest rates are determined by the Prescribed Rate of Interest Amendment Act 7 of 1997. An agreement to pay compound interest is enforceable. For payment of interest, the *in duplum*-rule applies, that the amount of interest payable may never exceed that capital amount of the debt outstanding. Interest can only become payable on liquidated amounts.[290]

386. In order to avoid the problems in recovering or quantifying damages, parties often include a penalty clause in their agreement that a predetermined amount of damages shall be paid in the event of breach of contract. Such a clause usually entails that a party who acts contrary to his contractual obligations will be liable to pay an amount of money, to deliver something or to make some other performance, which the other party would not normally have been entitled to. The penalty amount or value of the performance due could exceed the actual damages suffered by the injured party. The benefit of a penalty clause includes the wide extent of the claim and that the claimant does not have to prove damages nor comply with all the complexities of a traditional claim for damages. It has been held that a *rouwkoop* is not a penalty clause for purposes of the application of the Act.[291]

387. All penalty clauses, including forfeiture clauses are regulated by the Conventional Penalties Act. In terms of section 2(1) of the Act, the amount in terms of the penalty clause and damages as calculated above cannot be claimed cumulatively. A party may also not choose to waive his right to the penalty amount and elect to institute a common law damages claim instead. The parties can though agree that they can be claimed in the alternative. This will be of great benefit to the party who underestimated his potential losses when agreeing on the penalty amounts. In terms of section 2(2) no penalty may be claimed where the prejudiced party accepted a defective or partial performance and chose to continue with the agreement, unless the contract states clearly that the penalty is in addition to, and is aimed at compensating for, the defective performance.

388. In terms of section 3, a court may in its discretion reduce the penalty if it is of the opinion that the penalty is out of proportion to the actual prejudice suffered

288. *Schatz Investments v. Kalovyrnas* 1976 (2) SA 545 (A).

289. Bradfield, 650–651; Hutchison et al., 313–314; *Trustees, Two Oceans Aquarium Trust v. Kantey & Templer (Pty) Ltd* 2006 (3) SA 138 (SCA).

290. Bradfield, 657–658; Hutchison et al., 311; 363; 495–499; *David Trust v. Aegis Insurance Co Ltd* 2000 (3) SA 289 (A).

291. Bradfield, 607; Hutchison et al., 341–344.

by the creditor. The debtor has to raise and prove that the penalty exceeds the prejudice suffered by the creditor of the penalty. It should be noted that prejudice has a wider meaning than patrimonial damage. When determining the extent of the prejudice, the court takes the creditor's proprietary interest or that which was foreseen by the parties when entering into the contract into consideration, and also any legal interest of the creditor which is affected by the breach of contract. The court will, therefore, take into account everything that may harm the creditor in his property, person, reputation, work and other activities, as well as convenience and peace of mind.[292]

389. Because it was relatively easy for insurers to void or cancel contracts based only on the presence of the insured's misrepresentation or breach of warranty – no matter how trivial it was – provisions were introduced into both insurance Acts in order to protect policyholders. Section 59(1) of the LTIA and section 53 of the STIA state that an insurer cannot limit his liability in terms of an insurance contract or cancel the contract, or increase the obligations of the insured, based on a representation by the insured, unless the incorrect or false representation made by the insured probably *materially* influenced the assessment of the risk covered by the policy. As stated there is no unanimity on the question as to what should be regarded as *material*. The facts have to be examined objectively in order to determine whether the risk was substantially influenced by the misrepresentation or breach of warranty.[293]

390. Where the age of the insured is not disclosed correctly to a long-term insurer, the insurer may not void or cancel the agreement at all. The insurer must provide those policy benefits, against payment of the relevant premium, which would have been due had the insured disclosed his true age. Other adaptations to the policy in terms of statute for specific misrepresentations made by the prospective policyholder to the insurer are also possible.[294]

§3. Obligations in the Case of Insured Event

391. The moment a policyholder or other interested party alleges that a claim is due and payable, claims procedures are set into motion. The insured must comply with the prescribed claims procedure or preconditions (e.g., that due notice of a claim has been given) before a claim vests against the insurer for payment of policy proceeds. A claimant must prove on balance of probability in the first instance that a valid insurance contract existed. In the second instance, that the claim falls within the scope of the cover provided for by the policy. Where an insurer alleges that a special provision governs the relationship, the claimant will have to prove that it does not. On the other hand, where an insurer relies on an exclusion or exception clause, the onus falls on the insurer to prove the defence.[295]

392. Where a claim is not settled, a disgruntled party may use a number of routes to enforce his rights. As a matter of background: in South Africa there is primarily a distinction between statutory ombudsman schemes and voluntary ombudsman

292. *Van Staden v. Central South African Land and Mines* 1969 (4) SA 751 (C).
293. Nienaber & Reinecke, Ch. 23 at para. 9.
294. Section 59(2) of the LTIA.
295. Nienaber & Reinecke, Ch. 20, paras 5–10.

schemes. A statutory ombudsman scheme is a scheme is a scheme explicitly authorized by a statute. Often the statute will set out the powers of the ombudsman, procedures to be followed and jurisdiction. A voluntary ombudsman scheme on the other hand is initialized by stakeholders in a particular industry who not only fund the scheme but also agree amongst themselves to be bound by the decisions of the Ombudsman.[296]

393. In accordance with section 11 of the Prescription Act,[297] insurance claims are ordinary debts that prescribe three years from the date on which the debt is due. The creditor must furthermore be aware, or should have been aware by the exercise of reasonable care, of the facts regarding the cause and extent of his claim. One should note that there might be different triggers for insurance coverage. Prescription period will start running from the time when the loss-causing occurrence or event occurs where the cover provided is in terms of an 'occurrence' based policy. Where cover is provided under a 'loss occurrence' policy, the prescription period only starts to run on the date on which the damage or loss manifests itself and the insured knows or should reasonably have known about the damage or loss.[298]

394. Prescription must, in accordance of section 17 of the Act be pleaded specifically by a defendant or respondent, as a court cannot raise it of its own initiative. Prescription is interrupted by an acknowledgement of debt or by the serving of a summons, in accordance with sections 14 and 15 of the Act. Parties to an insurance contract can conclude a 'standstill agreement' in terms of which prescription is suspended. It is also general insurance practice to include a time bar clause in an insurance contract that extinguishes the insured's claim against the insurer where the claim is not brought within a specific period of time. In *Huyser v. Quicksure (Pty) Ltd and Another*[299] the policyholder instituted action against the wrong defendant and this mistake occurred primarily due to the bad drafting of the policy. When the policyholder discovered his mistake, the correct defendant (insurer) was identified and the policyholder attempted to join the correct defendant in the action. The insurer pleaded prescription. The court ruled that in terms of section 12(3) of the Prescription Act 68 of 1969 prescription only commences ones the correct debtor had been identified. *In casu*, as the policy document created confusion as to who the actual insurer was and this fact was only discovered after summons was issued against the incorrect party, the claim had in fact not become prescribed.

395. Prescription should not be confused with time bar or suit limitation clauses. It is important to note that agreements that limit prescription do not extinguish the insured's right of action, but only provide the defendant with a defence, whereas a time bar clause in an insurance contract extinguishes the insured's claim against the insurer. As was the case in *Barkhuizen v. Napier* discussed above, parties to insurance contracts often agree to time bar clauses. It should be noted that this type of agreement does not affect prescription, but is in its nature either a resolutive time period or condition, in that the right to claim lapses after a specific time period or an uncertain future event (in this case the failure of the insured to institute action within a specific

296. Millard, 141–142.
297. Act 68 of 1969.
298. Hutchison et al., para. 15.4.4.
299. Unreported Case No. 73006/2012; [2017] ZAGPPHC 24, [2017] 2 All SA 209 (GP) 93 Feb. 2017.

time limit). Other examples include that an insurer will provide comprehensive car insurance to a client provided that he keeps his car in a roadworthy condition at all times, or that an insurer will offer theft cover to an owner of valuable items provided that those items are kept in a safe. Although these terms are contractual duties of the insured, and non-performance can constitute breach of contract, they have the effect of a resolutive condition on the cover provided. The insurer's duty to pay on the claim is terminated. Parties to an insurance contract can conclude a 'standstill agreement' in terms of which prescription is suspended. It is also general insurance practice to include a time bar clause in an insurance contract that extinguishes the insured's claim against the insurer where the claim is not brought within a specific period of time.[300]

396. The laws that govern the contract are usually determined by agreement between the parties to the insurance contract, or by the general rules that apply to a conflict of laws in respect of contracts. The only statutory provision that exists on the jurisdiction on matters pertaining to insurance can be found in section 59(1) of the STIA. It provides that any claim against a Lloyd's underwriter under a South African short-term insurance policy will be cognizable by any competent South African court.

397. Generally speaking, the insurer's obligation to pay exists when the contract is current and the policyholder can prove that his claim falls within the four corners of the contract. Increasingly, insurance companies insert forfeiture clauses in insurance contracts to discourage policyholders from committing fraud. The recent case of *P K Harikasun v. New National Assurance Company Ltd*[301] confirmed the Roman-Dutch principle, namely that an insured cannot claim more than he is actually entitled to. Insurance companies often deal with insurance fraud by including fraudulent claims clauses into their contracts. Standard fraud clauses entitle the insurer to repudiate such claims and in some instances, the insurer may also be entitled to cancel the contract. These clauses confirm the parties' rights and where an insurer has for instance compensated a policyholder and it later transpires that the claim was fraudulent, the insurer has the right to recover benefits that were mistakenly paid to the policyholder. Forfeiture clauses, although by times patently unfair, are both valid and enforceable. It is however imperative that an insurance company cannot merely allege that a claim is fraudulent rather, allegations of fraud should be proven before claims may be repudiated. Such was the case in *Renasa Insurance Company Limited v. Watson & another.*[302] Regardless of the kind of fraud committed, the law states emphatically that the insurer who alleges the fraud must prove on a balance of probabilities that the insured's conduct amounted to fraud (*Santam Bpk v. Potgieter* 1997 (3) SA 415 (O) 422-3). In the absence of such proof, an insurer must pay.

300. Rule 7.4 of the PPR's in terms of the LTIA and the STIA.
301. Unreported Case High Court, *KwaZulu-Natal* nr 190/2008 of 12 Dec. 2013.
302. Unreported (Case No. 32/2014 [2016] ZASCA 13, 11 Mar. 2016).

Chapter 5. Obligations of the Insurer

398. In short-term insurance, the basic obligations of an insurer is to indemnify an insured against a loss proximately caused by the risks insured against. A claim vests in the insured when there is a valid contract of insurance; any suspensive conditions must have been fulfilled; the risk insured against should have materialized; the insured must have suffered a loss; and the loss must have been proximately caused by the risk insured against. The insured must prove that there was an insurable interest prior to the materialization of the risk and that the interest had been damaged. In addition, the insured must prove the extent of the damage or impairment and that the loss falls within the ambit of the contract of insurance.[303]

399. The basic obligations of a long-term insurer is to pay the sum insured on the occurrence of an event such as death which is a once-off occurrence or the payment of periodic amounts in the instance of a disability event such as the loss of a limb. A claim vests in the insured if there is a valid contract of insurance, if any suspensive conditions have been fulfilled, if the risk insured against have materialized, if the insured have suffered a loss and if the loss was proximately caused by the risk insured against and such loss refers to non-patrimonial loss. Certain forms of long-term insurance are not 'risk only' products and are use as savings vehicles. In those instances, a claim vests upon the maturity of the policy.[304]

§1. Non-life Insurance

I. Over- and Under-Insurance

400. Over-insurance occurs when the sum or sums insured are more than the total value of the insured's interest. For instance, if the insured's household contents are worth ZAR 200,000 and they are insured for ZAR 500,000, the insurer is still only obliged to pay ZAR 200,000 in the event of a total loss. Some policies describe the sum insured as the limit of liability and this is one of the factors used to calculate the premium. It is precisely because the premium is affected that it is necessary to ensure that a policy does not inflate the value of the property insured. Apart for the fact that the policyholder pays too much, over-insurance is in actual fact inconsequential.[305]

401. Under-insurance is however highly problematic for the insurer. In cases of under-insurance, conventional contracts stipulate that a person who is under-insured may recover only up to the amount of the sum insured or the amount of the loss, whichever is the lesser. This is not the case in marine insurance. The insured who under-insures in terms of a marine insurance policy is deemed to be his own insurer for the uninsured balance. This amounts to average. The fact that under-insuring reduces the amount a person has to pay their insurer explains why so many policyholders

303. Reinecke et al., 215–216; *Nafte v. Atlas Assurance Co Ltd* 1924 WLD 239.
304. Reinecke et al., 231.
305. J.P. Van Niekerk, *Under Insurance and Average*, MBL 125 (1981).

under-insure themselves. Individuals who under-insure often do so despite being aware that they stand to lose a great deal if the insured risk – the theft of the household contents, for example – materializes. However, insurers discourage the practice of under-insuring. In fact, short-term insurers have developed the practice of inserting standard clauses in contracts such as *pro rata* conditions of average. In order to prevent under-insurance in contracts other than marine insurance policies, policies often contain a condition which provides that if at the time of the loss the insured amount under the contract is less than the value of the property, the insured is his own insurer for the difference, which means that he must bear a rateable proportion of the loss accordingly. The effect of such an average clause is to incorporate the rule on under- insurance which is a *naturale* of marine insurance and an explicit clause in all other short-term insurance contracts. The suggested formula for average clauses constitutes limitations and it is imperative that prospective insureds should not only understand the importance of insuring property for the true value but also update their insurance annually. It is the responsibility of intermediaries, advisors or insurers themselves to draw the attention of prospective insureds to the existence of average clauses and to impress on them the importance of providing the correct values of the property they wish to insure. Average does not apply where the insurer opted to reinstate instead of compensate. It also does not apply to instances where there is a total, as opposed to a partial loss.[306]

II. Subrogation

402. The English law doctrine of subrogation was introduced into South Africa in 1918 by the courts in the judgment in *Ackerman v. Loubser*.[307] Subrogation is concerned solely with the insurer's right to be *dominus litis*. The insurer's right of recourse is then based purely on the grounds of unjustified enrichment or on an agreement with the insured. Most insurance contracts, however, contain a specific contractual subrogation clause to provide for this eventuality. In South Africa, subrogation often occurs in short-term (non-life) insurance. Subrogation provides for the reimbursement of an insurer who has indemnified its insured in accordance with the terms of a contract for indemnity insurance. Subrogation does not entail a transfer of rights but is simply a process of 'settling-up' between the insurer and insured where the insurer's claim against a third party has been successful.[308] Most modern-day insurance contracts contain express subrogation clauses that allow for the aspects discussed above. These clauses stipulate the common law rights and duties of the parties and may also contain additional provisions, such as the provision that full indemnity is not a prerequisite for the insurer's right to subrogation to become operative. The doctrine of subrogation has its shortcomings, most of which relate to the difficulty of applying its theoretical norms to practical situations.

403. Where the damage to the insured interest is caused by a third party, the insured has a choice either to claim from his insurer in terms of the insurance contract, or from the third party on the grounds of delict. However, the principle of indemnity

306. Millard 119–120.
307. 1918 OPD 31, 36.
308. Millard, *Modern Insurance Law* 122–123.

still applies, namely that the insured can never recover more than his actual damages. The insured cannot claim the full amount of his damages from both parties. If the insured does recover his damages from his insurer, the insurer by operation of law obtains the right to claim the amount paid out to the insured from the third party. The insurer institutes this specific claim in the name of the insured. No formal cession of actions by the insured to the insurer is required. Because the insurer has indemnified the insured, the latter loses all economic interest in his claim against the third party as the interest is transferred to the insurer.[309]

404. The following requirements exist for subrogation: (a) there must be cover under a valid insurance contract; (b) the insurer must have indemnified the insured; (c) the insured's loss must have been fully compensated by the insurer; and (d) the right must be susceptible of subrogation.[310]

405. Two situations have to be distinguished, namely where the insurer completely indemnifies the insured, and where the insurer only partially indemnifies the insured. In the first instance, the insurer becomes *dominus litis* of the claim against the third party. The insurer is entitled to any amounts recovered from the third party.

406. In the second instance, where the insurer does not completely indemnify the insured, the insured does not lose his economic interest in the claim as he has to carry some of the losses himself or recoup them directly from the third party. Splitting of the claim would be prejudicial to the third party. The insured therefore remains *dominus litis* of the claim and has to cooperate with the insurer to successfully claim the loss from the third party. The insured is entitled to any amount recovered from the third party. Any balance which the insured receives in total from the third party and the insurer, which exceeds the amount of loss or damage, has to be repaid to the insurer as the insured may in total never claim more than his actual loss. It is important to note that only one cause of action exists against the third party. The third party is entitled to use all the defences that were available to him had it not been for the subrogation, for example, that the insured waived his right to claim, or that the insured was contributory negligent as to the loss-causing event.

407. The insured may not in any way prejudice or frustrate the insurer's claim against the third party. This would, for example, occur where the insured waives his claim against the third party, or where a reaches a settlement with the third party for a lesser amount.[311]

408. The duties of the insurer under subrogation also aim to preserve the claim against the third party. The insurer must preserve the insured's claim and not to prejudice the position of the insured by, for example, accepting an unfavourable settlement offer by the third party. Any costs awarded to the third party regarding the proceedings are technically recoverable from the insured, yet as the action benefits the insurer, the position is that the insurer must bear these legal costs. For increased protection of the insurer's rights, it has become common practice for insurance contracts to contain an express provision providing for extended subrogation. This entails that the insured immediately transfers the full claim he would have had against third parties to the insurer, irrespective of whether the insurer fully indemnifies the insured or not.

309. Reinecke et al., 497.
310. Prozesky-Kuschke, in *Commercial Law* 369 (Nagel et al. eds).
311. *Visser v. Incorporated General Insurance Ltd* 1994 (1) SA 472 (T).

409. After paying out a claim, the insurer has the automatic right to salvage in cases of total loss, where the object of risk is totally destroyed, or where what remains is no longer an object of the type as insured originally. This will include where the insured has merely been deprived of his interest and its return is uncertain or unlikely. The parties may also reach an agreement on the insurer's right to salvage even though no total loss was suffered. The insurer has to pay the insured for total loss before he has a right to salvage whatever remains of the affected interest.[312]

III. Multiple Insurance

410. When a claim arises and there is more than one valid insurance contract in place, there is the occurrence of multiple insurance. The insured may choose to recover his loss from one or all of the insurers. However, an insured is not allowed to recover more than the actual loss. In South Africa, as in other jurisdictions, this simply means that if the loss amounts to ZAR 90,000, an insured who claims the whole amount from insurer A cannot also claim the whole amount from insurer B. Rather, insurer A can claim a contribution of 50% from insurer B. If there were three insurers, insurer A would be able to claim a third from insurer B and a third from insurer C, and so forth, The basis of contribution still rests on the all-important, underlying principle of indemnity, which means that the purpose of insurance is to make good a loss and not to make a profit. The right of one or more insurers to claim a contribution from another insurer or other insurers is a right of recourse. In addition, this right is a *naturalia* of a contract for indemnity insurance. This means that one of the legal consequences of the contract is that an insurer who has paid more than its rateable proportion of the loss may recover that excess amount from the other insurer or insurers. The right to contribution arises if the insurer who claims contribution has indemnified the insured and has paid more than his rateable proportion of the loss, if the payment to the insured was in respect of an interest which was the object of double insurance at the time of the loss and the double insurance must have been for an amount in excess of the loss.[313]

§2. Life Insurance

411. An insurer's main duty is to pay the agreed amount or to render the promised service as and when it falls due in terms of the policy. Usually, the insurer's performance is the payment of an amount of money but it may also be the rendering of a service, such as the arrangement of a funeral in the case of an assistance policy. The insurer's obligation to pay is dependent on the occurrence of the insured event and this event may be the maturity date of a policy or if it is a risk product, the death, birth, illness, injury, disability or retrenchment of the insured life. It is the duty of the insurer to pay to the policyholder, the nominated beneficiary or a cessionary. An insurer has the duty

312. Reinecke et al., 416.

313. Reinecke et al., 368–371; *Refrigerated Trucking (Pty) Ltd v. Zive (Aegis Insurance Co Ltd, Third Party)* 1996 (2) SA 361 (T), Millard 118.

to pay to the correct person and failure to do so may render an insurer liable to an aggrieved party.[314]

314. Nienaber & Reinecke, 243.

Chapter 6. Insurance and Third Parties

412. Both the LTIA and the STIA describe 'policyholder' as the person entitled to be provided with the policy benefits under a policy. The insurance benefits do not necessarily always accrue to the insured as policyholder. The rights under the policy may be ceded to another person, or a beneficiary may be nominated by the insured. A third-party beneficiary nomination may take place, for example, where a person receives a benefit from another person's insurance policy, pension fund or any other legal instrument. In insurance, these beneficiaries do not take part in the initial conclusion of the contract. A beneficiary nomination is not a cession, but a common law contract to the benefit of a third party or *stipulatio alteri*. In *Pieterse v. Shrosbree NO and Others; Shrosbree NO v. Love and Others*[315] the Supreme Court of Appeal explained the operation of a *stipulatio alteri* as follows:

> The legal nature of such a nomination is a stipulatio alteri (a contract for the benefit of a third person). In such a case, the policy holder (the stipulans) contracts with the insurer (the promittens) that an agreed offer would be made by the insurer to a third party (the beneficiary) with the intention that, on acceptance of the offer by that beneficiary, a contract will be established between the beneficiary and the insurer. The right to claim under a policy may thus vest in a nominated beneficiary. If the policyholder nominates a person to be the beneficiary of a life policy, the beneficiary does not become the new policyholder, but is only in future upon the death of the insured life or maturity of the policy, entitled to the policy proceeds. This is not necessarily a 'nomination of ownership', where the original policyholder replaces himself with a successor in title.[316]

413. According the general principles that apply to a *stipulatio alteri*, it is clear that the beneficiary acquires no rights until he accepts the benefit. *PPS Insurance Co Ltd and Others v. Mkhabela.*[317] Upon acceptance by the beneficiary a new legal obligation exists between the *promittens* (the insurer) and the beneficiary. On 295A-B the court authoritatively explained that the beneficiary only has an expectation or mere *spes* that would not pass to the executor of her estate if she died before the policyholder until he accepts the policy proceeds. The court also made a distinction here between accepting the beneficiary nomination and accepting the benefit being the policy proceeds. Accepting the nomination gives the beneficiary no enforceable right to the policy proceeds and he or she would continue to have only a *spes* until the time arises for acceptance of the policy proceeds.

414. The rights of the *stipulans* (the policyholder) against the *promittens* lapse upon the beneficiary's acceptance. Policy proceeds become payable to the beneficiary and not to the *stipulans*. In *Pieterse v. Shrosbree* at 313F-H the court highlighted that the legal nature of such a nomination of a beneficiary is a *stipulatio alteri* where the

315. 2005 (1) SA 309 (SCA) 313.

316. Nienaber & Reinecke, Ch. 18; M.F.B. Reinecke & P.M. Nienaber, *A Suggested Template for Beneficiary Nominations*, SA Merc LJ 1, 13 (2009).

317. 2012 (3) SA 292 (SCA) 294C-G, 295A-B.

intentions of the contracting parties are that the benefit, upon acceptance by the beneficiary, would confer rights that are enforceable at the instance of the beneficiary against the insurer, and not by the *stipulans* or policyholder. That intention is at the 'very heart of the *stipulatio alteri*'. This was confirmed in the subsequent case of *JR 209 Investments (Pty) Ltd v. Pine Villa*.[318] Cessions are often the subject of litigation. In *Malani & others v. Natalia Financial Brokers CC*[319] *In casu*, the appellants (children of the late Ahmed Ebrahim Malani) instituted action in the KwaZulu-Natal Division of the High Court, Pietermaritzburg, against the respondent, Natalia Financial Brokers CC (Natalia), an insurance brokerage. They claimed damages based on the alleged wrongful and negligent failure of one of its members, Bangaru, to substitute them as beneficiaries on a life policy which the deceased held with Old Mutual Life Assurance (Old Mutual) and that this constituted a breach of a legal duty owed to them by Bangaru, to submit a beneficiary appointment form signed by the deceased to the insurance company, in terms of which they were appointed as beneficiaries of the policy. The High Court (Koen J) dismissed the claim, finding that the appellants had failed to prove that they had suffered damages, and the quantum of the alleged damages. They had also failed to prove that any damages had arisen from the conduct of the respondent. The claim was similarly dismissed on appeal aby Theron JA and what is important is that the broker did not have the authority from the deceased as original policyholder to substitute the children with the beneficiary that was chosen and properly nominated by the deceased.

415. A beneficiary nomination can be either revocable or irrevocable. If it is clear from the policy that the right to revoke a nomination lies with the policyholder. It is important to note that a revocation of the benefit is possible as the beneficiary has no rights at all until his acceptance. His rights are not being revoked. It is the nomination that may give rise to his future rights that may be revoked. A revocation may be made tacitly or expressly. Express revocation occurs when the policyholder conveys this intention to the insurer at any time before maturity or the death of the life insured or acceptance by the beneficiary. An insurer may prescribe a form for express notification. An attempt to revoke a nomination that does not comply is invalid. Even though it places some form of restraint on the policyholder, it serves to notify the insurer of who the holder of the right to policy proceeds is once policy benefits become payable, and provides him with some protection against double payments in this regard. Where a policy permits the revocation but does not prescribe the manner in which the revocation should occur, the policyholder may revoke the nomination either expressly or by implication.

416. A nomination is irrevocable if the policyholder must acquire the consent of the insurer before revoking a prior nomination. The insurer may prescribe formalities and procedures regarding the application for and provision of the consent. A nomination made without the consent of the insurer in the prescribed format is thus ineffective. A nomination is deemed to be irrevocable unless the policy states otherwise. Reinecke

318. 2009 (4) SA 245 (SCA) para. [15]. *See also* Hutchison et al., Ch. 9, specifically para. 9.3.3; Reinecke & Nienaber, A Suggested Template for Beneficiary Nominations 2.
319. [2014] ZASCA 84, 31 May 2016.

& Nienaber have observed that usually life policies expressly stipulate the terms governing beneficiary nominations and are seldom silent on this issue.[320]

417. This position has been criticized as it infringes upon the policyholder's freedom of contract and constitutes a restraint of trade. Whether the restraint is contrary to public policy or not, will depend on the facts and circumstances of each case. Where a court must decide on the issue, it must take the principles of reasonableness and equity as discussed under the public policy requirement above into account. This viewpoint has been supported by some of the courts, who have held that a prior beneficiary nomination may be revoked by implication even if the insurer did require notice. Where a husband nominated his wife as beneficiary, then after their divorce indicated in his will that he wished to nominate his children, the revocation by the deceased was respected by our courts. This was even though the deceased did not obtain the insurer's consent or inform the insurer of the revocation.[321] The court reiterated that written notification is 'wholly for the protection' of the insurer and failure to comply did not affect the validity of the beneficiary revocation. However, in *Hees v. Southern Life Association Ltd*[322] the court found that a tacit revocation in a will had not revoked the prior beneficiary nomination and confirmed that the requirement for notification establishes certainty as to the rights arising from a beneficiary nomination and benefits not only the insurer but also the beneficiary. It appears that beneficiary nominations in most modern policies are revocable. In such a case the policyholder may unilaterally without any consent from the insurer revoke a prior beneficiary nomination.[323]

418. Some authors like Muller are of the opinion that ceding the rights under a life policy as security for a debt implies the revocation of a prior revocable beneficiary nomination. Due to this risk, life policies commonly contain an express provision that a previous beneficiary nomination is automatically revoked by a subsequent cession.[324]

419. On the question of whether a security cession could be an implied revocation of a beneficiary nomination, it is the opinion of some authors that, in the absence of a provision stating otherwise, a revocable beneficiary nomination cannot be impliedly revoked by a security cession. The first reason for this is because a cession of the rights under the policy and the revocation of a beneficiary are two separate and distinct acts. The second reason is that a cessionary must take cession subject to any contingencies. This means that a security cessionary of a life policy takes cession of the right to claim the policy proceeds subject to the right of any beneficiary already nominated, or who

320. Reinecke & Nienaber, SA Merc LJ 17–19 (2009).
321. *Wolmarans en 'n Ander v. Du Plessis en Andere* 1991 (3) SA 703.
322. 2000 (1) SA 943 (W).
323. Reinecke & Nienaber, 216.
324. E. Muller, *Life Insurance Benefits: The Setting Aside of Cessions and Nominations in Terms of the Insolvency Law and other Related Aspects*, De Jure 361, 364 (2005); P.M. Nienaber, *Some Problems Involving Security Cessions of Life Insurance Policies*, SA Merc LJ 83, 100 (2004); Reinecke & Nienaber, SA Merc LJ 30–31 (2009); Reinecke & Nienaber, 230; *Moonsamy and Another v. Nedcor Bank Ltd and Others* 2004 (3) SA 513 (D); *Ex Parte Calder Wood NO: In Re Estate Wixley* 1981 (3) 727 (Z) 729.

may be nominated in the future. The cessionary's right may have to 'yield' to that of the beneficiary depending on the policy provisions.[325]

420. The court has supported this viewpoint that a nomination could be revoked by implication, yet that unlike an outright cession where the beneficiary's expectation of the policy proceeds is extinguished, such an expectation remains intact with a security cession, since *dominium* of the life policy still vests in the policyholder's estate. Accordingly a security cession cannot revoke a prior nomination by implication.[326]

421. Sunkel is of the opinion that although this view is in accordance with the *ratio* in the *Moonsamy* case, the reasons submitted therefor are not entirely convincing. In both cases the cessionary and beneficiary are given rights in respect of the same policy proceeds, and in this sense the cessionary can also be viewed as a beneficiary. The difference is that the cessionary may claim the surrender value if necessary to satisfy an unpaid debt, but the beneficiary has no rights until death or maturity of the policy. This explains why an insurer would insert a clause in a life policy providing for the invalidation of a prior beneficiary nomination upon cession. Were it otherwise, the insurer would not know which 'beneficiary' to pay on death or at maturity.[327]

422. It remains important to keep in mind that at the time of the security cession, the beneficiary has no right to the policy proceeds as his right arises only on death or at maturity of the policy should he accept the benefit. Even though a cession is subject to contingencies, the right of the beneficiary to the policy proceeds cannot trump the rights of the cessionary. The security cessionary will always be first in time and must accordingly be preferred in right. Were this not the case, a cessionary may refuse to accept a life policy as security since it would hold little value. Cession and revocation should remain two separate and distinct acts and a security cession should not been seen to cancel or revoke a prior beneficiary nomination unless otherwise provided for in the policy. The nomination should remain in force, but should be subject to the cession. This means that on death or at maturity (or on surrender), the cessionary's claim must first be satisfied from the policy proceeds, and only then may any excess be claimed by the nominated beneficiary, provided he has accepted the benefit.[328]

423. When a policyholder surrenders a policy, the policy is effectively 'cashed in' before death or the date of maturity of the policy, and the surrender value calculated as a portion of the premiums so far paid, minus specific costs incurred by the insurer. The Supreme Court of Appeal remarked that the entitlement of a policyholder to be paid on the surrender of a policy is not one of the benefits of a policy, as '… it is no more than a separate entitlement that arises if the undertaking to pay benefits is terminated before the benefits accrue'.[329]

424. It is clear that a policy subject to a revocable nomination that is surrendered revokes a prior beneficiary nomination by implication. Where the nomination is irrevocable, the policyholder may, not demand the surrender value of a policy without

325. Reinecke & Nienaber, 230; Reinecke & Nienaber, SA Merc LJ 30–31 (2009).
326. *Moonsamy v. Nedcor Bank* 519–520A.
327. Sunkel (LLD), 39.
328. E. Muller, *Life Insurance Benefits: The Setting Aside of Cessions and Nominations in Terms of the Insolvency Law and Other Related Aspects*, De Jure 361, 364 (2005).
329. *Mungal v. Old Mutual Life Insurance Co SA Ltd, freeman v. Old Mutual Life Insurance Co SA Ltd* 2010 (6) SA 98 (SCA) at 106.

the prior consent of the beneficiary, because such a demand will amount to an implied revocation.[330]

425. Furthermore, extension clauses may provide for cover not only for the policyholder, but also for others under the policy. It is possible for a first-party policy to offer cover to a third person who is not the insured. This is usually done by the inclusion of a contractual extension clause that extends the cover to allow for claims under the policy by persons other than the insured. These are frequently included in a variety of insurance policies. An example would be where property or fire insurance cover also provides cover for the property of the insured as well as for the goods of third parties brought onto the insured property.

426. Extension clauses are often found in liability policies. This type of cover can be found, for example, where direct casualty insurance is taken out by a policyholder for the benefit of unnamed third parties. The exact structure of these clauses has been hotly debated in South African law for some time yet appears to have reached the end of its development as a *stipulatio alteri*.

427. An important statutory exception in the Insolvency Act[331] creates rights for a third party against the insurer of an insolvent insured or policyholder. Section 156 states: Whenever any person (hereinafter referred to as the insurer) is obliged to indemnify another person (hereinafter referred to as the insured) in respect of any liability incurred by the insured towards a third party, the latter shall, on sequestration of the estate of the insured, be entitled to recover from the insurer the amount of the insured's liability towards the third party, but not exceeding the maximum amount for which the insurer has bound himself to indemnify the insured.[332]

428. It is trite law as from the discussion above that where the clause is in effect a stipulation for the benefit of a third party, the third party obtains rights against the insurer upon acceptance of the benefit. Uncertainty, however, reigns on whether the third party receives rights from the original contract between the *stipulans* and the *promittens*, upon or even before acceptance, and becomes a party to that contract, or whether he receives rights only against the *promittens* upon acceptance of the benefit in terms of a second independent contract between himself and the *promittens*.[333]

429. Where the clause merely makes the proceeds payable to the third party as a beneficiary, the cover itself is not extended to include cover for the beneficiary. Where the intention is to extend the cover, it is proposed that the third party does not require an insurable interest at the time when the cover is obtained, but that he should at least have such an interest upon acceptance of the benefit that affords him the rights against the insurer. The fact that the third party does not pay a premium to the insurer for the insurance cover he receives, does not affect the nature of the contract. Reinecke is of the opinion that one cannot require the insured to have an insurable interest in the contingent liability of the third party were the contract intends to compensate the third

330. Reinecke & Nienaber, 2009 SA Merc LJ 28; Reinecke & Nienaber, 229.

331. Act 24 of 1936.

332. W.G. Schulze, *Extension Clauses in Insurance Contracts – Uncertainty Rules OK?*, 9 SA Merc LJ 64 (1997); also W.G. Schulze, *Extension Clauses in Insurance Contracts – A New Angle*, 9 SA Merc LJ 216 (1997). Reinecke et al., 46, 64, 88, 443–337.

333. Hutchison et al., 226. Nienaber & Reinecke, Ch. 18 at para. 8.

party. The exact construction will in each situation depend on the facts, the intentions of the parties and the construction of the contractual rights of the parties.

430. Generally, the insured who enjoys protection in terms of the policy is also the first holder of the policy. Any subsequent holders are cessionaries who obtain the rights by ways of a cession. The cessionary who will receive policy benefits in the stead of the cedent will not be a party to the initial conclusion of the insurance contract, and will only take up rights against the insurer at a later stage upon conclusion of a valid and binding cession agreement.

431. In brief, a cession can be out-and-out which transfers the right permanently and in full ownership to the cessionary. Where a right is ceded for security purposes, it may take one of two possible constructions. The first is the pledge construction where the parties intend the right to transfer only temporarily until the principal debt has been paid, upon which it reverts back to the cedent automatically. The second is the fiduciary cession, where the cession agreement is concluded in conjunction with an agreement that, upon the principal debt being honoured, the right will be ceded back by the cessionary to the original holder of the right. These two constructions for cession of insurance policies and the complications thereof are discussed in greater detail under the heading on cession below.[334]

432. Beneficiaries must be described in the contract or policy documents in such a way that they can be identified with legal certainty. It is also possible to name a class of beneficiaries, such as 'my grandchildren', provided that it is clear to whom reference is made. Beneficiary nominations are discussed in greater detail together with cession below.

433. In *Hlela v. SA Taxi Securitisation (Pty) Ltd*[335] the noting of the interests of a third party was discussed extensively. The appellants, who were mini-bus taxi operators required finance to purchase mini-bus taxis and they obtained money from SA Taxi Securitisation (Pty) Ltd (Taxi Securitisation) for loans. Taxi Securitisation provided the money and required the appellants to insure the vehicles with a registered insurer and on terms that were acceptable to Taxi Securitisation. The appellants, in terms of the finance agreements, ceded their 'entire right, title and interest in and to every insurance policy effected' in terms of the finance agreements to Taxi Securitisation. The appellants signed an application for insurance with the third respondent, Clarendon Transport Underwriting Managers (Pty) Ltd (Clarendon). According to the application for insurance, the broker was identified as the second respondent, SA Taxi Finance Holdings (Taxi Finance) and the insurer was the sixth respondent, The Hollard Insurance Company Ltd (Hollard). The certificate of insurance that was subsequently issued by Clarendon indicated that SA Taxi Risk Management Services (Pty) Ltd (Taxi Risk), and not Taxi Finance, was the broker. It is exactly the fact that Taxi Securitisation substituted the appellant's broker of choice with another broker that created difficulties. A dispute arose when the appellants asked South African Insurance Brokers CC to manage their insurance portfolios with Clarendon and to obtain more favourable insurance premiums. Taxi Securitisation refused to agree to the substitution of Taxi Risk with SA Insurance Brokers. Their argument was that as the cessionary of the respective insurance policies, they had the right to appoint a broker of their choice to

334. Hutchison et al., 368. *See also* Nienaber & Reinecke, Ch. 18, para. 86.
335. Unreported Case No. 515/2013 [2014] ZASCA 112 (26 Aug. 2014).

manage the policy for the duration of the finance agreements. Initially, Taxi Securitisation, as a registered credit provider in terms of the NCA, suggested to the appellants that they should insure the vehicles with Hollard, who are underwritten by Clarendon and they argued that section 106(1) of the NCA[336] does give them the power to do this. However, the choice of insurer does not lie exclusively with the credit provider because section 106(4) of the NCA provides that a consumer must be given, and must be informed of the right to waive the proposed policy and substitute a policy of the consumer's choice. More specifically, the court declared that while section 106(1) of the NCA aims to protect the interests of the credit provider, section 106(4) of the NCA, together with section 20(a)(i) of the GCC in terms of the FAIS Act confirms the notion that no person can be forced to use the insurer or the broker suggested by the credit provider. Although the credit provider had an interest in the insured vehicles and was entitled to demand that these were insured, their right as a third party is clearly limited.

434. Life insurance is a source of monetary consolation in the face of an adverse event such as death. Being a source of monetary consolation, life insurance is a valuable asset in the policyholder's estate, and can be used as a credit facility and for providing security, for example, where a trustee has to provide security for the trust assets under his management.

435. Because life insurance is also an asset, it can be used as security for credit facilities. Most financiers (or credit providers) extend credit only on the strength of some kind of security. Security serves to protect the financier in the event that the loan is not repaid. If the loan is not repaid, the financier can look to the security to satisfy the remaining indebtedness. Financiers would not be able to exist without a system of security.[337]

436. The cession of a life insurance policy as an instrument for providing security is still one of the most popular methods to secure credit. When a life insurance policy is used as security for a financial loan, for example, the financier acquires the right to claim the policy proceeds where the policyholder defaults on loan repayments. The proceeds of the policy aim to satisfy the outstanding balance under the loan. The transfer of the rights under the policy is intended to be temporary and for security purposes only. Cession straddles the law of property and the law of obligations. In addition to the diverging legal concepts of contract law, securities law, the law of cession and restraint of trade practices make the already complex situation even more complex.[338]

437. Legal uncertainty about the exact construction and consequences of a cession of a life policy when it is used as security for credit facilities prevails. Although academics have attempted to solve some of the issues and a large body of theory has emerged, a lot thereof does not consider trade practices and has been the source of discontent amongst practitioners and the financing sectors. The unsatisfactory situation prompted the South African Law Reform Commission to launch an investigation on

336. Act 34 of 2005.

337. *See* in general K. Sunkel, *Cession of Life Insurance Policies in* securitatem debiti*: A Practical Perspective* (LLD thesis, University of Pretoria, 2013).

338. Nienaber & Reinecke, Ch. 18 at para. 80.

the necessity of legislative intervention. The Commission eventually concluded that the issue was one which our courts would eventually have to solve.[339]

438. Due to alternative dispute resolution mechanisms very few plaintiffs and appellants approach the courts, with a result that very few cases on cession end in litigation. Two decades on after the release of the Commission's final report, the intricacies of security cessions of life policies have seen very little judicial development.

439. In South African law, the transfer method of a real right depends on the object of the right. Where the object is movable corporeal property, transfer takes place by delivery provided is in accompanied by the intention to pass and receive ownership. The court held in *Commissioner of Customs & Excise v. Randles Brothers & Hudson Ltd* that '[o]wnership of movable property does not in our law pass by the making of a contract. It passes when delivery of possession is given accompanied by an intention on the part of the transferor to transfer ownership and on the part of the transferee to receive it.'[340] Furthermore, due to the operation of the rule *nemo plus juris ad alienum transfere potest, quam ispe habent* one cannot transfer to another a right which he has not. Where the object is of the real right is immovable corporeal property, transfer takes place by registration together with an intention to pass and receive ownership. This is provided for by the Deeds Registries Act.[341]

440. Personal rights are capable of transfer yet not in the same way in which real rights are, because the object of a personal right is a performance, often the payment of a sum of money. Since this object is incorporeal in nature neither delivery nor registration can be employed to effect a transfer of a personal right, such as the right to claim policy benefits from an insurer. Personal rights are uniquely transferred by way of cession. In *First National Bank of SA Ltd v. Lynn NO and Others*[342] the court explained that cession is 'a particular method of transferring rights in a movable incorporeal thing in the same manner in which delivery (*traditio*) transfers rights in a movable corporeal thing. It is in substance an act of transfer by means of which the transfer of a right *(translatio juris)* from the cedent to the cessionary is achieved'.[343]

441. A cession differs from a beneficiary nomination, as with cession the right passes, whereas with the nomination, a new right is created for the beneficiary to claim from the insurer when he accepts the nomination.

442. A contract of cession in essence creates three different agreements simultaneously. It is, as highlighted in *Republikeinse Publikasies (Edms.) Bpk v. Afrikaanse Pers Publikasies (Edms) Bpk*,[344] not in itself merely a contract. The cession is an obligationary agreement that forms the *causa* or underlying reason for the subsequent transfer of the personal right that is being ceded. The obligationary agreement part of a contract of cession however, does not bring about the actual transfer of a personal right. A cession is also a real agreement or transfer agreement, namely the

339. J.P. Van Niekerk, 'Life Insurance: Cession' 1997 Annual Survey of South African Law 588.
340. 1941 AD 369, 398.
341. Act 47 of 1937. *See also Legator McKenna Inc and Another v. Shea and Others* 2010 (1) SA 35 (SCA) 44C-H; *Middleton v. Middleton and Another* 2010 (1) SA 179 (D) 183F-G.
342. 1996 (2) SA 339 (A) 345F-G.
343. P.M. Nienaber, *Cession* in LAWSA, paras 3–4 (2 ed. 2003) (updated by Lubbe G.F. 2013, paras 128–183).
344. 1972 (1) SA 783A-D.

act of transferring the personal right from the original cedent to the cessionary. Finally, it is also the absolving agreement that terminates the obligationary agreement by performance. All three take place simultaneously by the conclusion of a valid cession contract.[345]

443. The obligationary agreement can manifest itself in a number of ways, for example, where there are contracts of sale, lease, security or donation. No additional substantive or formal requirements for the validity of the obligationary agreement for a cession are necessary. The obligationary agreement is governed purely by the legal principles of the specific agreement that evidences the *causa*, or by formality requirements agreed upon by the parties. The case of *Glen Anil Finance (Pty) Ltd v. Joint Liquidators, Glen Anil Development Corporation Ltd (In Liquidation)*[346] serves as an example, where the obligationary agreement was governed by the provisions in the deed of sale.[347]

444. The transfer agreement evidences the transfer of the right from the cedent to the cessionary. It does not require nor depend on the existence of a valid obligationary agreement between the parties. The transfer agreement part of the cession does not generally require formalities, as it is a mental act.[348]

445. The only substantive requirement for a valid cession is a duly constituted agreement, either orally or in writing, in a manner that indicates that the parties are *ad idem*. This means that the cedent must have the intention to cede the personal right and similarly, the cessionary must have the intention to acquire it. The concurrence of the parties' intentions brings about the cession. A written deed of cession does not have to be drawn up, unless it is prescribed by statute or if it is the intention of the parties that writing is a requirement for validity. This is not a common law requirement for the cession of insurance policies. Where the cession happens to be evidenced in a document, for example, a share certificate, the document itself does not have to be delivered to the cessionary.[349]

446. The cession agreement, in addition to being an obligationary agreement and a real agreement, is also an absolving agreement in that it in itself is also the way in which the undertaking to cede the personal right is performed, terminating the obligationary agreement. The consequences of a cession are that cession brings about complete transfer of a right from the cedent to the cessionary and the cedent will be wholly divested thereof. The cessionary is subsequently the only person who may administer the right or enforce it.[350]

447. In accordance with the *nemo plus iuris* rule, the cessionary only steps into the shoes of the cedent and cannot be in a better or weaker position than that in which the cedent was. The personal right is transferred with all its attributes, benefits, privileges,

345. Hutchison et al., Ch. 14.
346. 1981 (1) SA 171 (A).
347. P.M. Nienaber, *Cession* in LAWSA, para. 28 (2nd ed. 2003) (updated by Lubbe G.F 2013, para. 171).
348. *Legator McKenna v. Shea* 2010 (1) SA 35 (SCA); *Botha v. Carapax Shadeports (Pty) Ltd* 1992 (1) SA 202 (A) 214F.
349. *Botha v. Fick* 778G-I, 779A-B.
350. *Trust Bank of Africa Ltd v. Standard Bank of South Africa Ltd* 1968 (3) SA 166 (A) 166 173D; J.P. Van Niekerk, *Life Insurance: Cession*, Annual Survey of South African Law 588 (1997).

defects and disadvantages. A cessionary obtains no greater rights against the debtor than the cedent enjoyed prior to the cession. Consequently the debtor of the corresponding duty may raise against the cessionary any defences to the original debt that he could have taken against the cedent.[351]

448. A cession may take the form of an outright cession or 'out-and-out' cession, or a security cession. When a personal right is ceded outright, the complete rights transfers to the cessionary. Nothing remains vested in the cedent and the cedent has no expectation of a re-cession by which the right reverts to him. The structure of this type of cession is clear and does not create as many problems as is the case with security cessions dealt with below.[352]

449. Complications tend to arise where a cession is *in securitatem debiti* – a security cession – where the intention is not to transfer the personal right permanently from the outset. The cedent always has the expectation that the personal right will be receded back to or revest in his estate once the principal loan for which the security serves has been repaid. In South African law a security cession may take one of two constructions. The first is the pledge construction, where a personal right serves the same function as a pledge of movable corporeal property. In this case the ownership or *dominium* of the personal right remains with the cedent and only the entitlement to enforce the right upon non-payment of the principal debt is transferred to the cessionary. Once the loan has been satisfied the personal right is reverts to the cedent's estate. The Roman-Dutch author Voet in his *Commentarius* 20.3.1 wrote that 'things can be given in pledge which are movable and immovable, corporeal and incorporeal'. South African courts have followed his viewpoint.

450. The second construction is called a fiduciary security cession. In this case the right is ceded to the cessionary or financier completely as an out-and-out cession. The intention of the parties in ceding a right in this manner for security purposes is that upon payment of the principal debt for which it serves as security, the right will be receded back to the original cedent. The intention is therefore that the cession is temporary until the principal debt is honoured. The cessionary gives an undertaking to recede the right to the cedent in future, when the parties conclude the cession agreement.[353]

451. Where the cession contract clearly stipulates the type of cession intended by the parties, the issue is moot. Yet where it is not clear which construction has been agreed upon the question arises as to which construction should prevail. Most courts including the Supreme Court (recently in the case of *Grobler v. Oosthuizen*) and in the provincial decision of *Retmil Financial Services (Pty) Ltd v. Sanlam Life Insurance Co Ltd*[354] have preferred the pledge construction. It appears as if industry prefers this construction as well and interprets its cession as being pledges.[355]

452. When parties employ the use of the pledge construction for security purposes, the intention of the parties at all times is that the object of security should vest in the financier only temporarily. The aim is for the object of security to revert to

351. *Van Zyl v. Credit Corporation of SA Ltd* 1960 (4) SA 582 (A) 587H.
352. Nienaber & Reinecke, para. 28.4; Reinecke et al., 456.
353. Hutchison et al., 369.
354. 2013 JDR 0864 (WCC) para. 26.
355. Sunkel (LLD), 32.

the debtor upon satisfaction of the debt. During the existence of the pledge the debtor or pledgee must retain possession and control in the object pledged until the principal debt has been extinguished. Loss of possession or control automatically terminates the pledge and security is forfeited.[356]

453. Where the cession is in the form of a pledge, the policyholder still retains the 'bare *dominium'* or ownership of the personal right that was ceded, yet cannot exercise his rights to claim under the policy from the insurer unless the parties agree otherwise. The creditor of the principal debt only obtain a *ius in re aliena* or right in another's property (the personal right to claim from the insurer) that enables him to claim under the policy only where the principal debtor and policyholder fails to honour the principal debt. Bare *dominium* still vests in the principal debtor or policyholder to whom upon discharge of the principal debt the personal rights revert. Davis AJ explained in the *Retmil* case that since the life policy was pledged, the position must be governed by the applicable principles: While the secured debt remained unpaid only the cessionary had *locus standi* to enforce the policy and receive payment. However, it is also true that because the policyholder retains the bare *dominium*, he retains an interest in the life policy even if he cannot for the time being enforce the policy. The cessionary was only entitled to demand payment of the policy proceeds if the policyholder defaulted with loan repayments.[357]

454. A pledge construction that functions well in the realm of corporeal property cannot simply be adapted to cession of incorporeal property. The court in *First National Bank of SA Ltd v. Lynn NO and Others* describes this challenge as follows: 'The fiction [of the pledge construction] has its origin in the practical needs of modern commerce but has caused much strenuous intellectual gymnastics on the part of scholars and lawyers in trying to prise one legal concept into the garb of another not ideally suited.'[358]

455. One may ask whether the pledge of a right is in fact a transfer thereof, and thus a cession. It is neither pledge in the traditional sense, or a true cession, and settles uncomfortably in both. Writers view it that a cession is necessary to complete or 'perfect' the pledge as the cession perform the delivery function required for the passing of the object of security from the cedent to the cessionary. 'Possession' of the policy document does not equate to possession of the right, because the policy document serves only as proof of the insurance contract and ensuing rights. Delivery of a policy document would serve the purpose only of proving the cession and thus transfer of the right. It may also serve the function that it informs the insurer who the holder of the right actually is.

456. The court held in *National Bank of South Africa Ltd v. Cohen's Trustee* that the policyholder 'need only demand the return of his property and a re-cession is not necessary to complete his title'. If the latter is not required, then one may ask how the right passed into the possession of the cessionary without a cession in the first place. The words of the court in *Cohen's Trustee* thus support the view that with a security 'cession' by pledge, a cession in the true sense of the word does not actually take place.

---

356. Hutchison et al., 370.
357. *National Bank of South Africa Ltd v. Cohen's Trustee; Retmil Financial Services (Pty) Ltd v. Sanlam Life Insurance Co Ltd* 2013 JDR 0864 (WCC).
358. At 350A.

457. One may ask whether it is possible to cede part of a personal right, that is, only the entitlement to realize or to enforce it and whether this does not defy the essence of cession. It has been submitted that 'a right cannot, at one and the same time, be transferred and retained'.[359] Similarly, the view has been expressed that ownership of a personal right cannot theoretically be divided and distributed amongst between various holders.[360]

458. There is no satisfactory way to explain how the financier becomes vested with the *jus in re aliena*. Sunkel recommends that one must simply accept that upon a pledge of the rights under a life policy, the financier has the right to enforce the policy until the secured debt has been satisfied. The acceptance of the pledge construction, however, does not eliminate the probability that no cession occurs. For this reason, the transaction should perhaps not be referred to as a security *cession* by pledge. Accordingly, it may be a misnomer to refer to the parties as 'cedent' and 'cessionary' yet this is the norm in practice.[361]

459. Where the policy proceeds exceed the outstanding loan amount and the financier is credited with a balance not due to him the beneficiary has no direct *locus standi* against the financier. It clearly cannot be expected of the financier to incur duties to pay out and distribute the policy proceeds to other persons. Sunkel advocates that in this situation it makes more sense if the insurer holds the policy proceeds in trust. In this way the insurer can pay the policyholder (or executor of his deceased estate) or the nominated beneficiary the full policy proceeds once the secured debt has been satisfied. Alternatively, the insurer can pay the financier if the policyholder defaults on loan repayment and can pay the balance to the policyholder (or executor) or nominated beneficiary as the case may be. Should the policy mature or the policyholder dies before the secured debt has been honoured, the solution is usually to be found in the obligationary agreements where the issue is usually expressly or tacitly addressed. If the obligationary agreement is silent on the issue, the insurer should hold the policy proceeds in trust until either the loan is repaid or the policyholder defaults on loan repayments.[362]

460. The courts prefer the pledge construction to protect the policyholder from the financier's insolvency prior to repayment of the loan. Because the policyholder retains *dominium* at all times, the right to claim from the policy does not fall into the financier's insolvent estate. *See Van Staden v. Firstrand* at 533C-D where the court said: 'With regard to the standing of the trustee, my understanding is that he proceeds on the basis that a cession *in securitatem debiti* takes the form of a pledge and accordingly the residual right (or bare *dominium*) remains an asset in the insolvent estate of the cedent despite the cession … .'[363]

461. Section 63 of the LTIA does however protect a portion of the policy proceeds in the event of insolvency, but protection is expressly excluded where the policy has been ceded as security regardless of the type of construction.

359. Hutchison et al., 371.
360. P.M. Nienaber, *Cession* in LAWSA, para. 53 (2nd ed. 2003).
361. Sunkel (LLD), 38.
362. Sunkel (LLD), 42.
363. Hutchison et al., 371.

462. If, however, it is the policyholder who becomes insolvent before the secured debt has been satisfied, the personal right to claim from the insurer falls into the policyholder's insolvent estate. In accordance with section 2 of the Insolvency Act 24 of 1936 the financier does acquire a secured claim for repayment against the insolvent estate, as a pledge is a statutory secured claim. In further support *see Van Staden v. Firstrand*[364] where the court stated that in a pledge 'the cessionary ... would be the holder of a real right of security and normally would be protected' and *Van Zyl v. Look Good Clothing*:[365] 'The effect of the cedent retaining *dominium* in the right ceded in the case of a cession *in securitatem debiti* is that, in the event of the sequestration or liquidation of the cedent during the currency of the cession, the trustee or liquidator in the insolvent estate has the right to recover and administer the claim which has been ceded on the basis of it being an asset in the estate being administered by him.'

463. In this manner the trustee of the insolvent estate may either enforce the claim against the insurer or realize the asset by selling it to a third party. The proceeds of the policy will be used to discharge the secured debt and any balance will be credited to the insolvent estate to distribute to the policyholder's creditors. In *Van Staden v. Firstrand* at 543C Murphy J pointed out that '[t]he trustee is accordingly the person entitled to recover the proceeds as part of his duty to realize the assets of the estate, but subject to the real right of pledge held by Nedbank [the cessionary] who consequently remains fully protected'. In *Leyds v. Noord-Westelike Koöperatiewe Landboumaatskappy*[366] the Appellate Division held that on the insolvency of the cedent, the pledge construction operates in the interest of both the cessionary and the creditors of the insolvent estate because the cessionary enjoys a preference in the proceeds of the personal right and any proceeds in excess thereof are distributed amongst the creditors.

464. Another advantage of the pledge construction is that it may be, in part, pledged to multiple pledgees. *Van Staden v. Firstrand* at 541F confirmed that as the *dominium* of the policy always vests in the policyholder, he is free to pledge his personal right under the life policy to the balance of the proceeds that are not needed to secure his prior secured debt. In this case the 'first in time strongest in right' principle will apply for division of the proceeds amongst the various pledgees. Academics however support the view that a security cession is preferable a fiduciary cession. In terms of this construction the policyholder cedes a personal right to the financier as an ordinary out-and-out cession together with a contractual undertaking, called a *pactum fiduciae* for the re-cession of the personal right to the policyholder once the secured debt has been paid. Furthermore, before the duty to cede the right back to the policyholder becomes due, the risk is that the cessionary may cede the right to another person. In order to prevent this, the *pacta fiduciae* do not only contain a duty to recede, but also a restraint of trade in the form of a *pactum de non cedendo*. This encompasses that the

364. 2008 (3) SA 530 (T) at 533D-E.
365. 1996 (3) SA 523 (SE) at 526G-H.
366. 1985 (2) SA 769 (A) at 780F-G.

cessionary may not transfer the personal right to any other person and evade his duties towards the policyholder.[367]

465. In *Merchant Bank of Central Africa v. The Liquidators of Tirzah (Pty) Ltd, G & D Shoes (Pvt) Ltd (All in Liquidation)*[368] the court agreed with and applied the following statement to its judgment: '... If the parties intended to effect an out and out cession, there are certain modifications which they will have to bring into effect by agreement. These are a *pactum fiduciae,* an agreement against further cession, and an agreement to that the cessionary himself will not institute action before the cedent's debt is due.' The agreement to cede the right back to the policyholder is a normal contract and the policyholder receives only a personal right to claim that a cession must be concluded with him. In view of the fact that a *pactum de contrahendo* (agreement to agree) in South African law is null and void, the enforcement of the *pactum fiduciae* becomes problematic. Breach of the duty is a breach of contract for which normal contractual damages could be claimed. A claim for specific performance will be difficult to enforce and the courts may be hesitant to give such an order. If the parties, however, inserted a *pactum de non cedendo* any further cession by the financier would be void and of no effect.[369]

466. It is clear that with this construction the cession brings about a complete transfer of the personal right to the cessionary who obtains full *dominium* of it. The purpose of a security cession that the personal right vests with the cessionary only temporarily appears to change to one where an actual out-and-out cession takes place. Sunkel correctly advises that:

> [a]ny provision in a contract that indicates that the parties intend a complete transfer of the personal right, but only until such time as the secured debt has been repaid, should be interpreted as a fiduciary security cession. In such an instance the pactum fiduciae and all the restrictions that it encompasses to achieve this objective should find application. Pending judicial clarification on this point the policyholder would be prudent to expressly include additional restrictions.[370]

467. Due to a lack of jurisprudence and statutory definition and regulation, the format, content and nature of the *pactum fiduciae* that applies *inter partes* will depend only on its contents and the intentions of the parties. Pertaining to insolvency issues, a fiduciary security cession has the advantage that it puts the cessionary in a stronger position where the policyholder becomes insolvent before the principal debt is honoured. The cessionary holds the full *dominium* of the personal right to claim from the insurer. As explained by Sunkel, the financier is technically entitled to be demand surrender of the policy and claim the surrender value. Where the surrender value exceeds the

367. J.C. De Wet & A.H. Van Wyk, *Die Suid-Afrikaanse Kontraktereg en Handelsreg* 415 et seq. especially 420–421 (Durban, Butterworths 1992) where the authors describe the pledge construction as a false doctrine ('dwaalleer'); S.J. Scott, *The Law of Cession* 246; C.G. Bradfield 538, 545–546; J.C. Sonnekus, *Sessie van saaklike sekerheidsregte?*, TSAR 772 (1997).

368. [2001] JOL 7532 [ZH] at 12.

369. K.D. Sunkel, *The pactum de non cedendo: A Re-evaluation*, 469, LLM Dissertation, University of the Western Cape (2009).

370. Sunkel (LLM), 469.

amount of the principal debt due, the problem once again is that the duty to pay and distribute the policy proceeds falls on the financier, and in addition, the beneficiary has no *locus standi* against the financier. In accordance with the submissions above, the correct payment procedure in the event of the policyholder's insolvency is for the insurer to pay the financier only the amount outstanding under the secured debt and to distribute the balance to the insolvent estate or the nominated beneficiary as the case may be. Conversely, the drawback to this type of security cession from the policyholder's perspective is that in the event of the financier's insolvency, the policyholder is left in an undesirable position. Because the right to claim the policy proceeds falls into the insolvent estate of the financier, the policyholder only acquires a personal right against the insolvent estate for re-cession once he has satisfied the secured debt.[371]

468. In the 1980s the South African Law Reform Commission embarked on an investigation on the effective use of corporeal and incorporeal property as objects for security purposes. In 1987 the Commission published a working paper, known as 'Working Paper 23' with its draft proposals. It supported a statutory regulation of cessions *in securitatem debiti*, expressly excluding the fiduciary construction as a preferred construction by enacting the Giving Security by Means of Movable Property Act. The report recommended that although the personal right remains vested in the insolvent estate of the cedent, it was suggested that the cessionary should acquire a secured claim in the form of a classic pledge construction against the insolvent estate. The proposal generated strong criticism in industry and from academics. Subsequently the Commission reported that '... neither the academics nor the commercial world is amenable to such a step'. Pressure was placed on the Commission to maintain the possibility of conclusion of a fiduciary cession *in securitatem debiti.*[372]

469. The Commission eventually decided that if the fiduciary security cession should not be abolished, it was not feasible to regulate only one construction of security cessions by statute and not the other, and scrapped work on the project. When the Security by Means of Movable Property Act[373] came into effect the use of incorporeal property as an object for security was expressly excluded the Act. As mentioned above the result was that it was finally up to the courts to find a solution on a preferred construction and to attempt to create precedents in law where insolvency of parties was at issue.

470. The only statutory contribution since 1993 to address cessions of insurance policies was in 2004 when the PPR were added as a schedule to the LTIA in accordance with section 62(5) of the Act.[374] Rule 18(f) provides that upon receiving notice of a cession, an insurer must inform the policyholder of the following: that the cession is recorded in the insurer's records; the exact nature of the cession and the name of the cessionary. Any contravention of this rule is an offence in terms of LTIA. Unfortunately, the brief amendment to the PPR does not prescribe a specific format and thus indicate the preferred construction for security cessions.

---

371. Sunkel (LLD), 52.
372. Giving of Security by Means of Movable Property Bill SALC Project 46, 124 (Annexure A para. 4).
373. Act 57 of 1993.
374. GN 1129 GG 26854 of 30 Sep. 2004.

471. The only other statute that enjoys some application is the NCA, which in section 106(1) of the Act stipulates that a financier may require the consumer (the moneylender) to maintain credit life insurance during the term of the credit agreement. Section 106(4)(a) allows a consumer to use an existing policy or a new one, and enables the financier to arrange for a specific policy should the consumer require a new one. The Act regulates the position slightly differently depending on whether a life policy was taken out a new or was pre-existing. Where the consumer uses a pre-existing life policy as security, section 106(6)(b) states that the financier could require the consumer to notify and instruct the insurer in writing by 'naming the credit provider as a loss payee under the policy up to the settlement value at the happening of an insured contingency, and requiring the insurer, if an insured event occurs, to settle the consumer's obligation under the credit agreement as a first charge against the proceeds of that policy at any time during the term of the credit agreement'. This would protect the rights of the financier. In the event that there has been a nomination of beneficiaries for the existing policy proceeds, the Act clearly does not require the financier to pay them directly.

472. Where it is a new policy, section 106(5)(d) stipulates that the financier 'must be a loss payee under the policy up to the settlement value at the occurrence of an insured contingency only and any remaining proceeds of the policy must be paid to the consumer'. This does create a duty that the financier must manage and pay credit balances on the policy to the policyholder. It would be unlikely that any other beneficiaries would be nominated as the cover would usually be the amount of the outstanding principal debt ensuring that the financier is the only payee. Where the product cover amount does exceed the outstanding principal debt and the policyholder decides to nominate a beneficiary for the balance, the same problem as illuminated above applies. The financier is not obliged by statute to pay any beneficiary other the policyholder.

473. Where the policyholder defaults on his duty to pay the principal debt, the financier must first comply with the strict notification provisions of section 129 of the Act, before he may cash in or enforce the rights in the policy that he holds as security. After due compliance with the provisions of this section, the financier may approach the court for enforcement of his rights in accordance with section 130 of the Act. If the policy that has been ceded is a life policy, the financier may in accordance with these sections enforce the policy before death of the policyholder.

Chapter 7. Termination of the Insurance Contract

474. Most contracts come to an end when all the parties perform properly in terms of their agreement. The contract is fulfilled as originally intended by the parties to the contract and reaches its end. Contracts are terminated in some cases by operation of law, an in other by agreement, such as where the parties agree to a resolutive condition or time period, waiver, novation, settlement or compromise.[375]

475. As a general rule, the debtor must deliver performance to the creditor. Any other person can perform on behalf of the debtor, even without the debtor's consent or knowledge, provided the intention is to perform on behalf of the debtor. There is an important exception to this rule. Where it is important for the creditor that the debtor should perform personally, no delegation of performance duties is allowed. Performance must be made to the creditor or his authorized representative. The parties may nominate a third party to whom performance must be made (a *solutionis causa adiectus*). Where the debtor makes performance to the latter, his obligation towards the creditor is terminated. The *adiectus* is not a party to the contract and cannot claim performance from the debtor. The debtor must deliver proper, complete and non-defective performance as intended in the agreement. The debtor is not entitled to make performance in instalments, unless agreed to either expressly or tacitly. A creditor could also, during the existence of the contract, consent to continue receiving performance in instalments. Payment of money must be effected by legal tender, that is, in cash (bank notes and coins issued by the Reserve Bank). The creditor is not obliged to accept payment made by cheque or other negotiable instrument, credit card or any other similar methods of payment, although he is free to do so. The debtor is entitled to a receipt and may refuse payment if the creditor does not issue a receipt. The receipt is prima facie proof of payment. Where the creditor disputes payment, the debtor can use the receipt to prove that payment was, in fact, made. Insurance legislation contains express provisions on the collection of premiums by the intermediaries, and the issuing of receipts.[376]

476. Partial performance by a debtor does not extinguish his contractual obligations, unless he delivers a partial performance in full and final settlement. This might be the case when an insurer offers to pay out a lesser amount on a claim, and the insured chooses to accept the payment, thereby waiving his right to claim the balance. If the debtor has the intention to make an offer of compromise or settlement of claim, his intention is that the whole debt will be discharged if the creditor accepts such offer.

477. The debtor must perform at the place agreed upon in the contract, expressly or where it is implied from the nature of the contract. Where this cannot be done, performance must be made at the place where the contract was concluded. Where money has to be paid, common law requires that the creditor must seek out the debtor and demand payment from him, unless the contract contains a fixed date for payment, in which case the debtor must seek out the seller and tender payment on or before such date.

375. Bradfield, Ch. 12; Hutchison et al., Ch. 15; *Alfred McAlpine & Son (Pty) Ltd v. Transvaal Provincial Administration* 1977 (4) SA 310 (T).

376. Bradfield, 471, 500–501; Hutchison et al., Ch. 15.

478. Where a specific day for performance is set, the debtor has until midnight on that day to perform, unless he has to make performance at the business premises of the creditor, in which case performance must be made during office hours. Where the day happens to be a Sunday or public holiday, the debtor may make his performance on the very next business day, unless it was agreed that performance must be made on a non-business day.[377]

479. Where a debtor owes a creditor various sums to honour different contractual amounts due, payments must be allocated as follows. Where the parties did not agree to the exact allocation or appropriation of payments, the debtor may make an allocation, except that he may not discharge capital before interest. Where the debtor does not allocate his payment, the creditor may make such an allocation, subject to the following order of precedence that is to the benefit of the debtor: (a) interest must be discharge before capital; (b) enforceable debts before unenforceable debts; (c) certain debts before uncertain debts; (d) a more onerous debt (for which security was provided or which carries interest, for example, before a less onerous debt); (e) an older debt before a newer debt; and (f) where all debts are equally onerous and of equal date, each debt is reduced proportionately.[378]

480. Parties may terminate a valid and binding contract through the conclusion of a new contract of either waiver, release, compromise or novation. Such a contract must meet all the requirements for contracts in general. Release from the contract is a bilateral act based on consensus between debtor and creditor. The creditor offers to release the debtor, who may decide to accept it or not. The offer may also be revoked prior to acceptance thereof. Should the debtor accept the offer, he is freed from his contractual duties. It often happens that the parties to a reciprocal contract mutually release each other (release in turn).[379]

481. Insurance contracts usually contain a clause stating that any party to the contract may choose to cancel or discontinue the contract by giving a unilateral notice of cancellation. In terms of Part V of the Long-term PPR, a policyholder may by written notice cancel a policy that is for longer than thirty days, within thirty days from date of receipt of the summary of the policy issued in terms of section 48 of the LTIA. The insurer has to refund all premiums or moneys paid, except for the risk cover actually enjoyed, and any market loss where the market value of the investments made has decreased due to prevailing market conditions. In terms of Rule 7.3 of Part V of the Short-term PPR, a short-term insurer may only terminate a contract by giving thirty days' notice to the policyholder, his independent intermediary or, where this is not possible, by publication in two editions of a local newspaper.

482. A compromise or settlement is an agreement between parties to settle an existing dispute between them. The original contract is terminated and substituted by the new settlement contract, which from then on determines the rights and duties of the parties. The original contract does not have to be valid for the compromise also to be valid – the validity of the original contract could be in dispute and depends on the compromise. Where one of the parties fails to honour the terms of the compromise, the injured party must sue him on the settlement agreement or compromise. The plaintiff

377. Bradfield, 498; Hutchison et al., Ch. 15.
378. Bradfield, 494–498.
379. *Schierhout v. Union Government (Minister of Justice)* 1926 AD 286.

may not revert to his cause of action in terms of the original contract unless this is provided for by express agreement or agreement by implication in the compromise.

483. Novation occurs when the parties to a valid and binding contract conclude a second contract with the intention of terminating and substituting the existing contract with the second. Unlike settlement or compromise, novation is only possible where the original contract that is renewed is valid. Where the novation agreement does not comply with the requirements for a valid contract, it does not replace the original contract, and the first contract is not terminated. Where parties conclude a novation substituting the existing debt with a new one, the novation discharges not only the existing obligation, but also all accessory obligations such as surety ships, pledges and mortgages. Novation which brings about a change in parties usually occurs when an existing debtor is substituted by a new one, in which case a delegation takes place. A novation comes into being between the creditor, the original debtor and the new debtor in terms of which the original debtor is released from his contractual obligations and the new debtor promises to perform in his place. This is the transfer of duties by delegation and the transfer rights. The latter are transferred by cession as discussed previously. Where a party is replaced by another where existing rights and duties are transferred to him, the replacement is a combination of cession and delegation and referred to as an 'assignment'.

484. Debts of same nature can be set-off against each other, and need not be equal in size. Only debts that are due and payable can terminate the debt by set-off. Debts must be liquidated to qualify for set-off. A debt is liquid if the amount thereof is certain (e.g., where the debtor admits the outstanding amount), or where the amount can be determined promptly and easily without the need for extrinsic evidence (such as the amount due under a cheque or a taxed bill of costs). The debts must be between same persons in same capacities.

485. Where the insured, at any given time during the contract, voluntarily waives the interest insured, the insurance contract is automatically terminated. As the existence of an insurable interest is one of the *essentialia* of an insurance contract, it follows naturally that an insurance contract cannot continue to exist without an insurable interest. Where performance becomes objectively absolutely impossible without the fault of any of the parties, for example, due to natural disasters, coincidence or acts of God and other instances of so-called force majeure, the obligation is terminated and the parties are relieved of their contractual duties. An order for the rehabilitation of an insolvent debtor discharges all debts which had arisen before his sequestration but it does not release a surety from his obligations.

486. The debtor is the one who must plead prescription. It is not within the inherent jurisdiction of the court to *meromotu* take notice of the prescription. A court will give judgment against a debtor even if it is clear from the documents before court that the debt has prescribed.[380]

487. Two different forms of prescription can be distinguished, namely extinctive and acquisitive prescription. In the case of extinctive prescription, legal obligations are extinguished through lapse of time, while in the case of acquisitive prescription ownership of another's property can be acquired after a period of thirty years. Only extinctive prescription is dealt with in this contribution. The Prescription Act applies

380. *Absa Bank Bpk h/a Bankfin v. Louw* 1997 (3) SA 1085 (C).

to debts arising after 1 December 1970. The Act provides for strong prescription, where a debt is extinguished upon completion of the period of prescription. The debt no longer exists and cession, novation or set-off of that debt becomes impossible. The time period for prescription of a contractual debt, such as a debt due in terms of an insurance contract is three years.[381]

488. In order to mitigate the strict consequences which strong prescription holds for the creditor, the Prescription Act provides for two exceptions to the general rule that debts are extinguished. Where the debtor pays the prescribed debt, it is deemed to be an effective payment. The debtor is precluded from recovery of such payment by means of an enrichment action, even if he was ignorant of the prescription or paid the debt by mistake.

489. The period is determined *de die in diem* in terms of the ordinary civil method. When the period of prescription starts on 10 December, it expires at midnight between 9 and 10 December of the appropriate later year.

490. The period of prescription commences on the day upon which the debt becomes due and payable.[382] Where the debtor conceals the existence of the debt or wilfully prevents the creditor from becoming aware of it, the period of prescription commences only when such knowledge is obtained by the creditor.[383] Section 12(3) also provides that a debt does not become due until the creditor knows or reasonably should have been aware of the identity of the debtor and the facts from which the debt arises. Where a claim for specific performance is combined with a claim for damages, the period of prescription in respect of both claims commences on the day upon which the cause of action arises, in other words, upon breach of contract. Where the creditor cancels the contract and claims damages, prescription in respect of the claim for damages commences at the moment of cancellation. Where a contract is reciprocal in nature, both debts will prescribe when the period of prescription of the last of the two debts due, has expired. Subsidiary debts, such as claims for interest, will prescribe together with the principal debt even if the period of prescription of the subsidiary debt has not yet expired.

491. In certain circumstances prescription can be interrupted, and commences *de novo* once the period lapses. This will be where the debtor expressly or tacitly acknowledges towards the creditor his liability to pay the debt (even where he only acknowledges liability for a portion of the debt). Prescription is also interrupted where the creditor serves process upon the debtor (such as a summons) and claims payment of the debt from him. The plaintiff must proceed with the process and obtain final judgment, unless the debtor acknowledges the claim. A new period of prescription then starts to run from the date of acknowledgement of debt, or from the date upon which the judgment becomes executable.

492. Prescription may in specific circumstances as set out in section 13(1) be delayed for one year. Prescription would in the ordinary course have been completed, but because of impediments, it is not completed before one year has elapsed from the date on which these circumstances or impediments have ceased to exist. These circumstances or impediments are the following: (a) the creditor is a minor, mentally

381. Bradfield, 560–579; Hutchison et al., 387–389.
382. Section 12(1).
383. Section 12(2).

incapacitated or under trusteeship or curatorship, or he is prevented by superior force (e.g., any law or order of court) from interrupting prescription; (b) the debtor is outside the Republic of South Africa; (c) the debtor and creditor are married to each other; (d) the debtor and creditor are partners and the debt arose out of the partnership relationship; (e) the creditor is a juristic person and the debtor is a member of its governing body; (f) the debt is the subject of a dispute subjected to arbitration; (g) payment of the debt is claimed from a deceased or insolvent estate, or from a company in the course of liquidation, or from an applicant to whom the Agricultural Credit Act applies; and (h) either the debtor or the creditor is deceased and an executor has not yet been appointed.[384]

493. After judgment in the case of *Barkhuizen* the claims procedures and time limits in insurance contracts have come under extensive scrutiny. From 1 January 2011 the time periods are statutorily regulated by the Long-term and Short-term PPR as follows:

(a) An insurer must accept, reject or dispute a claim within a reasonable period after receiving the claim, and then notify the policyholder in writing of his decision within ten days of taking the decision.
(b) Where an insurer rejects a claim or disputes the quantum of the benefit claimed, he must inform the policyholder in the written notification of: (i) the reasons for his decision; (ii) that the policyholder has a period of not less than ninety days from date of receipt of such a notification to make representations to the insurer in respect of the latter's decision; (iii) the right of the policyholder to lodge a complaint in terms of the Financial Services Ombud Schemes Act 37 of 2004 and the relevant provisions of the Act, in plain understandable language; (iv) any time limitation provision for instituting legal action and the implications thereof, in an easily understood manner; and (v) where the policy does not contain a time limitation, the prescription period that will apply in terms of the Prescription Act 68 of 1969 (at the moment a period of three years) and the implications thereof in an easily understood manner.
(c) The insurer must then, within forty-five days of receipt of such a representation, notify the policyholder in writing of his decision to accept, reject or dispute the claim. This notification must contain reasons for the decision, the facts that informed the decision and (iii) to (v) in (b) above, where the claim is rejected or disputed.
(d) Any time limitation provisions of the institution of legal action in policies concluded before 1 January 2011 may not include the time limits mentioned above.
(e) Policies concluded from 1 January 2011 onwards, may not include the time periods mentioned in (a) to (c) above, and must provide for a period of not less than six months after the expiry of the ninety-day period mentioned in (b)(ii) above.

494. Despite any agreement on a time limitation, a policyholder may request the court to condone non-compliance where good cause exists for the failure and where the clause is unfair to the policyholder.

495. Time bar or suit limitation clauses that change common law prescription periods are not foreign to insurance or other contracts. Their purpose is to curb inordinate

384. Act 28 of 1966.

delays, procrastination by the insured in submission of a claim against the insurer and the protraction of disputes. It aims to bring about economic certainty and business efficiency, all of which are crucial for effective insurance practice. It should be noted that the agreement to a time bar does not affect prescription, but is in its nature either a resolutive time period or condition, in that the right to claim lapses after a specific time period or an uncertain future event (in this case the failure of the insured to institute action within a specific time limit).

496. The effect of the Constitution on time bar or suit limitation clauses in insurance contracts in particular, is illustrated by the judgment handed down in the case of *Barkhuizen* that recently served before the South African Constitutional Court. In this case a time bar clause in an insurance contract reduced the prescription period for issuing summons against an insurer where the latter rejected an insurance claim, from the standard three-year prescription period to a period of only ninety days.[385]

497. This is standard industry practice for indemnity policies. The clause was tested for its constitutionality as it was claimed that it limited the insured's fundamental right of access to the courts in accordance with section 34 of the Constitution and in terms of his common law right to do so. This section states that: 'Everyone has the right to have any dispute that can be resolved by the application of law decided in a fair public hearing before a court or, where appropriate, another independent and impartial tribunal or forum.' It was claimed that the clause served no useful or legitimate purpose and was contrary to public interest, as the period of ninety days was an unreasonably short period of time.

498. In its judgment in *Barkhuizen*, the Constitutional Court held that the principle of *pacta servanda sunt* is not 'a sacred cow that should trump all other considerations', as it is subject, as all law is, to constitutional control. In terms of common law, contractual provisions will be illegal where they are contrary to public policy, yet public policy supports sanctity of contract that requires parties to comply with contractual obligations that have been freely and voluntarily undertaken. The right of access to the courts not only gives expression to the fundamental value of the right to seek judicial redress that is fundamental to the stability of an orderly society, but it also constitutes public policy.

Public policy is now deeply rooted in our Constitution and its underlying values, which simplifies its interpretation. It does not deny, but accommodates yet can limit the application of the principle of *pacta servanda sunt*. Public policy cannot be separated from the notions of fairness, justice and equity and reasonableness. The court stated that 'The proper approach to this matter is, therefore, to determine whether the relevant clause is inimical to the values that underlie our constitutional democracy, as given expression to in section 34 and thus contrary to public policy.' The majority of the bench in the *Barkhuizen* case held that the time bar clause did not deny the applicant his right to seek judicial redress, as it only limited the time within which he had to do so. This could not be seen as contrary to public policy.[386]

---

385. Section 11 of the Prescription Act prescribes an extinctive prescription period of three years for all ordinary debts unless stipulated otherwise by legislation.

386. *Barkhuizen v. Napier* 2007 5 SA 323(CC) paras 28–30. *See also* Hutchison et al., paras 1.1, 1.8 and 7.2. However despite this ruling, the PPR's in terms of both the LTIA and the STIA was subsequently amended to be more consumer-friendly.

499. However, the PPR's in terms of both the LTIA and the STIA was subsequently amended to be more consumer-friendly. The new Rule 7.4 stipulates as follows:

> An insurance party involved shall ensure that where any decision has been made as to the rejection of any claim under a policy, or as regards the quantum of a claim which is in dispute, the policyholder concerned is in writing informed of the reasons for the decision and that the policyholder may within a period of not less than 90 days after the date of the relevant decision make representations to the relevant insurer in respect of such decision.

500. The parties may include a provision in their agreement on governing law that would apply to their contractual relationship. In the absence of such a clause the governing law can also be determined by the general rules that apply to a conflict of laws in respect of contracts. The only statutory provision that exists on the jurisdiction on matters pertaining to insurance can be found in section 59(1) of the STIA. It provides that any claim against a Lloyd's underwriter under a South African short-term insurance policy will be cognizable by any competent South African court.

Part III. Property and Liability Insurance

501. The primary distinction of South African insurance business is between indemnity insurance (short-term insurance) and capital insurance (long-term insurance). Where indemnity insurance aims to compensate for patrimonial loss in the wide sense of the word, capital insurance is aimed at non-indemnity insurance. The use of the terms 'short-term insurance' for indemnity insurance and 'long-term insurance' for what is essentially non-indemnity insurance has been described as 'anachronistic', 'curious' and 'uniquely South African'.[387]

502. Even so, these terms serve to classify the products that are categorized under the LTIA and the STIA respectively. Following this classification, long-term insurance refers to assistance policies, disability policies, fund policies, life policies, sinking fund policies and policies that combine these policies.[388] By contrast, short-term insurance comprises engineering policies, guarantee policies, liability policies, miscellaneous policies, motor policies, accident and health policies, health policies, property policies, transportation policies or contracts that constitute a combination of any of these policies. Each of these policies has a statutory definition. It is evident from the uniquely SA classification that there might be conceptual differences between the headings as prescribed for this encyclopaedia and the types of insurance as mentioned I the LTIA and the STIA.

503. Other national chapters of this encyclopaedia will typically divide property and liability insurance in specified classes such as fire insurance; loss of benefit insurance; transport insurance; liability insurance (professional liability, product liability; environmental insurance private life liability insurance, etc.); motor vehicle insurance (*pro memoria*); legal aid insurance; aviation and space insurance; theft and embezzlement insurance; and agricultural insurance, hail insurance, livestock insurance and catastrophe insurance.

387. Reinecke et al., 8–9.
388. Reinecke et al., 11.

504. However, because of our strict statutory definitions discussed above, there is no narrow classification in South African insurance law, and it is safe to say that all property and liability insurance are generally classified as short-term insurance and subject to the STIA, hence the following discussion.

505. The STIA identifies a number of policies which are then managed under the general Act. These will be briefly discussed as they are dealt with in the STIA.

Chapter 2. Accident, Disability and Health Insurance

506. Accident and health policy means:

[A] contract in terms of which a person, in return for a premium, undertakes to provide policy benefits if a—

(a) disability event;

(b) health event; or

(c) death event,

contemplated in the contract as a risk, occurs.[389]

507. Both the STIA and the LTIA contain provisions relating to health and disability events and it is often challenging to determine which of the two statutes regulate a particular policy. One conceptual difference between the two pieces of legislation is that the LTIA deals solely with health policies while the STIA makes provision for accident *and* health policies. A further difference is that the STIA includes death events as a risk in accident and health policies but the LTIA does not. In an attempt to bring an end to the confusion between accident and health policies under the STIA, health policies under the LTIA and medical schemes under the MSA,[390] the Demarcation Regulations propose set categories of insurance that may be sold by long-term insurers and short-term insurers respectively. Although the new categories do not necessarily make a distinction between long-term insurance and short-term insurance, at least they contain a detailed description of the type of products that may be sold in terms of both the LTIA and the STIA and distinguish these from the business of a medical scheme.[391]

389. Section 1(1) of the STIA, *sv* 'accident and health policy'.
390. Act 131 of 1998.
391. Millard, 40–41.

Chapter 3. Engineering Insurance

508. An *engineering policy* refers to a contract in terms of which a person, in return for a premium, undertakes to provide policy benefits upon the occurrence of specific risks. These risks include, *inter alia*, the possession, use or ownership of machinery or equipment, other than a motor vehicle, in the carrying on of a business; the erection of buildings or other structures or the undertaking of other works; or the installation of machinery or equipment. The statutory definition also includes a reinsurance policy in respect of such a policy.[392]

392. Section 1(1) of the STIA, *sv* 'engineering policy'.

Chapter 4. Guarantee Insurance

509. A *guarantee policy* refers to 'a contract in terms of which a person, other than a bank, in return for a premium, undertakes to provide policy benefits if a person should fail to discharge an obligation'.[393] South Africa does not recognize caution insurance as a separate class of insurance cover.

393. Section 1(1) of the STIA, *sv* 'guarantee policy'.

Chapter 5. Liability Insurance

510. A *liability policy* denotes a contract in terms of which a person, in return for a premium, undertakes to provide policy benefits if an event relating to the incurring of a liability occurs. It also includes a reinsurance policy in respect of such a policy.[394]

394. Section 1(1) of the STIA, *sv* 'liability policy'.

Chapter 6. Risk Insurance: Legal Aid Insurance, Aviation and Space Insurance, Theft and Embezzlement Insurance, Agricultural Insurance, Hail Insurance and Livestock Insurance

511. A *miscellaneous policy* simply means a contract anticipating a risk relating to any matter not otherwise defined in section 1 of the STIA. Furthermore, it also includes a reinsurance policy in respect of a miscellaneous policy.[395] Motor vehicle insurance is perhaps the most common form of short-term insurance. This group also includes all property or asset insurance in the sense that it includes cover for risks caused by fire, theft, embezzlement; agricultural, hail and livestock insurance, transport insurance, loss of benefit insurance.

395. Section 1(1) of the STIA, *sv* 'miscellaneous policy'.

Chapter 7. Motor Vehicle Insurance

512. A *motor policy* simply means a contract in terms of which a person, in return for a premium, undertakes to provide policy benefits in the event of a risk relating to the possession, use or ownership of a motor vehicle, occurs. It also includes a reinsurance policy in respect of a motor policy.[396]

396. Section 1(1) of the STIA, *sv* 'motor policy'.

Chapter 8. Transportation Insurance

513. A *transportation policy* denotes a contract in terms of which a person, in return for a premium, undertakes to provide policy benefits upon the occurrence of a risk pertaining to the 'possession, use or ownership of a vessel, aircraft or other craft or for the conveyance of persons or goods by air, space, land or water'. In addition, the risk may pertain to the storage, treatment or handling of goods conveyed or to be conveyed in this manner. It also includes a reinsurance policy in respect of such a policy.[397] Aviation and marine insurance are two forms of transport insurance that deal with transportation by aircraft and ships respectively and contract of transportation insurance often forms part of a contract of carriage; the insurance contract may also contain terms that a particular to this type of insurance.[398]

397. Section 1(1) of the STIA, *sv* 'transportation policy'.
398. Millard, 49.

Chapter 9. Private Insurance

514. All the policies mentioned above can all be classified as private insurance. This means that these policies are concerned with the interests of an individual or a legal person. An individual can insure his life or his property or a business may procure insurance against liabilities. For private insurance, the individual takes the initiative to obtain the insurance and the obligation to pay the insurance is also the individual's responsibility.[399]

399. Reinecke et al., 11.

Chapter 10. Catastrophe Insurance

§1. General

515. Unlike the insurance industries in the EU and in other jurisdictions, South Arica does not distinguish small, medium, large and mass risks. The size and extent of the risk does not automatically affect or inform the classification of the insurance. The discussion on the nature of the risk and type of insurance as set out above alone will determine the classification of insurance.

§2. Nuclear Risks

516. Nuclear risks such as damage to the environment, damage to property or personal injury are not provided for specifically by insurance legislation. Depending on the actual risk, either the LTIA or the STIA applies. As was indicated in paragraph X above, mandatory insurance is required for operations and technologies that affect the environment. More specifically, liability for nuclear damage has been regulated by legislation since 1963 and is currently regulated by the National Nuclear Regulator Act.[400] Section 30(1) of this Act stipulates that the holder of a nuclear installation licence is strictly liable for all nuclear damage caused during his period of responsibility.[401] There is in principle nothing that prevents such licence holder to insure these risks. However, the question is whether there will be an insurance company who is willing to take on this risk. There is no such a thing as mandatory insurance or a national fund for nuclear disasters and depending on the kind of policy, the LTIA or the STIA will apply.

§3. Natural Catastrophes

517. South African insurance law does not provide separately for natural disasters or catastrophes. Rather, depending on the kind of risk, one of the other known categories of insurance (such as property insurance) may provide for this kind of peril. There is however social relief which is defined in the Fund Raising Act 107 of 1978 as the 'alleviation of need of persons by means of the temporary rendering of material assistance to them'.[402] Although this act provides for communities in crisis and principally include a variety of disasters such as the closing down of a mine and huge job losses, natural disasters such as flooding will also be included under this act. The relief is administered by a disaster relief fund that is available to all members of the affected community, regardless of their financial position. This is therefore a form of social

400. Act 47 of 1999.
401. J. Neethling & J.M. Potgieter, *Neethling Potgieter Visser Law of Delict* 400–401 (2014).
402. M.P. Olivier, N. Smit & E.R. Kalula, *Social Security: A Legal Analysis* 205–206 (2003).

security and as such, does not form part of private insurance. Individuals who require more than emergency relief against natural disasters must provide for this through private insurance.

Chapter 11. Credit and Caution Insurance

518. South African law does not recognize the concept of 'caution insurance'. Credit insurance on the other hand is prevalent and consumer credit insurance is the insurance that a consumer takes out as cover for the repayment of a debt that the consumer has incurred to a credit provider. It happens often that consumer credit insurance is sold as part of a package, in other words consumer goods such as cars are sold on credit and the credit provider initiates the further contract of insurance in order to safeguard against the eventuality of non-payment. Credit insurance as a wider category deals with risks such as the consumer (policyholder) becoming disabled or suffering critical illness or becomes unemployed before the debt is finally repaid. Usually, the sum insured reduces proportionally as the debt is repaid. These consumer credit products are usually short-term insurance products because an asset is insured against a risk. Credit life insurance is in fact a subcategory of credit insurance and the objective is to cover the outstanding balance of a policyholder's indebtedness in respect of personal loans, mortgage protection cover, overdraft facilities, student loans, credit card facilities and asset financing. This is a typical risk-only product and even though the insured event is actually the debtor's death, policies may be issued for disability, critical illness and retrenchment as well. The difference between credit life insurance and ordinary insurance is that the former does not provide for the payment of a lump sum to the insured if the insured event occurs but for the payment of the outstanding debt to the creditor.[403]

519. The LTIA and the STIA do not define 'credit life insurance'. This concept is defined in the NCA.[404] Accordingly, credit life insurance refers to cover payable by an insurance company if the following risks occur, namely the consumer's death, disability, terminal illness, unemployment or other insurable risk 'that is likely to impair the consumer's ability to earn an income or meet the obligations under a credit agreement'.[405] In addition, the NCA stipulates that credit life insurance may not exceed 'the total of the consumer's outstanding obligations to the credit provider in terms of their agreement'.

403. Reinecke et al., 569.
404. Act 34 of 2005.
405. Reinecke et al., 570.

Chapter 12. Technical Insurance

520. South African insurance law does not define the concept 'technical insurance'. Rather, the STIA provides for an engineering policy. An engineering policy refers to a contract in terms of which a person, in return for a premium, undertakes to provide policy benefits upon the occurrence of specific risks. These risks include, *inter alia*, the possession, use or ownership of machinery or equipment, other than a motor vehicle, in the carrying on of a business, the erection of buildings or other structures or the undertaking of other works, or the installation of machinery or equipment. The statutory definition also includes a reinsurance policy in respect of such a policy.[406] Other than it being so-called niche insurance that is marketed in sold by specialist insurers, there is nothing to suggest that engineering policies are subject to a different kind of dispensation than any other short-term insurance policy.

406. Reinecke et al., 533.

Chapter 13. Miscellaneous Insurance

521. A *miscellaneous policy* simply means a contract anticipating a risk relating to any matter not otherwise defined in section 1 of the STIA. Furthermore, it also includes a reinsurance policy in respect of a miscellaneous policy.[407]

407. Section 1(1) of the STIA, *sv* 'miscellaneous policy'.

Part IV. Motor Vehicle Insurance

522. A *motor policy* simply means a contract in terms of which a person, in return for a premium, undertakes to provide policy benefits in the event of a risk relating to the possession, use or ownership of a motor vehicle, occurs. It also includes a reinsurance policy in respect of a motor policy.[408] This is a very common type of insurance and it is often used in conjunction with a property policy. A policyholder may insure a vehicle separately or together with his household content. What is important to understand is that motor policies such as these do not cover an owner for personal injuries or death caused to another person. In South Africa, a system of compulsory third-party insurance exists in terms of a completely different framework. A form of fund compensation, in the form of the Road Accident Fund (RAF), is extensively regulated by statutory laws and regulations, that for example, introduce capping and thresholds for personal injury claims. The object of the statutory framework is to pay compensation in accordance with applicable legislations for personal loss or damage wrongfully caused by the driving of a motor vehicle. The government-managed, compulsory system is partly based on insurance principles (notably for the financial management of the system) yet also on social security principles, as it indemnifies the driver or owner of a motor vehicle against liability incurred as the result of the personal injuries or death wrongfully caused to another person in road accidents. This particular system is at the verge of a huge transformation. The proposed Road Accident Benefit System (RABS) will introduce a social security fund that functions on a no-fault basis. Although there will still be caps on benefits payable and thresholds, it will not be possible for a victim to claim the balance of his loss over and above what is payable by RABS from the wrongdoer. A victim who wants to ensure that he received full compensation must therefore privately provide and pay for health and life insurance with a private insurance company.

408. Section 1(1) of the STIA, *sv* 'motor policy'.

Part V. Insurance of the Person

Chapter 1. Workmen's Compensation and Occupational Disease

523. The most important statute that deals with workmen's compensation is the COIDA.[409] The workmen's compensation system is most probably the longest running system in South Africa that deals with the risks of occupational injuries and diseases in the workplace. Before the introduction of this system, the obligations of employers towards their employees were based on common law. Although employees have always had the right to a safe working environment,[410] the enforcement of this right in terms of Roman-Dutch principles or tort law (law of delict) have always been problematic, as employees who sustained injuries at work or who had contracted a disease had to claim damages based on tort law from their employers. This required employees to prove fault amongst other things.[411]

524. In attempting to overcome the glaring shortcomings of the tort-based system, a no-fault system was devised. The basic idea of this system is that, where a person carries on economic activities by using machinery and the labour of other persons, and in the process creates an organization that may harm workers, such employer should be responsible for providing compensation without any questions being asked about fault, since the employer gains the economic benefits. Another aspect of this approach is the fact that the employer is solely responsible for financing the scheme. The system is based on social insurance and private insurance plays no role whatsoever in this context. Therefore, where a person who falls within the definition of 'employee' in terms of COIDA becomes disabled because of an accident that occurs in the scope of his employment, or such an employee contracts a disease in the scope of his employment, COIDA provides for the payment of benefits to these individuals.[412]

525. Where an employee is injured in an accident that arises out of, and in the course of his employment, or an employee contracts a disease in a similar way, section 35 of COIDA provides that:

409. Act 130 of 1993.
410. Section 8(1) of the Occupational Health and Safety Act 85 of 1993 and ss 2(1) and 5(1) of the Mine Health and Safety Act 29 of 1996.
411. N. Smit, *Employment Injuries and Diseases and Disability in the Workplace*, in *Social Security Law: A Legal Analysis* 460 (M.P. Olivier et al., eds).
412. Smit, 474.

> [N]o action shall lie by an employee or any dependant of an employee for the recovery of damages in respect of any occupational injury or disease resulting in the disablement or death of such an employee against such employee's employer, and no liability for compensation on the part of such employer shall arise save under the provisions of this Act in respect of such disablement or death.[413]

526. Claims against the Compensation Commissioner in terms of COIDA are not based on fault. The aim of this particular system is to provide broad coverage for occupational injuries and diseases, substantial protection against loss of income and sufficient medical care and rehabilitation where an employee was injured or the employee had contracted a disease. Only employees that fall within the definition of the Act are protected in terms of COIDA. In this context, the Act defines an employee as a person who has entered into or works under a contract of service or of apprenticeship or learnership with an employer, whether the contract is express or implied, oral or in writing, and whether the remuneration is calculated by time or by work done, or is in cash or in kind.[414] Members of the security forces, independent contractors and domestic employees in private households fall outside the ambit of COIDA Furthermore, unless the context indicates otherwise, 'accident' means an accident arising out of and in the course and scope of an employee's employment and resulting in the personal injury, illness or the death of an employee.[415]

527. In terms of this system benefits are calculated with reference to a person's earnings.[416] The Compensation Commissioner also pays all medical costs upon the occurrence of an accident or where the employee contracted a disease. Protection against loss of income in terms of COIDA is of particular significance for this discussion. Legislation provides for compensation in those instances where an employee suffers either a temporary total disability or a permanent total disability. As far as compensation for permanent disability is concerned, there is a distinction between disability that is less than 30% and disability of more than 30%.[417] In the first instance, a lump sum based on fifteen times the employee's monthly earnings up to a specified maximum is paid out to the employee.[418] Where the disability is 31% or more, a monthly pension is paid to the employee. The monthly pension is calculated in the same way as the lump sum.[419] In calculating benefits for loss of earning capacity, the Compensation Commissioner makes use of a so-called meat list. This guideline contains a list of injuries and the corresponding percentage disability that is attached to specific injuries.

528. The issue of the assessment of permanent disability seems to be as problematic under COIDA as it is under any other system that provides for the assessment of disability. In *McLean v. Sasol Mine (Pty) Ltd/McLean v. Sasol Pension Fund,*[420] the

413. *R v. Canqan* 1956 3 SA 355 (E) at 357–358; *Jooste v. Score Supermarket Trading (Pty) Ltd* 1998 9 BCLR 1106 (E); 1999 2 BCLR 139 (CC); 1999 2 SA 1 (CC); 1999 20 ILJ 525 (CC).
414. Smit, 470.
415. Smit, 474.
416. Smit, 477.
417. Smit, 480–481.
418. *Ibid.* Where disablement is less than 30%, the lump sum is calculated proportionally.
419. Smit, 481.
420. 2003 24 ILJ 2083 (W).

court had to adjudicate a question of permanent disability. *In casu*, an employee was injured at work to the extent that he could no longer perform any work underground in the mine. However, he was able to do roughly 80% of clerical the work assigned to him above ground.[421] The plaintiff based his case on the fact that he was permanently unable to pursue his occupation or a similar occupation for which he was qualified by his training and experience.[422] This claim was repudiated on the ground that the plaintiff was not 'permanently' disabled in terms of the rules of the relevant pension fund. The same would have been true in terms of the COIDA provisions. It was common cause between the parties that as a result of a knee injury sustained at work the plaintiff was unable to perform his duties as an underground mining electrician. After undergoing a knee replacement procedure, he was employed in the employer's planning department in a temporary position.[423] During 1999 the plaintiff accepted a medical severance package in terms of an agreement between the company and the union.[424]

529. In adjudicating the plaintiff's case, the court held that the plaintiff was entitled to disability benefits in terms of the rules of the pension fund as he could be considered permanently disabled in terms of the rules of the fund. The court observed that a court should not easily interfere with the discretion exercised by the employer and the administrators of the fund. The court should exercise its discretion reasonably and in good faith. The court ruled that, *in casu,* the employer had not exercised his discretion in a fair, reasonable and honest manner.

530. Regarding the test for disability, the court ruled as follows:

> Where a rule or a practice makes generalisations about people solely on the basis of disability without regard to the particular circumstance of the specific class of individuals affected, then this is, in my view, entirely unfair to individuals. Moreover, in order for there to be true individualisation, a close assessment should be made of the individual in question since even persons with the same disability vary markedly in how they personally function and cope with their affliction, or vary in the degree of impairment because of different stages of their infirmity. I concede that this method may make matters somewhat burdensome for the employers. However, this is a small price to pay for the higher value society has placed on the rights of disabled persons. In any event, the employer is not without a proper remedy. The Code of Good Practice: Dismissals in schedule 8 to the Labour Relations Act 66 of 1996, specifically sets out grounds of ill-health or injury that may either be temporary or permanent, as the circumstances under which employees may be dismissed. In the present matter, there was clearly no investigation that informed a decision of placing the plaintiff in the position of a shift coordinator. Thereafter, in his capacity as a shift coordinator, the communication channels simply closed. There was no evaluation of his performance, nor any constructive training afforded. This led to the individual's frustration. The purpose of counselling is to motivate the employee to improve and to alert the employer to remedial steps that may be necessary. Here the employee

421. At 2087A.
422. At 2087H-I.
423. At 2089A.
424. At 2089B-C.

> participates and suggests ways in which the problem can be resolved. The extent of assistance in the form of additional tools or support or guidance that might be necessary should emerge from counselling. The appropriate assistance must be reasonable. This measure could have overcome the shortcomings plaintiff had developed as a result of his working environment. In my mind, upon a proper conspectus of the evidence, I am satisfied that the plaintiff suffered permanent functional limitations.

531. *McLean*'s case is noteworthy because it seems that, even though the employer attempted to retain the services of the employee in some form or another, his attempts were insufficient. In summary, although the protection for total disablement afforded in terms of COIDA plays a very important role, it is not above criticism. First, only those in formal employment who qualify as employees enjoy coverage. Second, little is done about the prevention of accidents and rehabilitation and reintegration and, finally, even those employees who do receive lump sums or monthly pensions merely receive defined benefits and will most likely not be in a position to maintain the same standard of living that they enjoyed prior to the employment accident. Those who do not fall within the definition of 'employee' must make use of private insurance to safeguard against loss of income because of the inability to work.

Chapter 2. Bodily Injuries

532. In South Africa insurance for bodily injuries is classified as long-term insurance and will be discussed in Chapter 4 under life insurance.

Chapter 3. Private Health Insurance

533. The MSA regulates medical schemes. Section 1 of the MSA defines a medical scheme as any such scheme registered under section 24(1) of the MSA, and the business of a medical scheme is defined as follows:

> [T]he business of undertaking liability in return for a premium or contribution—
>
> (a) to make provision for the obtaining of any relevant health service;
>
> (b) to grant assistance in defraying expenditure incurred in connection with the rendering of any relevant health service; and
>
> (c) where applicable, to render a relevant health service, either by the medical scheme itself, or by any supplier or group of suppliers of a relevant health service or by any person, in association with or in terms of an agreement with a medical scheme.

534. There is a distinct difference between medical schemes and products that insure certain risks pertaining to ill-health and disability. Despite this difference there is sometimes an overlap between the business of a medical scheme and some related insurance products. The business of a pension fund should be distinguished from insurance business.

Chapter 4. Life Insurance

535. The LTIA describes Long-term insurance business as the business of providing policy benefits under long-term policies. A long-term policy includes assistance policies, disability policies, fund policies, health policies, life policies and sinking fund policies. These different kinds of policies may also be combined with each other. The LTIA describes a life policy as a contract in terms of which a person, in return for a premium, undertakes to provide policy benefits upon and exclusively as a result of a life event or to pay an annuity for a period. A life event is in turn the event of a life of a person or an unborn having begun, continuing, having continued for a period or having ended. The different kinds of policies will first be discussed.

536. An *assistance policy* is a small life policy that may not exceed ZAR 18,000. This means that the value of the policy benefits or the amount of the premium for which an annuity should be provided, may not exceed ZAR 18,000.[425]

537. A *health policy* is a contract in terms of which the insurer undertakes, in return for a premium, to provide policy benefits on the occurrence of a health event. A health event is an event relating to the health or the mind or body of a person or unborn. Long-term health policies exclude benefits such as the payment of medical expenses, as these are managed in terms of the MSA.[426] The STIA also contains a definition of *health policy* and there is some overlap between the different kinds of benefits payable in terms of health policies. The discussion in paragraph 41 above explains this in more detail.

538. *Disability policies,* like health policies, may also be offered in terms of the LTIA or the STIA. The risk insured against is the impairment of the 'functional ability of a person or an unborn'. The distinguishing factor is possibly that long-term insurers offer lump sum payments and not indemnity benefits such as the defraying of the actual costs incurred by the policyholder.[427]

539. *Fund and fund member policies* are also defined by the LTIA. Here, the policyholder is a fund and not a private individual. More specifically, section 1(1) of the LTIA defines a fund policy as follows:

> [A] contract in terms of which a person, in return for a premium, undertakes to provide policy benefits for the purpose of funding in whole or in part the liability of a fund to provide benefits to its members in terms of its rules, other than such a contract relating exclusively to a particular member of the fund or to the surviving spouse, children, dependants or nominees of a particular member of the fund; and includes a re-insurance policy in respect of such a contract.

540. Accordingly, a fund policy provides benefits to a preservation, provident or pension fund and fund policies are taken out on a group basis, whereas a fund member policy is described by Nienaber and Reinecke as:

425. Nienaber & Reinecke, 69.
426. Nienaber & Reinecke, 70.
427. Nienaber & Reinecke, 71.

> [A]n individual policy entered into by the fund, with the fund as the policyholder and the member as the life insured, for the exclusive purpose 'of funding that fund's liability to the member' in terms of its rules. A fund member policy is designed to assist persons who do not qualify or wish to be members of a pension fund, such as farmers or self-employed persons running a business or practising a profession and who wish, for example, to take advantage of the tax benefits attached to retirement annuities.[428]

541. A *sinking fund policy* is defined in the LTIA as a means 'a contract, other than a life policy, in terms of which a person, in return for a premium, undertakes to provide one or more sums of money, on a fixed or determinable future date, as policy benefits; and includes a reinsurance policy in respect of such a contract'. As there is in fact no uncertain future event, it is suggested that these policies would be regulated under the law relating to investments rather than insurance.[429]

§1. Individual Life Insurance

542. With the above in mind, long-term insurance can primarily be classified into three products, namely whole life insurance, endowment insurance and term insurance. With whole life insurance, the insurance company pays the policy benefit is paid when the policyholder dies. It is usual for such a policy to build up a surrender value and if the policy is a so-called with-profit policy, bonuses are declared on the sum insured.[430] Endowment insurance is insurance where the policy has a term and a maturity date, which means that the policyholder is entitled to a lump sum payment regardless of whether he dies before or is alive at the maturity date.[431] This should be distinguished from pure endowment insurance, which provides no life cover and is actually a savings product. Term insurance is paid if the life insured dies within the term of the policy and there is no maturity value. This is the cheapest form of life cover available because the insurance company has no obligation if the insured is still alive at the end of the term.[432]

§2. Group Life Insurance

543. Group life insurance is made available to benefit a group of persons with so-called mutual or interrelated interests, such as the employees of a common employer. A 'group scheme' is defined in Regulation 3.1 of the regulations to the LTIA to mean a scheme or arrangement which provides for the entering into of one or more policies, other than an individual policy, in terms of which two or more persons without an insurable interest in each other, for the purposes of the scheme, are the lives insured.

428. Life Insurance, 71.
429. Millard, *Modern Insurance Law* 40.
430. Nienaber & Reinecke, 74.
431. Nienaber & Reinecke, 75.
432. Nienaber & Reinecke, 77.

A group life insurance scheme is brought about by an agreement between an insurer and a common denominator, such as the employer, as the policyholder. That common denominator (e.g., employer) insures all the members who belong to the group. These members are subject to the same basic contractual relationship and provisions. In practice, the policyholder collects the premiums and pays them over to the insurer. It is customary for group life schemes to be compulsory because it usually exists because of an employment relationship. Because it is compulsory, the insurer can ensure that the group life policy is actuarially priced on a group basis. Accordingly, there is very little individual underwriting of the mortality risk with the result that all members are accepted without proof of good health. This makes it an attractive option for individuals who would have faced limitations and exclusions or expensive premiums in individual life insurance. The rules of the group scheme determines the cover.[433]

433. Nienaber & Reinecke, 79–80.

Chapter 5. Pension Funds

544. Pension funds in South Africa are not administered by insurance companies, however, the retirement industry is structured in such a way that there are pension funds as defined by the PFA and then, there are annuities that are primarily marketed and sold by life insurance companies. Conceptually, there is a big difference between a pension in this sense, and an annuity. It is important to understand that pensions are not affected by the LTIA. Rather, a dedicated statute, the PFA 24 of 1956, deals with pensions. Accordingly, this statute does not define 'pension' but rather defines *pension fund organization as*:

> any association of persons established with the object of providing annuities or lump sum payments for members or former members of such association upon their reaching their retirement dates, or for the dependants of such members or former members upon the death of such members or former members; or
>
> any business carried on under a scheme or arrangement established with the object of providing annuities or lump sum payments for persons who belong or belonged to the class of persons for whose benefit that scheme or arrangement has been established when they reach their retirement dates or for dependants of such persons upon the death of those persons,
>
> any association of persons or business carried on under a scheme or arrangement established with the object of receiving, administering, investing and paying benefits that became payable in terms of the employment of a member on behalf of beneficiaries, payable on the death of more than one member of one or more pension funds,
>
> and includes any such association or business which in addition to carrying on business in connection with any of the objects specified in paragraph (a), (b) or (c) also carries on business in connection with any of the objects for which a friendly society may be established, as specified in section 2 of the FSA, or which is or may become liable for the payment of any benefits provided for in its rules, whether or not it continues to admit or to collect contributions from or on behalf of, members.

545. Conceptual difficulties may arise when the term 'pension' is used interchangeably with 'annuity'. The latter concept is explained in the insurance context as having a variety of manifestations. According to its primary meaning, it refers to a payment that is due in each year, which means that there should be a contract that provides for fixed and consistent periodic returns on a non-refundable capital amount that was invested.[434] It is in fact the Income Tax Act 58 of 1962 that defines a 'retirement annuity fund' as a retirement fund to which a member can voluntarily belong because he wants to invest money with the fund to save for his retirement. It is up to the fund to make investments in its own name or to invest in long-term retirement annuity policies with an insurer, and these are in essence endowment policies.[435]

546. In broad terms, one can say that retirement annuities and pension funds both aim at providing the beneficiary with money upon retirement. However, it is safe to say that pension funds are without exception established because of an employment relationship and the employer has no choice but to belong to the pension fund, whereas annuities are private savings that are taken out by individuals who either do not belong to a pension fund or who want to supplement their compulsory pension fund with private savings.

434. Reinecke et al., 555.
435. Nienaber & Reinecke, 78.

Part VI. Private Insurance: Social Security

547. Social insurance on the other hand refers to instances where there is a statutory obligation to belong to a fund and the aim of this fund is to address societal risks such as occupational injuries and unemployment. South Africa's social insurance legislation is not particularly integrated and well-developed, with the result that individuals mostly have to rely on private insurance to protect themselves against risks such as disability and loss of property. Social insurance legislation include the COIDA,[436] the Unemployment Insurance Act,[437] the Unemployment Insurance Contributions Act[438] and the RAF Act.[439] The respective risks covered are occupational injuries and diseases, unemployment and road accidents.[440]

436. Act 130 of 1993.
437. Act 63 of 2001.
438. Act 4 of 2002.
439. Act 56 of 1996.
440. Millard, 26.

Part VII. Insurance Intermediaries

Chapter 1. Law of Establishment and Supervision

548. An insurance contract exists primarily between an insurer and an insured. Because insurers are companies, they act through intermediaries, representatives and advisors. Therefore, before an insurance contract comes into existence, intermediaries, representatives and advisors provide services to insurers and potential policyholders respectively. These services are rendered in accordance with separate contracts which may be regarded as contracts entered into with a view to creating an insurance contract. These preliminary agreements are regulated by Roman-Dutch law and statutory law and it is important to consider which principles apply to these contracts in order to determine the rights and duties of the respective parties. This section discusses the common law position and subsequently the positions before and after the introduction of the FAIS Act.

549. Someone who performs a juristic act on behalf of another is generally referred to as a representative or an agent. Any person who renders a financial service to a client for or on behalf of an FSP, in terms of conditions of employment or any other mandatory agreement, excluding a person rendering a clerical, technical, administrative, legal, accounting or other service in a subsidiary or subordinate capacity is a 'representative'.

550. The law requires that a FSP must also maintain a representative register of all representatives as well as key individuals of such representatives. As is the case pertaining to the key individual register referred to above, the register of representatives must be submitted to the Registrar for reference or inspection purposes. In accordance with section 13(4) of the FAIS Act, such a register must contain every representative's name and business address and must state whether the representative acts for the provider as employee or as mandatory; and must specify the categories in which such representatives are competent to render financial services.

551. In the context of insurance and for purposes of this discussion, the term 'agent' is used loosely to refer to the representative, employee or broker who acts on behalf of either an insurer or an insured. This agent can execute the mandate of the principal, represent the principal in entering into a legal relationship and negotiate between different principals.

552. In insurance an insurance broker is an intermediary who acts independently of any insurer in mediating insurance contracts on behalf of a prospective insured. In any event, the conduct of all intermediaries is strictly regulated by the FAIS Act.

553. In accordance with the FAIS Act, 'intermediary service' means any act other than the furnishing of advice that is performed by a person for or on behalf of a client or product supplier that results in the client entering into or offering to enter into any transaction in respect of a financial product with a product supplier. Even if the client may only enter into any such transaction in future, it means that an intermediary service has already been rendered.[441] It can also mean any act other than the furnishing of advice that is performed by a person for or on behalf of a client or product supplier with a view to one or more of the following, namely buying, selling or otherwise dealing in, managing, administering, keeping in safe custody, maintaining or servicing a financial product purchased by a client from a product supplier or in which the client has invested; collecting or accounting for premiums or other moneys payable by the client to a product supplier in respect of a financial product; or receiving, submitting or processing the claims of a client against a product supplier.

554. In terms of section 1(3)(b) of the FAIS Act intermediary services specifically exclude the collecting or accounting for premiums or other moneys payable by the client to a product supplier where the bank merely acts as a conduit between a client and another product supplier. an intermediary service rendered by a product supplier who is authorized under a particular law to conduct business as a financial institution and where the rendering of such service is regulated by or under such law, is also excluded. Finally, the Registrar is empowered to exempt any other service from the provisions of the FAIS Act.

555. In the FAIS Act, 'advice' is described very broadly as any recommendation, guidance or proposal of a financial nature furnished by any means or medium, to any client or group of clients. The advice must pertain to the purchase of any financial product or an investment in any financial product. Advice also includes any recommendation, guidance or proposal of a financial nature 'on the conclusion of any other transaction, including a loan or cession, aimed at the incurring of any liability or the acquisition of any right or benefit in respect of any financial product' or 'on the variation of any term or condition applying to a financial product, on the replacement of any such product, or on the termination of any purchase of or investment in any such product'. These actions are regarded as advice for the purposes of the Act, regardless of whether the advice is furnished in the course of or incidental to financial planning or whether it results in any actual purchase investment, transaction, variation, replacement or termination. An 'adviser' is a person who gives the above-mentioned type of advice.[442]

441. Section 1 of the FAIS Act, *sv* 'intermediary service'.
442. Section 1(1) of the FAIS Act, *sv* 'advice'.

Chapter 2. Insurance Intermediaries and the Insurance Contract

556. Before the introduction of the FAIS Act, prospective policyholders could procure insurance in one of two ways, namely by making use of the services of a broker or by contacting an insurance company directly. Where the services of a broker was enlisted, the prospective insured could ask the broker to provide him with several quotations and to explain the different options to him. The prospective insured could either enter into a contract with an insurance company of his choice or where so agreed, could instruct the broker to enter into a contract on his behalf. Where the client contacted an insurance company directly, an employee of the insurer would provide the prospective insured with a quote. Upon acceptance of this quote, a contract of insurance came into existence. Agency governed the relationship between insurers, their representatives or employees, brokers and clients. Agency is when an agent performs a juristic act on behalf of another (the principal). However, in the context of insurance the term 'agent' is used loosely to refer to the representative, employee or broker who acts on behalf of either an insurer or an insured. It was often difficult to determine the exact nature of the relationship between the insurer, the insured (or potential insured) and the representative, employee or broker and to outline the rights and duties of the respective parties.[443]

557. The agent could perform a variety of functions, namely to execute a mandate of the principal, to represent the principal in entering into a legal relationship and to negotiate between different principals.[444]

558. As far as the execution of the principal's mandate is concerned, it could entail a go-between completing an application form on behalf of a prospective policyholder, to collect and receive information for an insurer on a prospective insured or to provide information on behalf of a principal. The principal in the last instance could be the prospective insured who needed information on the product or in the case of the renewal or variation of a policy, an insured who needed more information. In all these examples it is more correct to refer to the go-between as a mandatary and the principal who gave the instruction as the mandator. In addition, this is a typical contract of mandate which entails one person requesting another to perform a task which is not a juristic act. So even if a mandatary who performed one of these acts called himself an agent he was in actual fact a mandatary and as such had to carry out the mandate, not exceed the terms of the mandate, perform the mandate personally, act with care and skill, act with good faith and account.[445]

559. Representing the principal in entering into a legal relationship is however different from executing a mandate as it takes matters a step further. Where a representative, employee or broker could also accept an application on behalf of an insurer or complete and sign an application for insurance on behalf of a prospective

443. Millard & Hattingh, 17, 76; Reinecke et al., 507–509; P. Havenga, *The Law of Insurance Intermediaries* 1 (Juta 2001).
444. Reinecke & Nienaber, 201–202.
445. Reinecke & Nienaber, 201; Havenga 3–4; Millard & Hattingh, 76.

insured the picture changes and this form of representation is in actual fact a contract of agency. In order for a contract of agency to be valid, the following requirements have to be met, namely: The parties must have contractual capacity; the parties must have reached consensus on what needs to be done; the contract must not be illegal; performance must be physically possible; formalities must be complied with; and the agent must have the authority to act on behalf of the principal.

560. Again, regardless of what the representative, employee or broker called himself, if the requirements for a contract of agency was met, that person acted as an agent. Merely negotiating a contract on behalf of different principals on the other hand would be a contract of mandate and not one of agency.[446]

561. The obligations placed on agents and mandataries by common law are probably adequate in most instances where third parties act on behalf of principals. There are however complexities associated with financial products (of which insurance products form part) which prompted the legislator to draft the FAIS Act. These problems include *inter alia* the incorporeal nature of a financial product, the fact that standard-form contracts are often used without considering the individual relationship between the insurer and the policyholder, asymmetry of information where the intermediary is the knowledgeable party and the client the lay person and unprofessionalism in the financial services industry. There was a need for a stricter regulatory regime for insurance intermediaries. The next paragraph discusses the legal position in light of the FAIS Act.[447]

562. The FAIS Act came into operation on 30 September 2004. The Act's preamble informs that the purpose of the act is '[t]o regulate the rendering of certain financial advisory and intermediary services to clients; to repeal or amend certain laws; and to provide for matters incidental thereto'. The FAIS Act was enacted after the LTIA and the STIA and these three statutes should be read together because insurance products are financial products and as such these products may only be marketed and sold in accordance with the requirements of the FAIS Act. This means that insurance companies must comply with all the requirements of the FAIS Act as well as with the requirements of the statute which regulate their products.

563. The relationship between the FAIS Act and those common law principles pertaining to agency and representation that were discussed in the previous paragraph is an important matter. In South African law, there is a presumption that legislation does not alter the existing law more than is necessary.[448] As a starting point, one must understand that neither the FAIS Act nor the STIA and LTIA contain references to or definitions of 'agency' or 'representation'. Furthermore, a closer look at the functions entrusted to intermediaries in accordance with the three acts reveal that 'intermediaries' are more the brokers of old who may also perform juristic acts on behalf of clients and 'representatives' are more easily equated to mandataries because they perform tasks which exclude legal acts. However, one should guard against such a rigid and absolute distinction. In each situation it remains a question of fact whether an intermediary

446. Nienaber & Reinecke, 201–202; S.R. Van Jaarsveld 159 (); Millard & Hattingh, 76.
447. Moolman et al., 5.
448. Botha, 44.

or representative performed a legal act or not. Depending on that, the consequences of the contract of mandate or agency will apply to that contract.[449]

564. In practice, advice and intermediary services are often combined. Following the advice, a client will exercise an option and procure insurance. It is also possible that a prospective insured may phone an insurance company and seek advice from a representative. The representative may make suggestions and that may result in the client entering into a contract with a different insurer. The *actual* task performed by the intermediary or representative (with or without advice) may either be a contract of mandate or one of agency. However, where any individual limits his services to a consumer to the mere furnishing of advice on a financial product independently of any other services, the legal nature of that contract is probably one of *locatio conductio operis*. This contract entails a principal agreeing with a contractor to perform a specific duty. This contract is distinguished form an employment contract. According to *Colonial Mutual Life Assurance Society v. MacDonald:*[450]

> The contract between master and servant is one of letting and hiring of services (locatio conductio operarum) whereas the contract between the principal and a contractor is the letting and hiring of some definite piece of work (locatio conductio operis).

565. The independent contractor is obliged to perform a specified work or produce a specified result. In addition, the contract has the following distinct features, namely that the independent contractor may usually perform through others; the independent contractor must perform work within a period prescribed by the contract; the independent contractor is not under the control of an employer but is rather subservient to the contract; the contract does not necessarily terminate on the death of the contractor; and the contract terminates on the completion of work or the production of a specified result.[451]

566. Therefore, where a client approaches an intermediary or advisor with the sole objective of obtaining detailed advice, that contract is probably one of *locatio conductio operis.* It is submitted that the FAIS Act never changed the legal nature of this contract. Rather, the Act introduced minimum standards or requirements that need to be adhered to when providing advice. In addition, this contract comes into existence the moment advice is being offered, thereby invoking all the duties placed upon the adviser by the FAIS Act.

567. The purpose of a preliminary contract as described above is to broker a contract between an insured and an insurer. Insurers invest a lot of time and energy in presale negotiations in order to do business. Insurers can therefore not be ignorant of the practices and methods of intermediaries, advisors or representatives. Even though illegal acts perpetrated by third parties often do not come to the attention of insurers and those who are guilty of misconduct should be dealt with primarily in accordance with the FAIS Act, insurers should take care to offer adequate training to their employees

449. Millard & Hattingh, 76.
450. 1931 AD 412 at 433.
451. *Smit v. Workmen's Compensation Commissioner* 1979 (1) SA 51 (A).

and to ensure that compliance with the FAIS Act is used as a marketing tool to demonstrate their commitment to consumer protection.

568. Ultimately, preliminary contracts cannot be seen as independent from insurance contracts. Where a representative provided advice, asked questions, provided a quotation and proceeded to sell a product to a consumer, such an insurer is responsible for the intermediary service and advice as well as the duties as per the insurance contract. Role players in the insurance industry must therefore all comply with the standards set out by the FAIS Act in as far as it applies to them. The FAIS Act provides for extensive statutory sanctions where an insurance intermediary as a Financial Services Provider contravenes the act and related legislative measures.

569. Although South Africa is a developing or emerging economy, many multinational insurers and reinsurers operate in South Africa. Reinsurance is taken out with international reinsurers. Reinsurance is not mandatory. The attitude of the insurer is usually to reinsure nationally or internationally, depending on cover available.[452]

452. P.M. Nienaber & M.F.B. Reinecke, *Life Insurance in South Africa: A Compendium*, Ch. 7, 25.

Part VIII. Reinsurance, Co-insurance and Pooling

570. A reinsurance contract is an insurance contract in terms of which an insurer transfers a risk or several risks it has taken over under an insurance contract or contracts either wholly or partially to another insurer or insurers. The reinsurer receives a premium in exchange for assuming the risk from the direct insurer. The purpose of a reinsurance contract is for an insurer to relieve itself of the risk, either wholly or partially, and that is why reinsurance in fact involves the further spreading of risk. Insurers manage their exposure to those risks they have undertaken by further insuring these risks. Overall, this is a tool used to secure their financial solvency or at least to increase their capacity to assume further risks. Reinsurance is also a mechanism that is used by an insurer to protect itself against the event or a large amount of claims that may become payable at the same time. Reinsurance takes place at the initiative of the insurer and this should be distinguished from the situation where an insured takes out two or more policies with two or more insurers.[453] Where a reinsurer in turn insures his risks with another reinsurer, it is referred to as a retrocession.

571. Co-insurance takes place when several insurers underwrite a single risk. Normally, unless a contrary intention is evident, each insurer is responsible for his proportionate share of the loss. Insurers may attach a particular proportion to each one's risk, which means that there are several obligations and a co-insurance clause usually regulates the relationship between the parties. A co-insurance clause further stipulates that all the insurers are bound by the decisions of the leading insurer relating to the insurance.[454]

572. Risk pooling, although an internationally recognized practice in terms of which insurers come together to form a pool to safeguard against unusual risks, is not common in South Africa. Unusual risks are manages by way of reinsurance.

453. Reinecke et al., *South African Insurance Law* 504.
454. Reinecke et al., *South African Insurance Law* 227.

Part IX. Taxation of Insurance

573. Individual income tax (otherwise known as personal income tax) rates in South Africa are prescribed annually and range from about 18% to 42%. A prescribed annual tax threshold (e.g., depending on the age of the tax payer) means that anyone earning less than this amount pays no income tax. Individuals earning less than the specified amount do not need to declare their income and do not need to submit an income tax return so long as their remuneration is from a single employer, their remuneration is for the full tax year and no allowance was paid, from which PAYE was not deducted in full with regards to travel allowance.

574. Income tax is levied on residents' worldwide income, with appropriate relief to avoid double taxation. Non-residents are taxed on their income from a South African source. Tax is levied on taxable income that, in essence, consists of gross income less exemptions and allowable deductions as per the Act.

575. From March 2015, an amendment to the Income Tax Act standardizes the tax treatment of insurance policies that offer protection against death and disability. Currently, premiums on policies that pay out a lump sum on disability are not tax-deductible, but lump sums paid are tax-free. However, premiums on income-protection policies are tax-deductible, but monthly income on payout is taxed. The amendment removes the current tax deduction for premiums on income-protection insurance, and makes monthly income received tax-free; meaning claimants can expect a larger payout. The risk is that the amendment may encourage a reduction in cover as current premiums provide a pre-tax income rather than a tax-free income. It could also discourage the uptake of income-protection cover as individuals may value reduced taxes today more than potential future tax-free proceeds, particularly as chances are they may never claim on the policy.[455]

576. The Unemployment Insurance Fund (UIF) provides short-term relief to workers when they become unemployed or are unable to work because of maternity or adoption leave, or illness. It also provides relief to the dependants of the deceased contributor in terms of the Unemployment Insurance Contributions Act 4 of 2002. The bulk of contributions to UIF is collected by the SARS and transferred to the fund, which is administered by the Unemployment Insurance commissioner.

577. A deduction of medical lump sum payments is also possible. A taxpayer will be allowed to deduct from income derived from carrying on a trade, a lump sum payment: (i) to any former employee of the taxpayer who has retired from the taxpayer's employ on grounds of old age, ill health or infirmity or to a dependant of that former employee; or (ii) under a policy of insurance taken out with an insurer solely for one or more former employees or dependants mentioned in (i) above, but only to the extent that the amount is paid for the purposes of making any contribution, in respect of any

455. Association for Savings and Investment South Africa (Asisa) (www.asisa.org.za).

former employee or dependant, to any medical scheme or fund contemplated in section 18(1)(a)(i) or (ii).

Part X. Risk Management and Prevention

578. Generally speaking, risk management can be defined as the process of identification, analysis and prioritization or risks which is followed by a process of implementing strategies to avoid, reduce or transfer the risk. It is the transfer of risk that is essentially, in this context, insurance. However, not all risks may be insured. Unless the risk relates to a recognized insurable interest, it is not possible to insure that particular risk. *See* the discussions in paragraphs 116, 212, 214, 273–275, 398, 429, 485, 543, 588 on insurable interest.

579. As far as risk management in an insurance company is concerned, government has recently published the Governance and Risk Management Framework for Insurers of 2014.[456] This document applies to long-term insurers and short-term insurers alike and section 2(1) of this board notice stipulates that an insurer must adopt, implement and document an effective governance framework that provides for the prudent management and oversight of its insurance business and adequately protects the interests of its policyholders. This governance framework must include a risk management system that adequately support the board of directors in meeting its responsibilities with respect to the furtherance of the safe and sound operation of the insurer and the protection of policyholders, address risks on an enterprise-wide and individual business unit basis and should be embedded within the organization, in particular in the key operations and structures of the insurer. These new, detailed stipulations on the requirements for the risk management system have been formulated to ensure that insurance companies are aware of the risks within their organization and that these risks are managed effectively in order to ensure the solvency and liquidity of the company.

456. *See* Board Notice 158 in GG38357 / 20151219 of 19 Dec. 2014.

Selected Bibliography

Albertyn, C. & B. Goldblatt. In *Constitutional Law of South Africa,* edited by S. Woolman & M. Bishop. 2nd ed. Cape Town: Juta, 2008.

Botha, C. *Statutory Interpretation: An Introduction for Students.* 4th ed. Juta and Company Ltd, 2012.

Bracher, P. '*Gender Premiums and Discrimination*'. In NRSA Insurance Law September 2011 (update at www.nortonrosefullbright.com) (last consulted on 10 February 2015).

Bradfield, G.B. *Christie's The Law of Contract in South Africa.* 7th ed. Durban: LexisNexis, 2016.

Cassim, F.H.I. (ed.). *Contemporary Company Law.* Cape Town: Juta, 2012).

Combrinck, H. 'Testing the Boundaries: Women's Equality in South Africa'. In *The Principle of Equality – A South African and Belgian Perspective*, edited by J. Vandelotte, J. Sarkin & Y. Haecks. Antwerpen: Maklu, 2001.

Currie, I. & J. De Waal. *The Bill of Rights Handbook.* Cape Town: Juta, 2013.

De Wet, J.C. & A.H. Van Wyk. *Die Suid-Afrikaanse Kontraktereg en Handelsreg.* Durban: Butterworths 1992.

Havenga, P. *The Law of Insurance Intermediaries.* Cape Town: Juta, 2001.

Hutchison, D., et al. *The Law of Contract in South Africa.* Oxford University Press Southern Africa, 2013.

Joubert, E.P. 'Company law'. In *Business Law* edited by Nagel, C.J. et al. Durban: Lexis Nexis, 2015.

Kleyn, D. & F. Viljoen. Beginner's Guide for Law Students. Cape Town: Juta, 2010.

Kok, A. 'The Promotion of Equality and Unfair Discrimination Act: Why the Controversy?'. *TSAR* 5 (2001): 294.

Kok, A. 'Motor Vehicle Insurance, the Constitution and the Promotion of Equality and Prevention of Unfair Discrimination Act'. *SAJHR* 18 (2002).

Kuschke, B. 'Gender Equality in Insurance: Association belge des Consommateurs Test-Achats ASBL, Vann van Vugt, Charles Basselier v Conseil des ministres'. *De Jure* 3 (2012): 624.

Lewis, C. 'Interpretation of Contracts'. In *Southern Cross: Civil Law and Common Law in South Africa,* edited by Zimmerman, R. & Visser D. Cape Town: Juta, 1996.

Millard, D. *Modern Insurance Law in South Africa.* Cape Town: Juta, 2013.

Millard, D. Juta's Insurance Law Bulletin. Cape Town: Juta, 2014.

Millard, D. & W. Hattingh. *The FAIS Act Explained.* Durban: LexisNexis, 2016.

Moolman, J., Pillai, C., Bam, N.N. & J. Appasamy. *Financial Advisory and Intermediary Services Guide.* Durban: LexisNexis, 2010.

Muller, E. 'Life Insurance Benefits: The Setting Aside of Cessions and Nominations in Terms of the Insolvency Law and other Related Aspects'. *De Jure* (2005): 361, 364.

Neethling, J. & J.M. Potgieter. *Neethling Potgieter Visser's Law of Delict.* Durban: LexisNexis, 2014.

Nienaber, G. & D. Van der Nest. 'An Exploration of the Impact of a Claimant's HIV/ AIDS Status on a Personal Injury Claim'. *TSAR* 2 (2002): 290.

Nienaber, P.M. & G.F. Lubbe. 'Cession'. In *LAWSA.* 2nd ed. Durban: LexisNexis, 2013.

Nienaber, P.M. 'Some Problems Involving Security Cessions of life Insurance Policies'. *SA Merc LJ* (2004): 83.

Nienaber, P.M. & M.F.B. Reinecke. *Life Insurance in South Africa: A Compendium.* Durban: LexisNexis, 2009.

Otto, J.M. 'The South African legal System and Its History'. In *Commercial Law,* edited by Nagel, C.J., et al. Durban: LexisNexis, 2011.

Olivier, M.P., Smit, N. & E.R. Kalula. *Social Security Law: A Legal Analysis.* Durban: LexisNexis, 2003.

Prozesky-Kuschke, B. 'Introduction to Insurance and Insurance Contracts'. In *Commercial Law,* edited by Nagel, C.J., et al. Durban: LexisNexis, 2015.

Prozesky-Kuschke, B. 'Law of Contract'. In *Commercial Law*, edited by Nagel, C.J., et al. Durban: LexisNexis, 2015.

Reinecke, M.F.B. & P.M. Nienaber. 'A Suggested Template for Beneficiary Nominations'. *SA Merc LJ* 13 (2009).

Reinecke, M.F.B., Van Niekerk, J.P. & P.M. Nienaber. *South African Insurance Law.* Durban: LexisNexis, 2013.

Schulze, W.G. 'Extension Clauses in Insurance Contracts – Uncertainty Rules OK?'. *SA Merc LJ* 9 (1997): 64.

Schulze, W.G. 'Extension Clauses in Insurance Contracts – A New Angle'. *SA Merc LJ* 9 (1997): 216.

Scott, S.J. *The Law of Cession.* Juta: Cape Town, 1991.

Sonnekus, J.C. 'Sessie van saaklike sekerheidsregte?'. *TSAR* (1997): 772.

Sunkel, K.D. 'The pactum de non cedendo: A Re-evaluation'. LLM Dissertation, University of the Western Cape, 2009.

Sunkel, K.D. 'Cession of Life Insurance Policies in securitatem debiti: A Practical Perspective'. LLD Thesis, University of Pretoria, 2013.

Van der Merwe, C.G. *Sakereg.* Durban: Butterworths, 1989.

Van Jaarsveld, S.R. 'Agency'. In *Commercial Law*, edited by Nagel, C.J., et al. Durban: LexisNexis, 2011.

Van Niekerk, J.P. 'Life Insurance: Cession'. *Annual Survey of South African Law* (Cape Town: Juta, 1997).

Van Zyl, F. *Financial Advisory and Intermediary Services Manual.* Cape Town: Juta, 2000.

Wakefield, R. Reporting on South Africa. In *Getting the Deal through: Enforcement of Foreign Judgments in 28 Jurisdictions Worldwide,* edited by Mark Moedritzer & Kay C Whittaker. Law Business Research Ltd., 2012.

Wallis, M. 'What's in a Word? Interpretation Through the Eyes of Ordinary Readers'. *SALJ* 127 (2010): 673.

Index

The numbers here refers to paragraph numbers.

Index